The
G-String
Theory

by
Ilana Marks

The G-String Theory
Published in 2001

Copyright © 2001 Ilana Marks

Library of Congress Cataloging in publication data:
Marks, Ilana
The G-String Theory ; A New Wave of Being
ISBN 0-9715698-1-9

www.ilanamarks.com

Thank you to all those of you who have supported me on my journey and helped me bring THE G-STRING THEORY into form.

Clay, for your countless hours of help, reading, editing, and formatting.

Nadi and Anna, for the purity of your contribution and for your patience with the process.

Noreen, for holding and validating the true vision of what this book is, and for your beautiful, inspired background painting on the cover.

Vicki, for your constant support and for recognizing from the moment you read this, that God is working through us.

Chris, for all your helpful input with copyediting.

Norman and Joan, for your kind guidance and help with the interminable prepress work, especially on the cover.

Gizmo, for lying sweetly at my feet as I typed, and for giving up many walks so that I could get this finished.

Sai Baba, for the most beautiful initiation, and for calling me to India.

The Universe, God, Spirit, The Creator - Thank You.

Prologue

f

The G-String Theory came to life in a rather unusual way. I was invited to lecture in Hawaii, Australia, New Zealand, and England. I was excited to make this trip, but I didn't want to be away from my family for three months. So I took my children out of school, my husband took off from work, and we followed my Soul's guidance that the trip was the right thing to do, despite the many ego reasons not to do it.

The lectures, with anywhere from twenty to hundreds of people in attendance, were extremely well received all over the world. The response after each talk was the same. Many people said that they felt a Presence enter the room when I spoke, and that they received a deep healing. I got e-mails from others who wrote that attending the lectures gave them the courage and inspiration to make changes that they'd been trying to make for years.

One commonly asked question was, "Where can I buy your book?" I laughed because I didn't have a book, and I realized that there was a purity in traveling around the world to share a message simply because I felt guided to do it, even though I had nothing to sell.

Three days after arriving home I misstepped in my living room and injured my foot. I couldn't walk at all. I realized that I was supposed to slow down and regroup.

I sat at the computer to record some of my recollections from the trip. And then it happened...I found that I was writing a book.

As I wrote, I was completely back in the experience. I wrote non-stop for three weeks – the words flowed out of me with an ease and grace that astounded me. I felt as though I was taking dictation. I also started receiving beautiful teachings – the most obvious example of which is on the final page of this book. I felt a huge surge of energy move through me as I typed those words. The computer suddenly and spontaneously began typing in capital letters, and I knew that I had been gifted more than just words on a page.

People who have read those words have had a similar tangible feeling of a Presence moving through them. I encourage you not to go straight to the end, however, but to come to it through the process of reading the whole book.

I know that this book will provide you with more than just a humorous, spiritual romp through the craziness of India. When you read it, you will be gifted a healing as well. I know that it will effect change on a deep Soul level as it presents a new paradigm for experiencing life with joy, laughter, fun, gentleness, and love.

The G-String Theory is set against the backdrop of India. I include flashbacks to the rest of the trip, incorporate some teachings from my lectures, and describe my experiences at Sai Baba's ashram.

Sai Baba is widely considered to be the only living Avatar on the Earth today. He has millions of followers all over the world. On any given day, thousands of Westerners and Indians arrive at the ashram to see him. On his seventieth birthday, four million people arrived to celebrate with him. Other than Baba appearing to me in a very powerful dream a year ago, I knew very little about him before this trip.

My trip around the planet was transformational for me, much like the process that butterflies go through in their cocoons. It was also an opportunity for me to experience life in a state of total trust, and to witness a vision of the perfection of our Souls' sojourn upon the Earth.

I have always been inspired by Gandhi's words: "My life is my message". That is what I feel this book offers. I present, through my own example, a way of being that doesn't *prescribe* the right lifestyle, but rather *describes* my lifestyle and offers my experience as a way of inspiring you to follow your passions and your dreams. Perhaps the message of this book will give you implicit permission to wake up to the wondrous joy of Life.

Enjoy.....

Ilana

January 30

f

The plane landed at 10:30 PM.

The airport in Mumbai (Bombay) is without doubt the dirtiest "no-frills" airport that I have ever encountered. A couple of indolent government officials sat behind a little wooden table, stamping passports as weary passengers poured into the room. It took ages to get by immigration. They were in no hurry to let us through.

The baggage-claim machine circled around lethargically. Workers in drab uniforms leaned against the muddy walls, blending in perfectly.

I exited the building, walking into a sea of expectant faces. Not seeing John, I wondered if I would spend the night on one of the shabby airport seats, waiting for the next flight to Puttaparthi. I wasn't worried, though, partly because I was too tired after a full day of traveling, and partly because I was still in the glorious state of fullness and love that I had come to know as my constant state of being over the past couple of months.

I spotted John's suntanned face among the darker-skinned Indians. The man standing next to him held a small white board with 'Ilana Marks' written on it.

"John!" I called.

He heard me and came rushing over, clearly excited to see me. He seemed relieved that the arrangement we had made several months before, to meet on January thirtieth in Bombay, had actually come to fruition.

"Have you been waiting long? I wanted to be there the moment you stepped off the plane," he lamented.

"I've hardly waited at all; I just arrived," I assured him.

"Welcome India, Madame," said the man with the white board, smiling broadly as he relieved me of my bags. We followed him to the waiting taxi. John had booked us into a hotel called "The Sea Princess".

"A fitting name for my princess," he told me sweetly.

He had chosen that hotel because it was on the ocean, not for the view necessarily but rather for the air quality. It was marginally cleaner there because of the breezes off the Indian Ocean. Further into the city, where John had spent the previous night, the pollution was so thick that he hadn't been able to breathe.

We drove for about forty minutes and pulled into the circular driveway of a very grand-looking hotel. Immediately, I was surrounded by Indian men in white gloves and uniforms, eagerly grabbing my bags out the back of the taxi.

I walked inside feeling like a princess, albeit a bedraggled, exhausted princess, and we made our way up to the room.

I dropped my bags on the floor and flopped onto one of the beds. It felt good to lie flat after so many hours of flying, walking, pushing trolleys, and carrying heavy bags. I told John about some of my adventures over the past couple of months, and he filled me in on his life back in Boston.

"Do you feel like going to see the ocean?" he asked.

It sounded like a good idea to get some clean, fresh ocean air after breathing recycled air all day, so we walked out to the swimming pool on the terrace. Another uniformed, gloved security guard hovered around us. He was very interested in everything we had to say and was clearly trying to kill some time on his long shift by watching foreigners do whatever it is we do.

John told me about an adventure he'd had on the beach the night before.

He had been approached by a young Indian boy and his horse. The boy had asked John if he'd like to take a ride in the back of his horse-drawn cart.

"Only twenty rupees," the boy had promised.

Figuring you can't go wrong for fifty American cents, John jumped aboard. That was when the fun began. The boy took him down the beach for what felt like several kilometres.

Finally he stopped and asked, "You want go back now?"

"Sure," replied John.

"Is 400 rupees go back."

"Wait a minute," John retorted, "you said 20 rupees for the whole thing."

"No, no," said the boy, enjoying his captive's discomfort, "20 there, 400 back."

Recognizing his predicament, John had to think quickly, so he readily agreed to the 400 rupee ransom.

"Then, once back at the entrance," said John, recalling the excitement of the moment, "I jumped off the cart, and ran into the crowd with him chasing behind me. As I ran, I shouted over my shoulder, 'You told me 20 rupees! I won't let you cheat me!'"

I laughed at the image of John being chased for the ransom money, yelling as he disappeared into the crowded market stalls on the beach.

I was especially surprised, though, when minutes later John asked me, "So, should we take a horse ride on the beach?"

"Are you nuts?" I asked him. "After that experience? I

really don't feel a pressing need to experience it, too."

"Well, let's take a rickshaw ride down to the market area – that will be fun," he suggested.

Despite having woken in Australia and having spent a large portion of the day walking around Singapore, I decided that sleep could wait. I was ready to discover the sights and sounds of Mumbai's night life.

We went to the front of the hotel and hailed a rickshaw. Rickshaw rides in India are a special not-to-be-missed experience. A rickshaw is a tiny, black, three-wheeled vehicle with a driver on a small bench at the helm and the passengers squeezed onto a tiny black bench in the back. The sides are open, and, despite my small size, I needed to bend to fit under the roof.

As we drove, hunched over, rickshaws appeared from every direction, threading their way like drunken worker ants through Bombay's busy streets. Even at midnight, Bombay is busier and noisier than most cities are at rush hour.

The biggest drawback to being in that tiny vehicle was that, when the buses and trucks pulled up alongside us, as they so often did, the black diesel smoke choked our lungs.

After about ten minutes the driver stopped. "You want walk beach?"

"Okay," John said. "Will you wait here for us? We won't be too long."

There was no chance of him driving off because the few rupees we owed him ensured us a ride home.

We walked onto the beach front. It was my first real taste of Indian culture. Hundreds of people were crowded around food stalls, merry-go-rounds and other interesting stands.

"Come this way," John said. "I want to show you something funny."

We walked towards some red flashing lights, set up a little

way down the beach.

"This is really cool," said John. "You put on the headphones, and it gives you an astrological readout of your love life."

The young entrepreneurial owner of this device had quite a little set-up. A life-size human cardboard cut-out was flashing red neon lights. All kinds of astrological glyphs lit up on the cut-out's head. A pair of headphones hung off its body and connected to a tape recorder in the suitcase below. The suitcase also served as the foundation for the whole contraption.

"You try?" asked the vendor.

"No thanks," I replied. "We just look."

"You try this," urged the man again. "Only twenty rupees."

I wondered if it was twenty rupees to put the headphones on, and 400 to take them off, like the horse deal. In India, refusing a merchant who has your attention is no easy feat.

"If we put those headphones on, we are looking at an instant lice infestation," whispered John.

He quickly came up with a way to get out of the situation gracefully.

"Do you have any readings in English?" he asked, knowing full well that an English translation was not available.

"Ohhh....no English," sighed the man regretfully, realizing at once that 20 potential rupees were disappearing before his eyes.

We knew then that we were safe to just look.

Making our way back towards the market area, we came upon a young boy with his horses.

"Twenty rupees – I take you on horse down beach," called out the boy.

"No thanks," I said, John's story still fresh in my mind.

"Do you want to try it?" asked John.

"Are you joking?" was all I could come up with.

"No, it's fun," he said.

"Well, is it the same guy?"

"I don't know."

By now the young boy knew he had a sale. Standing close to him discussing the pros and cons for that length of time indicated a definite sale.

"Twenty rupees," he said again.

"How much does it cost to get back?" I asked.

"Fifty rupees," he replied, moving us closer to the carriage as he spoke.

"Fifty rupees there and back?" asked John.

We were assured that it would be a fixed, no-surprises-guaranteed fee.

So there I was, standing on the beach in Mumbai at midnight (actually five o' clock the following morning, for me). I climbed into the "chariot" in front of me, and sat down on the light blue, unpadded vinyl seat.

John jumped in beside me, and, with a quick flash of the whip, the two scrawniest of horses started running into the night.

Clinging onto the side railing, I longed for the comfort of the rickshaw as the wooden cart bounced its way over the uneven beach. I started to wonder if we were indeed being taken down the beach so that we would agree to pay any amount just to be returned to our waiting rickshaw.

Suddenly, a piercing whistle sounded from the driver's mouth, and the horses came to an abrupt halt. We held on for dear life, trying not to let inertia get the better of us.

"You want go back?" came the call from the front.

"Yes, please," I called without a trace of hesitation.

With another quick flash of the whip, we did a 180-degree turn on the sand and headed back up the beach.

Finally our bodies were jolted back to the starting point. I thought about the chiropractic adjustment Dr. John would owe me after that little adventure!

On our way back to the waiting rickshaw, John bought himself a mango-flavoured ice cream. I held true to my promise to eat as little as possible while in India, so I declined my favourite fruit-flavoured ice cream.

The driver took us back to the hotel, dodging cars, buses, and other rickshaws.

Back at the hotel, I decided that I'd had just about all the fun I could handle without any sleep for twenty-seven hours.

Just before I fell sleep, John said, "I have arranged a massage for you at seven o'clock tomorrow morning. I thought it would be nice after all the flying and traveling. If you want, a masseur who works in the gym downstairs will bring his table and set up in the room."

I definitely did want. Massage is one of my favourite things about being human.

"I got one from him yesterday," said John, "and for a full hour he only charged 150 rupees!"

An hour massage for under five American dollars sounded unbelievable to me.

"In the four days I've been here, I've already had three," said John.

I fell asleep looking forward to a good night's sleep, excited by the prospect of waking up to a good massage.

Δ

A couple of hours later, I was awakened by a strange sensation that I couldn't really define. It felt like the bed was shaking, but I assumed it was just my delirious exhaustion. I suddenly remembered that within the past few days one of the largest earthquakes ever to rumble this planet had occurred only 300 miles north of us.

As I sat up in the dark, my mind filled with images of collapsing cement buildings I had seen on the TV news. I wondered if it was possible that the building was indeed shaking from earthquake tremors. I had vague memories of the same sensation from my childhood in Cape-Town, when several earthquakes shook the area. I remembered having to run out of the house in the middle of the night, waiting in the street for things to calm down.

"It can't be that," I convinced myself. "You're just overtired."

In a semi-lucid state, I wondered why I'd decided to come to India. I had no idea why I was guided to be there, but the circumstances leading up to the trip were synchronistic enough to make me pay attention.

John had been talking to a patient about the patient's upcoming trip to Australia. John asked him what the time difference was between Boston and Australia, but the man didn't know. Just then the phone rang and John picked up. The operator asked if he would accept reverse charges on a call from Australia, and told John what time it was there. The timing of the call was impeccable.

The call was from a man John had met at Sai Baba's ashram several years earlier. He was calling John after at least a year with no contact. The man, Rijeva, was living in Australia and was getting married in Sri Lanka. He was calling to invite John to the wedding.

Just after they hung up, I arrived at John's house.

"Guess what?" I'd said very excitedly. "I booked to go to Australia!"

"That's great," said John, telling me what had just

transpired with the phone call. "Do you want to go with me to a wedding in Sri Lanka?"

"Okay!" I answered, picturing a map of the world in my mind and deciding that it could work.

"Then we could visit Sai Baba's ashram," he said.

"That sounds like a good idea," I answered.

Thus my trip to India was born. I decided to go to Perth instead of Sri Lanka, so John and I arranged to meet in Bombay after the wedding. I had no idea why I was including India in the trip, but I've decided to say "yes" whenever my Soul tells me that something is right, regardless of whether it makes any sense to my ego.

Lying in the dark shaking hotel room, however, my ego was in definite conflict with my Soul. I felt, however, that something wonderful was happening, and I looked forward to finding out why it was that my Soul included India in my journey.

Finally, desperate for sleep, I dozed off.

January 31

f

As soon as I awoke, I told John about my nighttime adventure. He hadn't felt a thing, so I dismissed it and went to have a shower before the masseur was to arrive.

Promptly at 7 AM, there was a knock at the door. A thin young man, dressed all in white, and looking no older than a teenager, came into the room. He told me that his name was Pakua and asked if I was ready.

As John walked out the door, he whispered to me, "I'll be back in an hour. Remember this is no time for inhibitions. In India anything goes, so don't be shy."

He walked out, handing the man 300 rupees, which included a rather generous tip.

I was left alone with the young man. I had no idea what the protocol was, and I was confused about John's "warning" on his way out. I realized that it must have had something to do with the upcoming massage.

"Where is the massage table? I asked.

"I no bring table. Lie on bed," he informed me.

"Do you do Shiatsu?" I asked, remembering that the Shiatsu massages I've had in the past allowed for clothing to be left on.

"I do Shiatsu, and oils. You want I use you cream or my?"

"Mine," I said, realizing that my clothes would certainly have to come off if cream was to be applied.

I walked over to the bed, hoping that he would turn around so that I could take off my shirt. There was no chance of that. He was not about to miss the fun of watching his client undress. So, with his eyes burning into me, I turned around, took off my shirt, and quickly lay face down on the bed.

I left on my shorts and underwear knowing that underpants were definitely part of the massage protocol in America.

"No pants," he declared as he pulled off my shorts and underwear with one quick, well-rehearsed tug. John's words of warning rang in my ears.

So there I was, lying naked in my hotel room in India, with a strange man hovering over me, and my protector somewhere downstairs working on his biceps and push-ups.

"Okay!" I decided. "I am not going to be a prude. When in Rome..." and I relaxed ever so slightly, waiting to see what would follow.

Pakua started to smear the lotion on my body, rubbing my skin in a circular motion as he went. After a while, my cream ran out. Pakua pulled a bottle of some cheap pink cream from his pocket. It looked like it was several years past the expiration date. As he poured the cream onto the palms of his hands, the heavily perfumed smell wafted down towards me. I knew then why I had suggested the use of my non-scented, environmentally-friendly cream in the first place.

That became the least of my concerns as Pakua's hands started becoming a little more adventurous, making their way to the top of my thighs. He pretended to focus on acupressure points on my legs, but I felt his eyes fixed on my body.

I began to see the humour in the situation. I pictured

Pakua going home to his high-rise apartment at the end of the day and telling his drooling, envious friends that he had earned his rupees that day by rubbing cream into the naked body of an American tourist. I wondered if perhaps it wasn't back to front, and that actually I should be the one getting paid for this.

"Maybe you could put a blanket over me," I said, trying to sound nonchalant. "Lying here so relaxed, I'm starting to feel quite cold."

Reluctantly, he picked up a blanket from the floor, and, getting one last look, he draped it over me. I felt a lot better, and actually a lot warmer too.

"Okay. Now I can relax and enjoy this," I thought.

Little did I know that the real massage was just beginning.

"Turn over," came the order.

I did a quick flip without disturbing the blanket. Pakua moved his hands up beneath the blanket and continued to work my thighs from the front, all the while regaling me with a story of how he had fallen in love with a woman from a caste below him. Their families had prohibited them from having any contact.

"I Brahmin," he said proudly. "That is highest caste, but her family no happy because not allowed to marry out of caste. I hate this. I hate this caste system even though I have highest caste. I love India but I hate caste. Now I no more girlfriends. I no marry."

"Pakua, how about you do my neck and shoulders instead? That area is bothering me the most," I said, moving my attention away from his love life, and back to the moment.

Pakua obediently moved around the bed to my neck, and placed his hand lightly on my shoulder muscles. He rubbed them for a few minutes.

"No tightness here, Madame," he exclaimed. "I go back to legs. Skin dry by pelvis – you need more cream."

"Oh I don't think so!" I blurted out. "How about you do some reflexology? I love reflexology."

"Reflexology take too long," he explained apologetically. "How you like I do a breast tonement?"

"A what?" I asked, wondering if it was his thick accent that was interfering with my comprehension, or if he was simply mistaking the English word for breasts.

"A breast tonement," he repeated matter-of-factly. "All women love it. It help muscles firm. No sagging after I tone women breasts."

I couldn't believe it.

"Are you telling me that Hindu and Moslem men allow their women to come to you for a breast toning?"

"Oh they love it," he assured me. "I very professional. I turn away clients when I find out they just want breast toning only. They cry on phone beg me for breast tonement, but I say no."

"Oh right!" I thought. The B.S. metre had just shot off the charts. I could just hear Pakua turning down poor Salaama, who was begging for his strong hands to massage her breasts. "Sorry! No can do," he would say in Hindi, "I know what you want – I too professional to give it to you. Sorry. Find yourself another massage therapist and don't come in here begging for that again!"

Somehow that conversation seemed completely unlikely.

"I'm sure you are very professional, Pakua, but I will pass on the offer. Let's do the reflexology instead."

"Oh! I see clock – hour is finish! I must go now."

I rolled over, and, much to Pakua's disappointment, managed to pull my T-shirt and shorts back on under the blanket.

"How you feel?" Pakua asked me. "Relax?"

"Yes, quite relaxed. Thank you."

13

I was especially relaxed knowing that John would be knocking on the door any minute.

"You give me your e-mail. Dr. John give me e-mail, but I like e-mail friends all over world," he said, handing me a piece of paper and a pencil.

I wrote my e-mail address down next to John's. I knew that e-mail addresses are untraceable, so I didn't mind giving it to him. Pakua asked me one last time not to let hotel management know that he had been in the room.

"Big trouble for me I come up guest room," he explained. "Only allow work in health club downstairs. No say Pakua in room."

Smiling, he grabbed his cream, shoved the money in his pocket, and slipped out of the room as quietly as he had entered.

John came back into the room beaming. He had just worked out and relaxed in the hot tub downstairs.

"How was it?" he asked me.

I looked at him and started to laugh.

"Okay! Let's go down and have breakfast," he suggested, "then you can tell me all about it."

John reminded me that we would have to eat quickly, as our next adventure for the day was about to begin. This one entailed a visit to Punji, the Banana Leaf Akashic Record Reader who lived in the centre of Mumbai.

We walked into the dining room, and I saw my favourite vegetarian foods spread out in front of us on beautiful silver platters. I knew then that it was going to be extremely difficult to restrict myself to the muesli bars and apples which I had brought with me from Australia. The temptation was too great. I decided that I would eat just a little and keep away from anything raw.

I took a plate and found myself in front of uniformed, gloved men with serving spoons, who were eager to heap plentiful portions onto my plate. I walked back to the table grabbing a freshly squeezed mango juice. The food was really delicious. I decided to trust that I was being sent to India for a particular purpose and that I would be protected while there. So, although I didn't eat as much as I would have back home, I had more for breakfast than I had planned on eating the whole trip.

"Well? How was the massage?" John asked once we had settled down to eat.

"It was interesting. I know now what you meant when you warned me not to be inhibited."

"There are no boundaries here. Anything goes," said John as he tucked into some very strange-looking curry sauces poured over a white, compressed rice-like cake.

"That's for sure!" I said. "He just pulled my clothes off. It was very different from any other massages I've ever had. Definitely more sexual."

"Really?" said John. "Was it bad?"

"No, it wasn't that," I said. "It was...how should I say? Well, for example, he tried to convince me to let him do a breast tonement." I started laughing again as I thought back on it.

John started laughing, too, and said, "Now that you mention it, he did massage me in places I never would have thought of either."

"Like...?" I asked.

"My scrotum!"

I burst out laughing. "He did? Really? You got the scrotum tonement!"

"Yeah," said John, laughing more now, too. "I wondered at the time if that was normal for India. I'm sorry. I didn't really think he would be like that with you. Actually, come to think of it, I started thinking maybe he was gay."

"Well, he doesn't seem very gay to me. Maybe he goes

15

both ways."

We swapped more information about our respective experiences, and then we hurried to the front desk to have them call us a taxi.

We were told that the same driver could take us to Punji, wait for us there, and then give us a ride to the airport so that we could catch our flight to Puttaparthi. Puttaparthi – the whole reason we were in India in the first place.

The woman behind the counter assured us that the driver would be there in just a couple of minutes and that, in the meantime, a porter would bring our luggage down from the room. I wasn't used to that type of service. It did not in any way resemble what someone traveling in the Western World on my budget would experience.

We waited and waited, watching the time tick by. I knew that I couldn't possibly be on time for my appointment with Punji if the driver didn't arrive immediately. Time is completely inconsequential in India – it was my first experience with "two more minutes" really meaning "somewhere between fifteen and forty-five minutes from now."

Trips to the front desk were futile. They kept assuring us that the driver would arrive imminently. A couple of times they even squelched our attempt to get a different cab by pointing to a non-existent taxi and insisting, "That must be him now."

Eventually, the taxi arrived. John had requested air conditioning to try to keep some of the diesel fumes out the car. It wasn't that the weather was hot; it was just that the fumes from an hour long ride through the maze-like streets of Mumbai could kill you, if the oncoming trucks and buses didn't do it first.

Perhaps the big mistake was telling the driver that we were in a hurry. Taxi drivers in India need no encouragement to drive fast, and the almost explicit permission to drive like a maniac inherent in the words "We are running late" is not a mistake you repeat too often.

After about half an hour of weaving around the sidewalks and potholed streets of the inner city, I asked the driver, "How much longer?"

Another futile question.

"Fifteen minutes," he said.

Our appointment was supposed to be in ten minutes.

"You phone?" asked the driver, holding up a modern little cell phone. It seemed so incongruous to be handed a cell phone amidst such poverty. Beggars were surrounding the car at each traffic light, while John was calling our Akashic Records Guru to say that we were running late.

John had been to see him the day before and was looking forward to seeing what my impression of the man would be.

"I don't know what you'll think of him," John said. "I think he's a bit whacked."

"Well, why are we sitting in this traffic, busting our butts to get over there, if he's whacked?" I asked.

"Well...see what you think. Besides, there is entertainment value in all this."

I agreed. I saw it as another experience and another piece of the whole colourful jigsaw of which we were a part.

Fifteen minutes later I leaned towards the front seat and asked again, "How much longer now?"

"Fifteen minutes," came the reply.

"Fifteen minutes?" I said to John. "That's what he said twenty minutes ago."

John pulled out a daily English newspaper that had been delivered to the hotel room earlier that morning.

"Look at this!" he said, pointing to the lead story.

I read, "...ten more tremors shook the area last night, being felt throughout Mumbai."

"Wow! It really was the aftershocks of the earthquake I was feeling," I said.

"You should have woken me," said John.

"Luckily, I'm only finding this out today. I wouldn't have slept at all if I'd known that the shaking was not just my delirious imagination."

Ten more minutes passed, and John asked, "How much longer now?"

"Nearly there," he said. "Fifteen minutes."

So we drove some more, looking out at the less than aesthetically pleasing views. We felt extremely grateful to have air conditioning, as we watched thick clouds of black smoke wafting by the closed windows of our cab.

Another ten minutes went by, and I started to wonder if we shouldn't go directly to the airport. We had squeezed the appointment in quite tightly, so there wasn't much time left.

"Only one more kilometre," the driver volunteered.

"Good," I thought. "That means it will only be about fifteen more minutes."

Finally, the taxi pulled into a side street, went up a driveway, and parked outside a whitewashed cement apartment building.

We jumped out of the car, asking the taxi driver to wait with our luggage until we were done. We both laughed at how funny it was to leave our luggage with a total stranger. It was so antithetical to the advice we are given about traveling, especially in Third World countries.

"Do you think our stuff will be okay?" John asked, as we made our way up the winding stairs.

"I don't know, but I don't have anything worth stealing, so I'm not worried."

I kept following John until we were standing in front of a plain white door. I knocked tentatively. I had no idea what to expect.

A man in his late sixties or early seventies opened the door. He was dressed in a white punjabi. His thinning hair was also white and brushed back over his skull. He welcomed us and commented on how late we were. We told him about the traffic, and there seemed to be a tacit understanding of the problem.

"Come with me," he said, wasting no time.

The apartment was very clean and sparsely furnished. I noticed a young boy who appeared to be a servant standing in the kitchen. John found a couch in the living room and plunked himself down.

The old man led me onto his back porch. He took a metal ruler off a hook that was hanging on the porch wall and motioned me to stand against the opposite wall. I did what I was told. He seemed to be measuring me.

Then he took the measuring stick and ceremoniously threw it on the tiled floor, like an African Witch Doctor throwing bones. He didn't say a word; he just motioned me to go back with him into the room that served as his study. He sat in the lotus position on the chair in front of his desk and again motioned me to sit in the opposite chair.

"Write birthday here," he said, pushing a piece of paper in front of me.

I wrote down my birthday and slid it back towards him. He looked at it knowingly and reached to the side of the desk, his hand disappearing into a thick pile of papers made from banana leaves.

He pulled one of the papers out of the pile. It was about one foot long by six inches wide. It was covered in what I assumed was Sanskrit or Hindi writing. The letters looked somewhat like Hebrew characters in their design, but I had no idea what they meant.

"Thirty-eight," said his voice.

"Well not quite," I said. "Still a couple more months."

"Yes. March you thirty-eight."

"So far I'm not impressed," I thought to myself. "That's a pretty simple deduction, given that I have just written my birthday on the piece of paper he's holding. I really hope it gets better than this."

At that point Punji handed me scraps of old paper. Apparently he was about to come out with something worth writing down, and I was to make notes. I looked on the back of the carbon-like paper and saw that it was an invoice pad.

I do believe in the psychic realm, and I get messages myself all the time. I know the messages come from other dimensions, so I didn't need this man to prove the existence of Akashic Records or the psychic realm to me. I have learnt from my years of interviewing many people who have jumped on the New Age bandwagon that we need to be discerning, and not give away our power to someone just because they call themselves psychic. It is a fine line between being judgmental and being discerning. Perhaps it is one of our more difficult lessons to learn as humans.

We need to always remember that the greatest con-artist and the highest healer are just two sides of the same coin. In both cases they are gifted at tuning in to someone's energy; the difference lies in how each chooses to use that gift.

We need to remain conscious of that choice in each moment. We decide whether to use our talents and gifts, whatever they are, for the highest and best expression of our Soul's evolution, or to use them in pursuit of our ego's expression.

So, with that racing through my mind, I sat before the old Hindu man, who was dressed all in white, in an upstairs apartment, somewhere in the Indian subcontinent.

I decided to enjoy the whole experience, rather than

concern myself with whether or not there was any value in the information which was about to come forth.

For about half an hour, Punji looked intently at his banana-leaf Sanskrit page. Every now and then he looked back at me, declaring something in an English that was coated in such a heavy Indian accent, that making out individual words was almost impossible. I speak several languages and am usually able to understand thick accents, but his was particularly unusual.

"You spatial an telen," Punji said, a grin baring his semi-toothless mouth.

I assumed, by the smile on his face, that it was a compliment, but I had no idea what it meant to be "spatial an telen".

"Could you say that again, please?" I asked, craning my ears towards him to try to make better sense of it all.

"Spatial... Spatial... "

I stared at him blankly. I felt like a devotee who had just climbed to the top of the Himalayas to discuss the meaning of Life with a great Guru, only to find out that I couldn't understand a single word of his wisdom.

"Believe Sai Baba," he finally offered in explanation.

"Oh! I get it! Spiritual."

"Yes, yes spatial," he said, so happy that we could now understand each other.

"So what is telen?" I asked.

"You much good art, write, create," he said.

"Oh. Okay – talented, creative."

I was pleased that we could move onto the next part of the reading. At this rate we would be there a long time if I was to get my entire Akashic Records read. We still had a plane to catch and Bombay's traffic to weave through.

"You much money, success, radio and television," he went on.

"When is that going to happen?" I asked.

"Not two year."

"Do you mean before two years are up?" I asked.

"Yes, before two year much travel with work. Very good. You need learn many yoga and meditation for relax so much success. I teach you mantra. You say mantra every day. Write mantra."

I began writing down the words he was saying. I had no idea what they meant or how to spell any of it, so I wrote it all down phonetically. Afterwards, he had me repeat the mantra with him a couple of times to make sure that I had transcribed it correctly. For all I knew I could have just written down his favourite recipe for masala-dosa.

Satisfied with my attempt at the pronunciation of the Hindi mantra, he continued, "You many books write. Many language read books. You many language learn speak."

"I already speak four languages."

"Must more learn. Also Hindi. Need eight language learn speak," he said smiling.

Punji continued to give me the details of what he told me would be a long and prosperous life. Who can ever feel bad after hearing all that? So, happily, I paid him the rather high price (even by American standards) of a thousand rupees, and John and I headed back down to the waiting taxi.

I couldn't get over how patiently taxi drivers sat and waited for their customers, whether it was midnight on the beach front, or midday in a Banana Leaf Reader's Bombay apartment.

During our long drive through the streets of the city, I told John about Punji's reading.

"Did he tell you if you'll get an interview with Baba?" asked John.

"Yes. He said not this time – when I'm forty-two."

"He told me that I'll get one in four more years," said John.

"That's funny because, in four more years, I'll be forty-two. Maybe we're coming back here together," I laughed.

"Let's see if Punji's right. If we do get an interview this trip, it will bring into question everything else that he said," replied John.

We finally arrived at the airport. The driver carried our bags to the door of the building; this was starting to feel somewhat natural to me, and I hadn't even been there twenty-four hours.

We found the primitive blackboard with the flight departure times. I searched for Puttaparthi. I felt excited that I was going to see Sai Baba and the ashram, and witness the stories I had heard from other people.

"Canceled...?" said John, screwing up his eyes to see if he was reading correctly.

"Where do you see that?" I asked.

"Look at the second board – the third row down says 'Puttaparthi – canceled'."

Sure enough, there it was in black and white. Our flight was canceled. My first thought was that the information couldn't possibly be correct. There are only two flights a week from Mumbai to Puttaparthi, and I didn't think it possible that we would have to spend four more days in Mumbai waiting for the next flight. There had to be a mistake.

John ran over to the ticket counter, to find out what was going on. In the meantime, I found an office with the words "Airport Manager" on the door. I went in, and found a young woman dressed in a beautiful blue sari seated behind her formica desk.

"Excuse me," I ventured, "is the flight to Puttaparthi canceled?"

"Puttaparthi...let me look. Yes, that flight is cancel."

"Well, what should we do? We have tickets to travel there. Are you putting on a later flight?"

I had hoped that the reason for their putting "canceled" rather than "delayed" on the black board was due only to a shortage of letters needed to spell out the word "delayed". Maybe they had used up all the D's or Y's.

Once again, I had to accept that things were done differently in India. Reasons were unnecessary, and the expression "Time is of the essence" was not part of the culture. The woman told me that I should go and speak to another woman behind a different desk. The second woman was severe and harsh, and she had no interest in discussing the inconveniences that some tourist might be experiencing at the airport.

"Take a different flight," she told me, barely looking up.

"There isn't one until Sunday. That's several days from now," I explained.

"Take a flight to Bangalore," she sneered.

"How do I get from Bangalore to Puttaparthi?"

She had no interest in continuing the conversation. That was made very clear by the scowl on her face as she went back to the papers she was shuffling around her desk.

Just then, John came running up, "Let's take a flight to Bangalore!" he said, almost out of breath. He saw the puzzled look on my face. "There's a flight leaving in a couple of hours for Bangalore. Once we get there, it's a few more hours by bus to Puttaparthi."

At that moment I didn't really mind where we went, as long as we didn't spend any more time in Bombay than was absolutely necessary.

We threw our bags onto the ancient x-ray machine, got an orange sticker for having gone through successfully, and made our way over to the ticket counter.

After checking in, we had a two-hour wait for the flight.

We figured that the flight to Puttaparthi had probably been canceled because it wasn't full enough. Only Sai Baba bound devotees use the tiny airport at Puttaparthi, so we thought that perhaps not enough people had bought tickets.

Just then I spotted the Airport Manager coming out of her office. I decided to try to find out the reason for the cancellation.

"It's the earthquake," she said. "They using many planes take supplies to area."

After my shaking-hotel-room experience the night before, I bought the explanation. I thought that it would be a very good use for the plane. John immediately dropped his eyes in what looked like an extreme case of Catholic guilt, as he whispered to me, "Can you believe we were were being so indignant, and they are actually using the plane to save people's lives?"

His guilt didn't last long, though. It disappeared as soon as his eyes moved over to the "Restaurant" sign overhead.

It did seem like a good idea to spend the time eating, because there was absolutely nothing to do or see at Bombay's airport. It was difficult to find a clean place to sit down. I dreaded having to use the toilets after I saw what the rest of the building looked like.

We went downstairs and saw a very similar style buffet to the one the hotel had set up for breakfast. Silver serving dishes were heated over tea-light candles on a long trestle table. The buffet hadn't officially opened for lunch yet, so there were no uniformed men with ladles.

"You know what? I don't think I am going to eat," I said, looking around at what would not pass the sanitary code in many other countries.

The seats were full of people waiting hungrily for the buffet to begin. We found a table to sit down and, after a few minutes, a waiter approached us.

"Are you on flight to Bangalore?" asked the waiter.

We nodded yes.

"Show me your boarding cards," he said.

I thought it a little unusual to have a waiter request boarding cards at a restaurant table, but we pulled them out of our pockets and handed them to him.

He quickly stamped them with a little green stamp and said," You eat free."

With that he walked off.

"Okay. I can do that," John said as we tried to figure out what had just happened.

I still didn't want to eat, although the enticing smell of spicy curries were starting to fill the room. Waiters took up their posts behind the tables. All of a sudden, there must have been some secret message broadcast, because everyone jumped up and ran to stand in line. After a while John joined them. He came back smiling, carrying a heaping plate of lovely vegetarian food. As he started eating, I realized that my attempt at fasting for the week was not going to work. I decided to include airports on my places-where-it-was-probably-okay-to-eat-in-India list. So far, I had five-star hotels and airports on the list.

Encouraged that breakfast hadn't produced any stomach cramps, I walked over to the buffet table and filled a plate of food for myself. I was ready to throw caution to the wind once again.

Δ

A crackling announcement over the intercom let us know that it was time to board the Indian Airlines flight to Bangalore. This was not my favourite part of the trip. I was definitely reluctant to fly with a company that could, for all I knew, have the same maintenance record for their planes that most Indian companies seemed to have for their buses and trains.

I had seen the way hundreds of people were packed into the buses. They were so overloaded with human bodies that they couldn't balance. The result was that buses drove at 45 degree angles, spewing smoke though the windows of those vehicles not fortunate enough to have air conditioning.

Once again it was a relax-and-know-you-are-fine thought process, that kept me happily chatting and laughing during the ninety-minute flight. John made many jokes about the dangers of flying Indian Airlines, pointing periodically to the wings and asking questions like, "Are they supposed to be bouncing up and down like that?" Sometimes he would wonder aloud if the duct tape holding the seats and arm rests together was the same quality tape that was used to hold the plane together. This type of humour is only funny in retrospect.

A German man was sitting at the window of our three seat row. We started conversing with him in pigeon German. After a while, we could understand enough to know that he was a Baba devotee. He told us that Baba was not at the ashram in Puttaparthi. He was at his other ashram in Whitefield, which is only a 45 minute drive from Bangalore.

It all came together then. I knew that "Central Headquarters" (as my friend Vicki calls it) always takes care of the details. This was a perfect example of needing to move with the flow, and getting our egos out of the way. How perfect that they had canceled our flight to Puttaparthi, and that we were sitting next to a devotee who knew that we should stay in Bangalore. If they had not canceled the flight to Puttaparthi, we would have flown there, only to take a long cab ride back to Bangalore.

The lesson was well taken. There is no reason to doubt the perfection of any apparent inconveniences that show up in our day-to-day lives. There is a greater plan, and it reveals itself all the time in small ways.

Δ

Outside the airport in Bangalore, hundreds of taxi drivers stood waiting desperately for business.

"You need taxi? Excuse me, taxi? You need taxi?" were the only words I could make out above the din of the cars and crowds who filled the place.

"Whitefield..." John said to an eager man who had approached us. "How much to the Whitefield ashram?"

On the plane we had decided to go to the ashram in time for darshan and afterwards look for a place to stay, possibly back in Bangalore.

Darshan means seeing or catching sight of a Holy Person. It is the time of day that Sai Baba comes out of his house. He either walks amongst the thousands of people who flock to see him every day, or he stands on the stage in front of them. Darshan is usually at 7 AM and 4 PM. To get a good view, however, it is necessary to line up hours beforehand.

We agreed on a price and jumped into the back of the taxi.

"Isn't this exciting? Imagine, you are about to see Sai Baba for the first time," said John, hardly able to contain his great excitement at once again being in the presence of the Avatar he had traveled thousands of miles to see.

"Yes. I am excited," I said, looking through the window at the scenes outside.

The roads were narrow and only partially paved. There were no sidewalks, only red, dusty earth baking in the sun. There were people everywhere I looked. In addition, there were thousands of street vendors with colourful market stalls set up to display their wares. Chickens, cows, and goats were grazing near the side of the road.

Huts constructed from banana leaves were clustered together, like some sort of Third World condominium complex. Clearly, those tiny "houses" had no plumbing or electricity. There were several rows of them built up against the edge of the road. The dust and diesel particulate which settled on them created a black-stuccoed-paint effect on the outside. Lines of washed clothing hung everywhere. I wondered how the laundry could possibly get clean with all the soot and dust falling on it as it dried under the hot sun. Little children played in the streets with stray dogs and newborn puppies who seemed to appear from everywhere.

Suddenly, the shock-absorber-free car came to a sharp jolting halt. I looked over to see why we had stopped so abruptly. A cow was standing right in the middle of the road. A large tan coloured bull, with horns painted bright orange, stood next to her eating garbage. We waited until they moved on.

I came to learn that only cows are capable of bringing cars to a stop in India. Trucks coming at you on the same side of the road, or buses hurtling towards your little Morris Minor, do nothing to frighten the taxi drivers. But a cow – now that was a different story altogether! Cows are sacred to the Hindus. In India they are not eaten or even contained. They are free to wander the streets at their own slow pace.

"If you have to be a cow, this is the country to be one in," I said to John, thinking of all the horrible cattle ranches in America where unsuspecting animals are bred like potted plants. The babies are pulled from the womb and stuck in metal cages within twenty-four hours, only to be consumed later at all-you-can-eat buffets with the leftovers thrown out like useless candy wrappers. It is such depravity that we humans have descended to that level. How can we still call ourselves a caring, highly evolved society?

I really like that Sai Baba decries the eating of animals. Actually, I am told he has three requirements at the ashram: no meat, no smoking. and no alcohol.

Δ

We arrived at the ashram about an hour later. A high, pink cement wall formed the perimeter of the ashram. It stretched for what would be the equivalent of several city blocks. At the entrance, there were two blue wrought-iron gates. One for men and the other for women. A third gate allowed cars in, but it was seldom opened because cars were not allowed on the ashram grounds without permission. John and I entered our respective gates and met up again on the inside. I saw that hundreds of people were already seated across the cement yard, waiting for Baba to make his entrance.

We hurried into a little white building at the gate, and a sweet-faced old man said that he would watch our bags. I put my passport, camera and money in a small purse which hung around my neck. John hurriedly put on the white punjabi trousers he had brought with him from his last trip to India.

"Why don't you run ahead without me?" I said. "I can't go inside with shorts and a T-shirt, and I don't have a punjabi. It's better if I wait behind,"

"No. You are here, it would be a shame to miss darshan," he said. "I can run across the street to buy you one."

"No, John. That's sweet, but I don't want you to miss darshan because of me, and apparently Baba is about to come out any second."

"I can be quick. Wait here. I'll be right back."

Within seconds, he had run back out the men's gate and was lost in the crowds of peddlers and gerry-rigged market stalls. I stood waiting patiently. I knew there was a whole routine that went along with darshan, but I didn't have a clue what to do or how to do it. I noticed that there were piles of shoes lying against the curbside, so I took off my sandals and left them with the others.

John came running back, somewhat out of breath.

"Here," he said, pushing a plastic bag with white clothes towards me.

I ripped open the bag and found a pair of long white cotton pants with a drawstring top and a matching white, long sleeved shirt. I decided that, in the interest of time, I would slip the punjabi over my clothes. Within a few seconds anyone could have mistaken me for a long term ashram dweller. The shirt came down to the middle of my thighs – overlapping the baggy pants.

Then John handed me a beautiful purple silk shawl with black glyph-like prints on it.

"I bought this for you as well," he said. "Wear it over the whole thing."

I glanced at it as I threw it over my shoulders, admiring his taste in women's clothing. We set off across the cement courtyard towards the open-sided hall where all the activity seemed to be happening.

We separated as we got closer. I remembered that men and women were not allowed to sit on the same side of the room. I had stumbled upon a Mahashivaratri celebration at a huge Hindu temple in London the previous year. Walking in, I found thousands of men and women seated on either side of an aisle which ran down the middle of an enormous, elaborate hall.

Plush red carpeting served as the only form of seating.

There was no such luxury at the ashram, though. Everyone appeared to be seated directly on the black stone floor, with a centre aisle of white stone serving as a divider between the sexes.

I made my way up the few stairs at the back of the hall and had my first experience with "seva dals". Seva means service. Hindu men and women of all ages did service at the ashram. They all wore similar looking saris with triangular scarves tied around their necks. On the back of each scarf was a yellow and orange design of a rising sun spilling its rays in all directions. Three or four seva dals were spread out across the steps, blocking the entry.

"Walk around," they hissed.

I walked in the direction they were pointing, wondering why it was taking so long to get from the front gate into the covered prayer area. Suddenly I was pulled over by yet another seva dal.

"Any bags?" she asked me, whipping out a weird metal object that looked like an ungainly coat hanger. She started frisking me.

"I have this," I announced, taking off my shawl and the punjabi shirt I had spent so much time trying to put on. I was once again dressed in just my T-shirt. Hanging against it was the little money purse.

"Open!" she commanded.

The chances of making it into the hall before Baba were growing slimmer by the minute.

"Camera!" she exclaimed, incredulous that someone would have the nerve to try and sneak one through the metal detector.

"I keep my camera, passport, and money with me all the time," I told her. "I don't want to leave my purse at the gate."

"No camera in darshan!" she stated officiously. "Take

camera to house."

She pointed to the place where our bags were being kept. I knew that the only way past this lady was to relinquish my camera. I wondered how there could be so many photos of Baba everywhere, if cameras were considered a cardinal sin.

"What about money and passport?" I asked.

By the dismissive look she gave me, I assumed that I might get by with those items if I was willing to leave the camera behind.

I ran back across the large courtyard. I handed my camera to the man at the door, hoping that I would see the little camera again; I had purchased it especially for this trip. I turned around and ran back across the courtyard. I was starting to get very hot dressed in so many layers of clothing, albeit it cotton and silk clothing. All the running back and forth under the hot Indian sun was heating me up.

I stood once again under the severe gaze of the seva dal. She opened my purse again to make sure the offending camera had been removed and then made me walk through a rinky-dink metal detector. It was the kind of contraption that they set up at airports, only this was a very primitive version. I passed the inspection and was finally free to enter the sacred space where the sea of bodies was still waiting patiently for Sai Baba to enter.

After being directed by yet another saried seva dal, I found a place to sit at the back of the hall. There was complete silence in the hall, despite the thousands of people seated obediently on the floor. I sat and waited. And waited. Half an hour must have gone by.

A middle-aged woman leaned over and whispered to me in an European accent, "Maybe Baba's not coming today."

"After all this, it would be really nice if he would make an appearance," I thought, but, instead of voicing that, I asked,

"Why wouldn't he be coming?"

"Baba was outside the ashram today. Maybe he got back too late."

We sat some more, and, after about forty-five minutes, someone must have been signaled that Baba would not be doing darshan that day. Everyone stood up and filed out of the hall. I had hoped that I would at least catch a glimpse of him, but it was not to be.

I waited for the hall to empty a little more, and then I joined the crowd moving across the courtyard. I spotted John and made my way over to him.

"We should go and find a place to stay. Do you want to see the ashram accommodation first?" he asked me.

"Okay, I am curious to see what it looks like," I said.

After asking a couple of people for directions, I found the women's sleeping quarters. The rooms were all in a row similar to what you might see at a monastery, and the doors opened onto a courtyard. Inside, the rooms were small, with half a dozen little straw mattresses filling all the space on the cement floor. All around the rooms I noticed little shrines set up with books and photos of Sai Baba. Candles were burning, and the smell of incense wafted through the open windows and doors. It was obvious that none of the rooms had private showers or toilets.

I went back to find John.

"I don't want to sleep here," I said.

"Neither do I. Let's go and find a hotel," he suggested.

We retrieved our bags, completely intact with the camera balanced on top, found our sandals, and headed out the ashram gates into the chaos outside.

"Taxi! Taxi! Yes, please, taxi?" yelled the ever-hopeful drivers, who became particularly excited when darshan was over. That was when business began in earnest.

We looked across the street at the dilapidated buildings behind the frenzied market area. The constant stream of trucks, buses, rickshaws, and taxis was partially obscuring our view. There was nothing inviting about the scene, and we both thought that our best chance of getting a clean room was probably to head back to the city.

"How much to Bangalore?" John asked one of the drivers.

"You come back?" the driver asked.

"No, just one way," John responded.

"250 rupees one way. 400 both way."

I was starting to get the drift of the do-you-want-to-come-back routine. It was something John would have done well to know about his first night on the beach with the horses.

"Are there any hotels around here?" asked John.

"No hotel here. No good quality," came the reply.

"Okay, then why don't you take us to Bangalore. 250 rupees, right?"

"Yes sir," he replied, quickly grabbing our bags and putting them in the boot of his car before we had a chance to change our minds.

We jumped in the back seat and braced ourselves for the treacherous drive back to the city. As the driver was about to get into his seat, John suddenly piped up, "Do you have A/C in the car?"

"No A/C sir," he said. "A/C very expensive."

John turned to me and said, "Should we try to find a taxi with A/C?"

"We're already sitting in here," I answered. It wouldn't be right to get out now. He carried our bags and has spent all this time with us."

"That doesn't matter. It's terrible with the fumes and no A/C," John argued.

"I know, but let's just stay here now. Next time, we can get

A/C. How bad can it be?"

I later regretted having uttered those words, as we sat in Bangalore's rush hour diesel nightmare. Once again, we were asking, "How much longer?" every twenty minutes, only to be told, "Another twenty minutes, sir." I was learning that an hour in India is divided into at least fifteen equal twenty-minute segments.

John was starting to choke on the fumes. In between gasps he blurted out, "This is all your fault."

I wasn't sure which part of India's craziness was my fault, but I suspected it had something to do with not agreeing to change to an air-conditioned car.

Just then we heard the loud sound of a train coming towards us. Our driver came to a quick halt behind dozens of other cars, as the old metal gates fell down across the tracks.

At this junction, the traffic was truly unbelievable. The two lanes had narrowed to one thin path across the tracks, and as far as the eye could see, there were cars in both directions. Each driver seemed to be hoping that he'd be the one to gain dominion over the single-lane path, after the old metal gates would lift. I couldn't imagine how the logistics of the traffic jam would play out, not to mention the simple physics of needing to squeeze so much metal through so little space. We waited, with the diesel spewing though the windows and drivers hooting even though they knew full well that there was no place to go.

Once again John looked over at me and said, "I knew we should have taken an air-conditioned car. Now we're choking to death here all because you didn't want to offend the driver. Do you feel guilty about this?"

I started laughing as I took my long dark brown hair and put it over my mouth and nose, using it as a breathing filter. I didn't want to imagine what my lungs would look like at the end of the trip.

"Actually I don't feel guilty at all," I said. "I would only feel guilty if I had intentionally tried to deprive you of oxygen. I will listen to you in the future, though, and I promise I won't choose a car without A/C again."

Finally, the old caboose passed us by, and the heavy rusty gates started to lift. As I had expected, the first cars on each side of the "road" made a mad dash towards the middle of the tracks, hoping to get jurisdiction over the path. I was fascinated watching the cars lurch back and forth in a game of metallic chicken, each one seeing who would get centre stage first. The car that made it onto the road first started hooting crazily at the oncoming car. The loser declared defeat by reversing out of the way to let the victor squeeze by. Then, the whole maneuver started up again as the next two cars, poised head to head, raced towards each other like two stallions ready to do battle.

I noticed that trucks and buses took priority. Even if they didn't get to the middle line first, they were given a certain respect because of their size. Frankly, as a passenger in the back of a tiny 1970s car, I was extremely grateful for this etiquette.

After at least twenty minutes at that junction, we finally got our turn to go head to head with the oncoming car. I actually don't know how it played out, because I closed my eyes when another taxi started heading towards us with the determination of a general marching towards the front line.

"Tell me when this is over," I said to John, my eyes closed.

John, still protesting my choice in vehicles, had stopped breathing, so I wasn't sure he would ever be able to tell me anything ever again.

A little later, as we swerved through and around sidewalks, pedestrians, and cows, I turned to John.

"You know it's really funny that your mother called Clay, crying and scared that her little Johnny might have been involved in the earthquake. This is what she should be worrying about! Driving through these streets has to be as close to a near-death experience as any earthquake."

"It's a good thing she's not here," laughed John. "Maybe I should write and tell her, 'Ma, there's good news and bad news. The good news is that I survived the earthquake. The bad news is that I'm spending a lot of time in Indian taxi cabs...'"

We laughed about how dangerous the driving was. We would come to see that laughter was key to getting through the day in India. We had to keep our focus on the bigger picture, trusting Spirit all the time.

"Remember that guy you interviewed on your show about near-death experiences? What was his name?" John asked.

"Oh, yeah, you probably mean Raymond Moody," I said.

"Yeah...him. We should write and tell him how we're having near-death experiences every fifteen minutes. He could write a whole book just with this material."

As John said that, the cab hurtled to an abrupt stop once again. We both lurched forward, wishing that seat belts had been mandatory thirty years ago when these cars were manufactured. Once again, my hands flew up in front of my eyes. I had no interest in seeing what had caused the sudden screeching stop. I heard our driver shout angrily out the window.

"You can look," said John.

I saw a young family on a scooter inches from the bonnet of our car. They were headed towards us, having just overtaken a stationary bus on the wrong side of the road. It was literally a whole family riding on one little scooter. The father was driving with his five-year-old son on the handlebars, his wife side-saddled behind him so that she could ride in her long sari, and their little daughter hanging off the back of the scooter. The incredible thing was that none of them were wearing helmets, and they seemed completely unfazed to be meeting a car head-on in the middle of a busy city road.

After some more yelling, we continued on.

"Which hotel you live?" called the driver over the noise of the outside traffic.

"We don't know. Maybe the Atria," said John, remembering a pleasant stay there nine years before. "Do you know a good hotel in Bangalore?"

In the rearview mirror, I caught the driver smiling happily at my question. I knew he must have had something to recommend.

"I show you three hotel. You choose. I wait. You look to room and I wait. Yes?"

"That sounds good," said John.

After what felt like hours more, the driver finally pulled up to a sleazy-looking building on a busy street.

"This hotel very good. Good price. You look. I wait."

"I don't like the feel of this place, John. I don't even want to go in. I can tell we won't want to stay here." I wasn't about to choose a place that would send me back into the it's-your-fault category again.

"You're right," agreed John. Then to the driver he said, "We won't look at this hotel – we don't like it. Can you take us to the next hotel?"

"No, you look first. Good price," came the reply from the front seat.

"We don't want to look," I told him. "We don't want to stay here."

The driver had no interest in what we wanted and what we didn't want. He wanted us to look, and he was driving, so we were going to have to look. He pulled into the underground parking structure, and told us that he would watch our bags while we ran in. Somehow, it didn't feel right to leave our things with a man who appeared to have such an agenda for us.

"Why don't you go and take a look, and I'll wait here with the luggage," suggested John. "We're only doing this so that he'll take us where we really want to go."

"Okay. I'll be quick," I said, running off towards the entrance. I went to the front desk, and asked if they had a room for the night.

"Yes. Madame see room?" replied the man behind the dirty counter.

Before I could explain that I had no real interest in seeing a room, and that I was only asking to see one to appease a crazy taxi driver, I found myself in the lift with a young man who was carrying the keys to the room.

"This way," he said, leading me down a corridor that had not seen paint or breathed fresh air in decades.

Just then I heard John calling my name. I turned around and saw him coming towards me from the elevator.

"What about our stuff?" I asked, wondering what he was doing there.

"He insisted I come in. He needs me to look, too. We agreed that he'd lock the car and come in with me."

I started laughing as I thought about how we were allowing this taxi driver to manipulate us like marionettes. We arrived at the room. With little ceremony, the bell hop opened the door. I thought I would gag from the smell of stale cigarettes, must, and who knows what else.

"Thank you. We've seen the room. Now we can go back downstairs," I said, not venturing further than the threshold.

"You like?" he asked optimistically.

"No I don't like," I said. "But thanks for showing us anyway."

"Good price," he said.

"We aren't interested," said John.

"How much you want pay?" he continued, ignoring our

obvious displeasure with the room.

"Nothing," I said. "We don't want the room at any price. It doesn't smell good."

"Oh!" he said excitedly. "I show you different room."

I realized my mistake immediately. I had given him something to counteroffer. A definite no-no in any sales situation, but especially in the land of merchants and bargaining.

"No, thank you. We don't want a different room. We are not staying here," I said emphatically.

"Good price. How much you pay?" he called one last time as the lift doors closed behind us, giving us a temporary respite from the sales pressure. The respite only lasted a few seconds though, because, waiting at the lift's door in the lobby was our taxi driver.

"You like?" he asked hopefully.

"No. We want to leave," John said.

"Good price," he said, walking after us.

"You know, I might be really tired and a little slower than usual," I said to John, "but this really seems like a big set-up. I don't like how he's pressuring us to stay here. Does he get kickbacks?"

"Of course he does. That's what this is all about," said John.

"Okay. Let's just tell him that we don't want to see his other hotels. Let's go to the one you know is good," I suggested.

Easier said than done. John passed my message along to the driver, who responded by assuring us that we would definitely like his next choice in hotels.

"I'm sure they are very nice, but we're tired, and we want to go to the Atria. Okay?" I said, not interested in his games anymore.

It was hard to believe that it was still the same day that had begun with Pakua up in my Mumbai hotel room. It was already dark as we drove by the next of the recommended hotels.

The driver pointed to a shabby building from the road, and said, "This one very good hotel. Very nice price."

"No," said John. "Please take us to the hotel we asked for. We're not looking at any more of your hotels."

"Atria very expensive. This hotel very nice price," he insisted.

"We don't care how much it costs," said John. "Just take us there, please."

There was no point in trying to find a different cab because it was dark, we had no idea where we were, and our bags were locked in the boot. Also, there was no guarantee that the next guy who'd pick us up wouldn't also insist that we take a tour of his favourite hotels.

Finally, and much to our relief, we pulled into a driveway surrounded by lovely gardens set back from the street. I saw the sign "Atria" above the large glass doors. Uniformed porters stood on the steps, waiting to help weary travelers.

"I like this place," I told John. "Let's stay here. I'll see if we can get a room."

Before I could even get up the front stairs, John called me back.

"Let's tell him we are going to stay here whether or not there are rooms," he said. "If there aren't any rooms, we can get a different cab to take us somewhere else. Let's just pay him and get him to leave."

That sounded like a brilliant idea to my very tired brain, so we went to the driver's window and asked him to open the boot.

"You stay here?" he asked, trying to hide his disappointment.

"Yes, we're staying here. Can we please have our bags out the back?"

"Maybe no rooms," said the driver, who was in no hurry to

return our bags.

"We are staying here," said John emphatically. "Please open the back so we can get our bags out."

The driver slowly moved to the back of the car, and asked, "You come back to Whitefield tomorrow?"

"Yes. But we'll get a taxi from the hotel. Please open the back," answered John.

"I come back get you tomorrow morning," the driver said.

"No. We will get a cab from the hotel. Here, let me pay you the 250 rupees so that you can go," said John.

"No 250 rupees," said the driver. "400 rupees."

"You said 250 one way. 400 is there and back," John quickly reminded him.

"One way and return same price," said the driver.

"You told us 250 rupees. Why are you now putting up the price? That's not right," I said.

"400 rupees, and I pick you up tomorrow morning at hotel."

"No. We aren't going to get back in your cab tomorrow. Please open the back and give us our luggage."

"400 rupees!" he insisted stubbornly.

John started to get angry. I wondered how we were ever going to retrieve our luggage, and get the man to accept the price he had quoted us. We stood there, on the steps of the hotel, and burst into laughter once again. We recognized that we were arguing about five dollars, but it didn't seem right to be held ransom by the taxi driver.

"Look! Just give us our bags, okay? We want to check into the hotel," said John, after we had collected ourselves.

The laughter must have energetically cleared the air, because the driver opened the boot, and John quickly pulled out all our bags. I went into the lobby, leaving John to sort out the taxi fare. I made my way to the front desk.

"We need a room for four nights. Do you have anything?" I

asked the man behind the reception desk.

"Hmmm. We are quite full. Definitely no rooms from tomorrow. Just for tonight we can give you a room." His English was very good and easy to understand.

I was excited at the prospect of checking into a clean hotel, having a hot shower, and getting some sleep. I didn't care if they were full the following day. I only cared that I wouldn't have to get back into a decrepit taxi, and drive around for hours breathing more diesel fumes.

"Okay," I said. "I'll take the room for tonight."

The man glanced over to a different desk across the lobby. Seated behind that little desk was a man who looked like an FBI agent. He was sitting there, making ever such slight gestures with his head and hands.

"Uhm, one moment. I check to see if we have rooms free for tonight," he said, picking up a telephone.

"I thought you just said you have a room for tonight only," I said, confused at the apparent change of heart.

"I need to check," he said.

As he spoke into the mouthpiece, I saw that the FBI agent was also on the phone, looking over in our direction.

John walked over to me with a "well???" look on his face. I explained what was going on.

"Sorry, we have no rooms," said the young man, hanging up the phone.

Just then, I spotted the dreaded taxi driver entering the hotel.

"What is he doing here, John? Didn't you pay him?" I asked.

"Yes. I gave him 300 rupees. I don't know what he's doing in here."

"Sorry, we have no rooms tonight," repeated the receptionist.

"Wait a minute," whispered John. "Let me get rid of that guy. I don't like his energy. I'm sure they have one room free. Just wait here." He headed off towards the driver.

After standing at the desk for a while longer, I walked over to where John was begging the driver to leave us alone. I heard him insisting again, "We do not want to ride with you. I gave you more money than you quoted us, so please leave. We'll find our own taxi tomorrow. Leave us alone."

None of it deterred the driver, who refused leave. He insisted on taking us to a different hotel and picking us up in the morning. He also demanded the full return fare of 400 rupees.

John headed for the exit, knowing that the man would follow him out. He didn't want to make more of a scene than we'd already made, given that we very much wanted a room.

I looked around the lobby and noticed that everyone was dressed in business suits or evening dresses. I suddenly realized that I was still in my T-shirt and shorts, overlaid with the punjabi and silk shawl. I stood against the wall keeping an eye on our luggage which was in a heap near the front door. I tried to visualize a room with a shower and clean sheets. I could see John out of the corner of my eye, trying desperately to shake the incredibly pesky man off his back. I knew that, after this whole episode, John would really want me to feel guilty that I didn't jump out of the taxi back at the ashram, while we still had the chance.

Just then an Indian man in his late forties, who was squeezed into his business suit, walked over to me. "What's the problem?" he asked.

"I need a room but the hotel seems to be full," I said.

"Where you come from?" he asked.

"Sai Baba's ashram."

He looked me over a couple of times and asked, "Where you live?"

"America," I answered.

"You been India before?"

"No. This is my first time. We just got to Bangalore today, but it seems the hotel is full," I answered.

"Wait here. I help you get room," he said, with far too bright a sparkle in his eye. He walked over to the desk where the FBI look-alike was seated. I watched him talk briefly with the the man who'd vetoed our initial attempt at securing a room.

He came back to me, sporting a wide grin. "I can get you a room."

I wondered what exactly the quid pro quo was for that little favour, but I knew that once John and I were settled in the room we'd be fine.

"Really? Thank you. Do you work here?" I asked.

"No. We have a big convention here," he said, pointing to a few other executives hanging around the lobby. He told me that they were all there on business. I assumed that that was how he was able to pull rank.

John returned after a few minutes without the driver.

"Guess what?" I said. "This man can get us a room."

When my new best friend saw John, however, the look on his face told me that my prospects of getting the coveted room had faded.

"Just a minute. I check again," he said walking back towards the FBI agent at the desk.

I quickly told John what was going on. He said that he thought we were finally rid of the taxi driver, at least until the morning.

The businessman returned, shaking his head regretfully. "They really are full – no more rooms. Sorry. Go and ask at reception. He will call a different hotel for you."

And our friendship was over faster than it had begun.

John felt sure that the interaction with our taxi friend was the reason the FBI agent had vetoed the availability of the room. I thought it also had something to do with our bedraggled appearance. I knew, however, that had John shown up a few minutes later, my businessman friend would certainly have secured a room for me. After that, it would have been hard for management to claim the room didn't exist.

"Let's go and ask the receptionist to call for us," I said. "They must have a competitor in town that they hate enough to recommend us for the night."

They did.

The man at reception made a call and found us a room. It seemed that there was some kind of large convention in town. It was also "The Auspicious Days".

The Auspicious Days are certain days in the year that are considered to be lucky for getting married. Many people consult with a Vedic astrologer before planning any sort of ceremony. That may have explained the shortage of rooms in Bangalore.

We asked the receptionist to get us a hotel taxi to avoid being accosted by our last driver, who was most probably lurking behind the bushes in the hopes that we would need his services again.

Δ

We arrived at the Chancery Hotel. It was not quite as plush as the Atria, but it appeared to be very nice and clean.

We checked in at the front desk. The porters brought in our luggage from the taxi and led us to our room. I immediately went to wash my hands and face in the bathroom. When I came out, John was staring uncomfortably around the room.

"Don't you think we should get a room with two beds?" he asked, looking at the double bed in the middle of the room.

"Yes," I answered, "let's call the front desk and ask if they have any rooms with two singles."

John called reception. Before he hung up, there was a knock on the door. Two men were waiting outside to help facilitate the move to our new room. Room 309.

I apologized for having used the towels in the first room, but the smiling porters assured me that it wasn't a problem.

The phone rang as I was about to step into the shower.

"Is this room good for you?" asked a pleasant voice.

"Yes, thank you. This room is perfect," I said.

After my nice, hot shower, I collapsed on the bed. It had been so many weeks since I had slept more than four consecutive hours, but I was buzzing and didn't feel very tired. John wanted to shower, but there wasn't a second towel. So he dialed the front desk and asked if they would send one up. Minutes later there was a knock on the door. A young man handed me two clean towels. I thanked him, and he left.

A few minutes later there was another knock on the door.

"Do you get towels, Madame?" asked a different porter.

"Yes, thank you. Someone already brought them," I answered.

While John was in the shower, I called the front desk to find out if they had e-mail services available. I thought it would be nice to send my husband, Clay, and my daughters an e-mail. I wanted to let them know that I had made it safely to India, and that we were not going to be in Puttaparthi after all.

There was another knock on the door. I opened it and found a smiling porter holding up a five-litre bottle of water. It was apparently my water bottle, but it was hardly recognizable because it had been tightly wrapped in silver duct tape.

"Oh thank you! I forgot that," I said.

"It broken on lobby floor. Water fall out. I fixing it," he said, smiling proudly.

I thanked him again and went downstairs. I found a plush lounge with a computer sitting impressively on a shiny desk.

"What a contrast to Whitefield," I thought.

John and I agreed that it was worth paying the extra money to stay in a place that had hot running water, clean sheets and no apparent infestations.

I sat down and wrote a long letter to Clay, describing our adventures thus far. I enjoyed recalling the details of the past twenty-four hours. It seemed more like a month had gone by than a day.

After writing for almost an hour, I pressed "send". Nothing happened. I heard the modem dialing up, but nothing seemed to be happening. I pressed "send" again and waited some more. Still nothing happened.

I found a button on the hard drive and pushed it. That button did nothing either, so I decided to print the letter on the snappy looking printer sitting adjacent to the computer. I dug out some old paper from the desk drawer and pressed "print". The printer groaned for a while and looked as though it might do something useful. Then, with a strange whining sound, the whole system shut down!

Just like that, I had managed to erase my entire letter. An hour's worth of prose disappeared into cyberspace with the push of a single button. I knew, though, that it was not meant to be. Rather than attempt the whole thing again, I went back to the room.

"This is particularly irritating because I wrote such a long letter which was filled with so much detail," I told John.

"What do you mean 'so much detail'?" asked John.

"Well, I told Clay about the earthquake tremors last night, about Punji's reading, about the massage, and the near-death experiences in the taxi cabs."

"You did? Why did you do that?" asked John incredulously.

"Why not? It's funny," I answered.

"I know it is, but it won't be that funny for your husband to read about it from five thousand miles away."

"Oh, he won't care. As long as I'm alive to tell him about it, he'll see the humour in it. Besides, I didn't actually let Pakua do his 'breast tonement'."

"You're too much!" said John laughing. "The last thing Clay said to me on the phone when I called him yesterday morning was, 'Take good care of my girl!' Now you're blowing it by talking about earthquakes, crazy taxi drivers, and breast massages. I am supposed to be protecting you! Clay's going to wonder how someone could fail so miserably in their task in less than twenty-four hours."

We started laughing at how funny it would be to get a letter like that, without any context of the feel, taste, smell, and energy of India.

"Some e-mails are better left unsent," said John. "Besides, what if my mother calls Clay again and asks how her Johnny is doing? What would he say?"

"The poor woman," I said. "She'd probably fly out here immediately and take you home."

"You know," said John, still laughing at how revealing my letter was, "the Universe always takes care of the details."

"Well, I'm not irritated anymore. I know that for some reason it wasn't supposed to send."

We realized that it was already after 9 PM. Although I hadn't eaten since the buffet at Mumbai's airport, I didn't feel particularly hungry. John wanted some ice cream.

"Do you know what Sai Baba calls ice cream?" he asked as he looked over the menu.

"No," I said.

"Frozen love. Isn't that a great description?"

John liked the pistachio, the mango, and the strawberry. He couldn't decide which one to get, so he rang the front desk and ordered one bowl with three small scoops.

"They must know Room 309 by now," he said, laughing at how often we had already called the front desk.

While we were waiting for the ice cream to arrive, I took out the lettuce and tomatoes I'd bought two days prior in Australia. I knew that I wouldn't buy fresh produce in India, so I brought along salad fixings to prevent an attack of scurvy. There were no bowls or plates, so I emptied the water out of a pitcher that had been sitting out ever since I arrived; it was the closest thing to crockery that I could find. The prewashed vegetables from Perth and the plastic cutlery at the bottom of my bag (with kind regards from a restaurant in Singapore) created a feast fit for a king.

There was a knock on the door. A waiter arrived, carrying a huge tray laden with glass bowls, serviettes, and silverware.

"I thought you ordered three scoops of ice cream. What's all this?" I asked, watching the waiter skillfully flip the huge round tray onto the coffee table.

"I did," said John, also surprised by the volume of paraphanalia and food on the tray.

They must have thought John was ordering three scoops of three different ice creams. Given that the serving sizes were generous to begin with, there were mounds of different coloured scoops.

"Lots of frozen love in this room," I said. "Baba would be pleased with you."

John began eating in earnest. I declined his offer to taste the various flavours.

The phone rang. I picked up, and the voice at the other end

asked, "Did you get ice cream?"

"Yes, thank you. We got it."

It felt so good to be in a comfortable, clean room. Having showered and eaten, I was looking forward to a good night's sleep, even though we needed to wake up at four o' clock for darshan.

There was another knock on the door. The waiter reappeared to collect the tray. He gathered up the empty bowls and left.

"Maybe we should order the taxi tonight," suggested John. "Given how early we are leaving for the ashram, it might be difficult to find one. Besides, it's better if the hotel organizes it so that we don't get stuck with the type of guy who held us hostage today."

"Okay. I'll call up and ask them to book it," I said, happy to defer to any suggestions John made about taxis.

I dialed the front desk.

"Can we get a cab for 5 AM, please? This is Room 309."

They assured me that a cab would be waiting but suggested that 4:30 might be better.

"I think 5 is fine," I said, noticing how late it was already. I hung up.

"We should ask for a wake-up call," said John, picking up the receiver.

"Hello. This is Room 309. Could we please get a 4:30 wake up call?"

Just then there was a knock on the door.

A hotel worker walked in and asked, "Is air condition work now? We change control for whole hotel so cool you better."

"Thank you very much," I said, having already forgotten about our earlier request to fix the A/C in our room.

He looked around for a few moments and left. The room-service thing was starting to seem like a gag from a Marx

Brothers movie.

"You know, with all the traffic, and given how unreliable the taxis are, maybe we should ask for a 4:30 cab," said John.

"You call, John. I'm not calling them again!" I said.

John picked up the phone. I couldn't stop laughing as I heard the familiar, "Hello, sorry to bother you again, but could we change our taxi to 4:30 AM instead of 5 AM?"

After he hung up, I realized that we would have to call back! With a 4:30 cab arrival time, we needed a four o'clock wake-up call. We had to change the wake-up call, and I knew it was my turn!

By then, we were laughing so hard that I could hardly dial the number to the front desk. I felt like a child who needed to keep calling someone just to experience the wonderment of using a telephone for the first time.

"Hello...," I tried to stop myself from laughing, "this is Room 309..."

"We know which room you are!" said the unamused voice on the other end.

Something about the way he said it struck me as so funny that I couldn't speak anymore. I pictured them sitting at the front desk, fists banging the table, screaming, "Why did we ever agree to let them in here? We should have known better once the Atria recommended them!"

John took the phone from me. Although he was laughing, too, he was able to control it long enough to sputter, "We need a 4 AM wake up call please, not 4:30. Thank you. Sorry about all this." And he hung up.

"They might ask us to leave if we call again," I said.

I went to brush my teeth in preparation for going to sleep. The bottle of spring water was sitting next to our toothbrushes as a reminder that we needed to brush with filtered water only. (From my trip to Mexico the previous year, I knew not to brush my teeth with tap water.) I finished brushing and, for some reason, I rinsed my mouth out with the tap water. The bottle glared at me. No sooner had I finished rinsing than I realized my mistake.

"Oh no!" I said, hurrying back into the room. "John, you won't believe what I just did. I rinsed my mouth with tap water!"

"Probably not a good move," said John, stating the obvious.

"I know that. What should I do?" I asked.

"Wait," said John.

I decided not to ask, "Wait for what?" I already knew the answer. Instead, I put my energy towards feeling healthy and imagining myself waking up feeling fine the next morning.

"It's deceiving being in a clean hotel. Because you feel like you're in a Western country, you aren't as cautious. If we stayed in those places that we passed along the way, I wouldn't have forgotten that the water was recycled sewage," I said, realizing how ironic it was that the cleanliness had proven a disadvantage.

Just before getting into bed, I thought that I would refrigerate the remainder of the tomatoes. I opened what looked like a refrigerator door, and a big brown blanket fell out at my feet. I looked over and saw that the blanket was missing from my bed.

"What's my bedding doing in the refrigerator?" I asked John, knowing that there had to be a service-related answer to my question.

I was right.

"Well, the guy who checks on the guy who came to check on the air conditioner arrived after you went down to use the e-mail. After he fiddled around with the system for a while, he noticed that your blankets were still on your bed. He must have thought that it was his duty to rearrange the bedding, so he pulled your blanket off and stuffed it in that cupboard that looks like a refrigerator."

I remade the bed and pulled my pillow out my bag. I snuggled my head into it and fell asleep wondering if my dreams could possibly be any more surreal than my awake state.

February 1

f

Both of us were already awake when the phone rang at 4 AM. It was still dark, and there seemed to be little movement outside as the city slept.

We were downstairs by 4:30, dressed in our punjabis. We waited on the steps outside the hotel. A uniformed night-watchman came over to where we sat.

"Is better inside wait," he said.

"We can wait here," I said. "The taxi will be here soon."

"Better inside wait," he repeated, opening the door to emphasize his point.

I couldn't tell if there was a reason why it was better to "inside wait," or if he was just bored from standing there all night with no one to talk to. Telling us to move gave him a purpose for being in a starched uniform outside a hotel lobby at four-thirty in the morning. So we moved inside and waited for our cab driver.

By 4:45 there was still no sign of the taxi. I walked over to the front desk. I had tried to be invisible until then because I knew that they knew we were Room 309. An early morning encounter with us might have proven too much for the desk clerk, who had been awake all night minding the reception.

Finally, John and I walked over together.

"We are from Room 309," I stated bravely, knowing that the introduction was totally unnecessary.

Without so much as a glimpse in our direction, the man said, " I know who you are."

"We ordered a cab for 4:30. Do you know when he's coming?" I asked, ignoring his irritation.

Still he didn't look up from the magazine he was reading.

"He come soon. I call wake him up."

"Wake him up?" asked John, "Where is he sleeping?"

"He's asleep," he repeated, still not making eye contact with the denizens of Room 309.

Later we would learn that it was common practice for taxi drivers to sleep in their cars. In fact, we would also learn that most shopkeepers, porters, petrol station attendants, and a host of other workers all spent their nights on straw mats on the floors of their workplaces.

"Well, could you let him know that we were supposed to have been picked up fifteen minutes ago? We would like to get to Whitefield in time for darshan," I said.

As I was walking away, the previous night's memory of brushing my teeth with tap water came to mind. I couldn't resist. I needed to ask the receptionist another question, even though he had no interest in further communication.

"Excuse me," I ventured, "is it okay to use the tap water for brushing teeth?"

"We filter all hotel water," he said, without looking up.

I was relieved that I had made that mistake in a five-star hotel.

We went back to wait at the door.

After ten minutes there was still no sign of the driver or the cab. We decided to go back outside and wait. Once again, the guard told us how much better it was to wait inside.

"Could you call us a cab, please?" I asked. "Our cab driver is asleep somewhere in the city, and we need to get to Whitefield."

He walked off, pleased to have something to fill the time. He reappeared after a few minutes, proudly telling us that the driver had indeed been asleep in his cab in the underground parking garage but that he was now awake and would be with us shortly.

Fifteen minutes later, a bleary eyed man pulled up in a small white car. We jumped in the back and told him where we wanted to go. He looked disheveled and not particularly happy to be awake at that time of night.

Despite the early hour, the roads were starting to come alive. It was a bit unnerving that the driver didn't turn the headlights on. There were cars, buses, trucks, and scooters heading towards us in our lane, yet no one, except for a few drivers, was using his headlights.

There were no streetlights either, so it was even more risky driving in the dark than in the day.

"Should we ask him to put on his lights?" I asked John. "Why do you think they drive at night without any lights?"

"They try to conserve every ounce of fuel. That's also why they charge us extra for a car with A/C," he explained.

"I hadn't really thought about headlights using extra fuel. I thought they ran off the battery. I know A/C uses extra petrol, but I didn't realize headlights do too," I said.

It's incredible to be in a country with a population of close to a billion people, where they drive around like maniacs in the dark just to save the extra few pennies it would take to illuminate their way. It made me think about the quantity of food, fuel, and other natural resources that we waste on any given day in the Western World.

"I do think headlights are in a unique must-have category, though," I said, not at all pleased with this particular driving custom.

Just then the driver abruptly pulled into a dark, vacant lot. He drove to the back of the lot and, turning to face us, said," You give money now."

"Do you think he's taken offense at my request to turn the headlights on?" I whispered to John.

I imagined a scene that would fit perfectly into a Seinfeld episode. Something in the same vein as the "Soup Nazi". Our driver would pull open our car door and yell, "You! Spoilt American tourists! Out! No ride for Room 309. Out!"

I wasn't sure what to do, when suddenly a young boy appeared out of nowhere and stood at the driver's window. I looked out again and saw something that vaguely resembled a petrol pump standing all alone in the dark. The young boy took orders from the driver and started filling the tank. Relieved that that was the reason for our diversion, we happily handed the driver the fare.

I found out that, in India, cab drivers often wait until their customers are in the car before they buy petrol. Then, they only put in the barest minimum necessary to get to their destination.

"Do you think he'll turn on the lights now that he has some petrol in the tank?" I asked optimistically.

As we headed back into the night, I realized that there was no chance of that happening. "Headlights! Who needs them anyway?" I thought, surrendering to the flow once more.

Bouncing around in the back seat, over pot holes and around cows, John squinted at his watch in the dark. "Can you believe it's over an hour since we arrived in the lobby this morning, and we're only a couple of kilometres from the hotel?" he said.

"This cab routine is becoming a little too familiar.

Maybe we should try to find a place to stay nearer the ashram to avoid this craziness," I said, wondering if we would get to darshan on time.

Δ

The familiar pink walls of the ashram appeared in front of us. We jumped out of the cab.

"You come back?" asked the driver.

"No. This is just one way. Thank you," said John.

"You come back?" he asked again.

"No. We're not coming back. We're staying here until this evening," I told him.

"I wait here," he said, getting back into the cab.

"No. We'll find our own way back to the hotel. You can leave, " I repeated.

I marveled at the selective lapse in understanding that overcame taxi drivers when they weren't hearing the words they desperately wanted to hear.

We filed through our respective gates. The scene which lay before me was entirely different from the afternoon before. The courtyard which I had been running across in the previous day's heat was filled with thousands of people sitting in neat rows on the cement ground. It was still dark and, considering the number of people filling the place, really quite silent.

"Go over to the women's side," said John. "You need to line up. The seva dals will tell you when you can go into the main hall. I will look for you around this area after darshan."

He gave me a quick hug and said, "Enjoy your first darshan!" and he disappeared into the throng of men who were sitting patiently in their rows.

I took off my sandals as I had done the day before and left them at the curb. I made my way over to the women's area and sat at the back of a long line.

Within minutes, a seva dal approached me saying, "Sai Ram. Please. Sai Ram. Please."

I had no idea what she wanted. I hadn't brought my camera with me, so it couldn't be that.

"What do you want me to do?" I asked her.

"Sai Ram. That line!" she said, pointing towards a shorter line at the edge of the courtyard.

I stood up and went to sit in that line. I looked around me at the sea of women. Everyone was dressed in either a bright sari or a punjabi with a silk shawl like mine. There were many Hindu women of all ages. The older ones were all dressed in lovely, brightly coloured saris.

I noticed that there were hundreds of Western women as well. Most of them had on some sort of ribbon or scarf embroidered with the name of their country. It was fascinating to see such a diverse group of people, representing almost every country in the world, sitting on a cement floor in the middle of the night somewhere in India. Almost everyone was seated on a cushion, with or without a vinyl back support. I made a mental note to bring myself a pillow for the next darshan. The hard cold cement was already becoming uncomfortable, and I had only been sitting there for twenty minutes.

I also noticed various activities were occupying the waiting crowd. Some women were reading books about Sai Baba, while others were writing something over and over again in little journals. Still others were sitting with their eyes closed in deep meditation, and there were those who were repeating some sort of mantra over and over again under their breath. A lot of women were just chatting with the people around them. I watched all of it, intrigued by the whole scene. The row behind me quickly filled up. Very efficiently, the seva dals moved the latecomers into a new line next to me.

All I could hear coming from them was, "Sai Ram. Please Madame. Sai Ram. Sai Ram," as they directed the sea of bodies with a no-nonsense air. They were extremely busy and definitely very aware of everything that was happening around them. Each row had its own seva overseer, and the rest of the seva dals lined the perimeter of the crowd.

The women who had filled the row to my left each wore a white scarf embroidered with the word "Argentina". There were still empty spaces in their row, so the seva dals quickly directed women of other nationalities to fill that row.

Two women sat down. One was a lovely young woman with the word "Peru" sewn onto her red scarf. In front of her sat a fellow landsman, who looked to be in her seventies. No sooner had they sat down than the leader of the Argentinean group walked over to her and said something in Spanish.

The Peruvian answered her but clearly not to the Argentinean's satisfaction, because the Argentinean's voice got louder and louder. Then she went towards the next few people who were seated in the line and started shouting at them, too.

One of the women looked up and said in a British accent, "I don't understand what you're saying."

The Argentinean said in broken English, "You no sit here. This line Argentina only."

The Brit looked up and calmly stated, "We were told to sit here."

"No! No sit here. Argentina only this line."

The Brits ignored her, not at all interested in the discrimination.

The Argentinean became quite irate. She kept moving between the Peruvians and the Brits telling them the same thing over and over. Getting louder each time, she finally shouted,

"Argentina only! Argentina only this line!"

Finally, a seva dal came over to inspect the noisy situation.

The Brits and the Peruvians explained to the Indian that the Argentinean didn't want them to sit there. I wondered if this was the type of incident that could begin a world war. Almost every country was represented somewhere in the courtyard.

The seva dal decided that the British and the Peruvians could remain in their seats, a decision which infuriated the Argentinean.

I knew that the Argentinean hoped to be in a row which would secure her an interview with Baba. Getting an interview is the greatest prize any devotee could hope for. I also knew that, if Baba does select someone from a group, only those wearing the identifying scarf of that group would be allowed in. So I couldn't understand why she wanted the British and the Peruvians to leave her row.

Finally, the young Peruvian turned to me and said in very good English, "Do you mind if we squeeze into your row? I am here with this seventy-five-year-old woman. She's having a difficult enough time sitting on the ground. We don't want to be involved in this."

"Yes, of course you can," I said to her, not at all sure where exactly they would fit.

The rows were so tight that we were almost sitting on the laps of both the people in front of and behind us. There was no wriggle room whatsoever, but I understood that she didn't want to be seated in a spot where she wasn't wanted. So, much to the dismay of the two women surrounding me, I let the Peruvians squeeze into our line.

"Gracias. Muchas gracias," said the older woman appreciatively, as she tried to get her aging body back onto the hard ground.

"My name is Kathy," said the young Peruvian, introducing

herself. "This is my friend Chilita. Thank you for letting us in. I really don't understand why that woman is being so rude."

"It makes you wonder where God is in this experience. If people are here to be at peace and to have a direct experience of God, why is this kind of rudeness going on?" I said, referring not only to the Argentinean woman, but also to the seva dals and the many people I had watched pushing and elbowing to get a better seat.

"I have been here for eight weeks this time," Kathy said. "This is our third visit to India. There are some people like that here. Even some who live at the ashram. In fact, that Argentinean woman is living at the ashram now."

"What does Baba say about this?" I asked.

"Someone once asked Baba why those types of people are here. He said that they need to be here, because nobody on the outside loves them. Swami is so sweet. He loves everybody. He also loves those who find no other love," said Kathy, her eyes tearing from the love and kindness she felt from being in Baba's presence.

I wondered what motivated people to be here. Why do millions of people fly across the globe, leaving the comforts of their homes? They sleep on straw mattresses on concrete floors, with as many as six strangers in a cell-like room. They line up for hours on end in the dark every morning, and again in the heat of the afternoon sun. All of this simply to be in the presence of a seventy-five-year-old man, who is about five feet tall, weighs 108 pounds, and shows himself for ten minutes to an hour, twice a day.

It's incredible. He doesn't advertise, and he tells people that they can't live in the ashram permanently. He sends them back into the world, telling them to follow their own individual religion, whatever it is.

He talks about there being as many paths to God as there

are people on the earth. So how is it that this little man, who claims to be a human manifestation of God, can attract that type of a crowd every single day of the year?

I remembered how a friend of mine had compared Sai Baba's approach with the methods of Alcoholics Anonymous.

"In both instances," she'd said, "no advertising of any kind exists. They both draw people in by attraction, not by promotion."

I recognized the obvious power of the concept of attraction rather than promotion in everything that we do. If something is our absolute truth, and we speak it from our Soul, it will naturally draw in those people who resonate with the vibration of the message. It will draw in those people who resonate with that higher vibration of truth.

If, however, our motivation comes from our egos, we can easily become attached to external pleasures like making money, selling a particular product, getting on a best-seller list, recording a platinum hit, getting married, or whatever it is our egos tell us we *need*. When this happens, we cannot resonate with our highest vibration of Soul truth.

I thought about the analogy of music. If you're in a room filled with guitars and you pluck the G-string, every other guitar in that room will resonate with that G-string frequency. They will each begin to sound the same note, with no one playing them or even touching them. The other guitars involuntarily resonate with the same beautiful note that they heard coming from the lead guitar.

That is why an Avatar, or any human who is on his Soul path, is able to attract thousands of others to come and join him in sharing the beauty, the fullness, the love, and the resonance of his truth.

The only reason any of us need to sit at the feet of a Guru, an Avatar, a holy person, or any teacher is that, when we look into the eyes of that person and are in his or her presence, we see our own Divinity reflected back to ourselves. We see a reflection of the highest expression of our Self. It is like a divine mirror into which we can gaze. If we choose to be open and receptive, we will begin to resonate in harmony with that chord which has been struck by someone who is already expressing his Divinity.

"This is the G-string theory," I thought to myself as I sat and watched the brilliant orange sun rise over the pink and blue buildings of the ashram.

Δ

All of a sudden, a line of women stood up.

"What's going on?" I asked Kathy.

"Their line has been picked first. It's random. Each day the order is different. That's why it really doesn't matter where you sit."

I watched the women move forward. They were ecstatic at being the first line called. Being the first line to get inside the hall meant that they would almost be able to touch Baba as he made his way, barefoot, down the deep red carpet that is laid out for him each day.

Everyone filed through the metal detectors and submitted to a frisking. Getting seated in the hall was a long, slow process. The excitement began to mount as lines were called one after the other. The seva dals worked diligently to stop people from sneaking out of their original line and into the line that was being called. The shouts of "Sai Ram, please, Sai Ram, you not in that line. Sai Ram!" filled the morning silence, as saried seva dals ran after perpetrators. As far as I could tell, nobody ever got away with it, no matter how many times they tried.

Finally, with about eight lines left to call, my line was told to stand up. I couldn't help noticing that we were called before the "Argentina only" line.

Once we were past the metal detector, mayhem ruled as the women around me broke rank and ran into the hall, trying to get a seat on the aisle. An aisle seat, even at the back, seemed to be the next-most-coveted location once all the front row seats were taken.

The running and pushing to secure an aisle seat led me to believe that Baba must walk all the way down the aisle to the back of the hall. I wasn't at all interested in getting involved in the mania.

"If Baba is an omnipotent, omniscient, omnipresent Being," I thought to myself, "then he knows that I'm in this hall right now. If he wants to speak to me, he will find me. If he doesn't know that I'm in the hall without me sitting right at his feet, then it isn't worth flying halfway around the world to see him in the first place."

So I chose a spot near the back, trying to avoid sitting behind the pillars which blocked all views of the throne-like seat that was set up on the stage. It was a long way to the front of the huge hall, but I could see larger-than-life colour photos of Baba hanging on the back wall of the stage. White handkerchiefs were lying neatly folded over the arms of the red velvet chair. There were thousands of little crystals (the kind that you find on chandeliers) all around the perimeter of the stage's ceiling. Bulbs lit up the crystals which shone brightly, waiting expectantly to shine their light on the man everyone was waiting to see.

We waited silently while the rest of the people filed into the hall. I couldn't believe how tightly we were all packed together. Women continued to busy themselves with the same activities as they had outside. I sat quietly watching, having no idea how it all worked and wondering what it would be like once Baba arrived.

After about half an hour of waiting, a sudden rush of energy filled the room. Nothing apparent had happened, but everyone was craning their necks to see something. It was as though an electrical current was surging through the room and everyone was plugged in.

"Swami! Swami's coming!" people whispered excitedly.

The mantras got more intense, and people started scribbling on their pages at a frantic pace. From somewhere, music started. At first it was only instrumental; then later vocals were added. Everyone in the room started singing along. I looked in the direction most heads were turned, and, in the distance, walking through a pair of huge wrought-iron gates, I caught a glimpse of Sri Sathya Sai Baba.

I smiled as he made his way towards us. "This is it," I thought. "This is the moment everyone talks about. Darshan with Baba in 3D and colour – walking towards us."

As he reached the top side entrance to the hall, he turned and headed towards the crowd. The elderly women were seated on raised cement ledges that lined the edge of the hall. I could tell that Baba had to walk by them first. He stopped and spoke briefly with a white-haired woman. She sat huddled in her sari, looking adoringly at Baba. As Baba moved towards the front of the hall the energy coursing through the room became palpable.

Every so often, Baba would stop and take a letter from the outstretched hand of a devotee. Many people had letters that they held out, praying for Baba to take them. I was told that, if Baba takes your letter, anything that you request in the letter will come true. He apparently knows exactly what the letter says before he ever reads it. He decides which letters he will take, based upon their content, without ever opening the envelopes. People sitting a few rows back were almost falling over the people in front of them in an attempt to get their envelopes closer to Swami. Baba kept walking very slowly along the front aisle towards the middle of the hall.

"He's probably going to make his way down the centre aisle now," I deduced. More hands stretched out and more necks craned, as people tried to sit on their knees for a better view. Next, Baba walked on the carpet between the men and the women. He occasionally stopped to chat with a devotee, sometimes touching their foreheads, sometimes choosing one person's letter yet ignoring the letter of their neighbour.

As Baba reached the middle section of the room, all the bodies seated up front turned backward in unison to keep him in view. The excitement of the people further down the aisle grew as Baba neared them. I found myself swiveling around on my aching feet and ankles, grinding them into the stone floor as I turned.

I didn't get a close view of Baba, but I was struck by how very small he was. His brilliant orange robe hid his frail little body. What also stood out was his wonderful full head of dark brown frizzy hair that rings his full face like a halo.

He stood at the back stairs, where the seva dals blocked latecomers from entering, and he waved out to the empty courtyard area. Perhaps there were people working there whom he wanted to acknowledge. He then made his way behind the back row of the men and continued his walk up the far side of the men's section. All I could make out at that point was the light filtering through his hair in the distance.

He finally returned to the front of the room and carefully climbed up the stairs to the stage. Two male seva dals followed closely behind him, periodically relieving him of the piles of letters he had accumulated.

Once up on the stage, Baba stood still in front of his chair. I felt excited thinking that he was about to deliver his darshan message, or possibly materialize something.

He ceremoniously picked up one of the large white handkerchiefs that was draped over the arm of the red velvet chair behind him and began to mop the sweat off his brow and blow his nose.

"This is so funny," I thought, laughing to myself. "I am sitting here waiting for God to perform a miracle, or materialize something, or at least speak, but instead he's standing in front of the adoring crowd blowing his nose!"

Baba sat in the chair and looked out over the crowd. The music continued as Baba conducted the bhajans by moving his hand around in the air.

After a while, he stood up. Immediately, a bell started ringing, its full sound filling the hall. Two young Indian boys, dressed all in white, ran onto the stage and prostrated themselves at Baba's feet. Then they got up and stood before Baba, performing some sort of short ceremony that involved a little glass bowl with a flame burning in it. Then Baba turned around, and a large door at the back of the stage opened as though by magic. Baba disappeared through it into the lush tropical garden behind the hall.

A last chant was sung. The only words in the chant were "OM" and "Shanti". Then people stood up and filed out. Some women ran to the side of the hall, hoping to catch a last glimpse of Baba leaving.

I sat still, absorbing everything I had witnessed and wondering what, if anything, had just transpired.

Δ

After the hall cleared, I made my way back to the

courtyard. There's a large statue of the Indian god Shiva in the middle of the courtyard. I stood there for a while waiting to see if I could spot John. I didn't see him, but I did see Kathy.

"Where are you staying?" she asked me.

"In a hotel in Bangalore," I answered.

"Why don't you stay here?" she asked.

"I don't know of any places around here. Can you recommend one?"

"I can show you a few places if you'd like. How much are you paying in Bangalore?" she asked.

"Almost 3000 rupees a night," I answered.

Kathy almost fell over. "No! This can't be. We have a very nice clean apartment behind the ashram, and we pay 500 rupees per night. Do you want me to take you over there? Maybe the landlord has extra rooms available."

"Okay. Thank you. I need to find my friend, and then we can go over there," I said.

John and I both wanted clean accommodation but the cab routine was getting really tiresome. I realized that we would have to drive back after morning darshan and return a few hours later for the afternoon session. That meant doing the nightmarish ride four times each day. I hoped John would want to stay in Whitefield. Besides, I liked Kathy, and I thought it would be fun to hang out together.

Just then, John walked up. I introduced the two of them, explaining that Kathy would take us to look at hotel rooms. John was receptive to the idea, so the three of us walked off together in search of a new place to call home.

"What did you think of darshan?" John asked me, excited to hear my first impressions.

"It was interesting," I said, not yet sure how I felt about it.

"Did you get a close look at Baba?" he asked.

"No, I was really far back. I couldn't see much of

anything," I answered.

"That's too bad. Maybe tomorrow morning you'll get a bit closer," he said.

I described how Kathy and I had met.

"From what I'm told, the women are notorious for pushing and clambering to the front, " he said. "The men are more laid back. No one pushes, and everyone sits patiently in line. It's actually a nice, relaxed atmosphere on the men's side."

Kathy told us that, in order to get to the apartments, we needed to walk through the market. There was so much to stimulate the five senses that it was hard to follow her quick step. Beautiful silk scarves and shawls hung everywhere. Wooden carts were laden with shiny silver jewelry and piles of semi-precious stones. Ropes strung up like washing lines held exquisite fabrics for making saris. Heaps of shoes, plastic household supplies, photos of Baba, incense, and all types of other exotic paraphernalia filled our path. It was difficult to walk without tripping over young children playing in the dirt. Old people sat stooped over on the ground, their wares displayed on their laps. Their wrinkled brown skin and toothless mouths gazed up hungrily hoping for a few rupees to be tossed their way. More aggressive beggars pulled on our clothing trying to get our attention, and energetic market vendors ceaselessly called out prices.

As we followed Kathy in single file through the narrow alleys, I decided that I would only brave the market once we were better settled into the rhythm. We passed doorways that led into cave-like shops and little restaurants that were nestled at the back of the path. Kathy pointed out the good ones, although they did not look like places I wanted to add to my okay-to-eat-here list.

Kathy stopped and turned to face us. "This is the bad part," she said.

I soon saw what she was referring to. We had to walk over a dusty little bridge that, for some reason, had become both the rubbish bin and the urinal for the village. The smell was so bad that I couldn't breathe. Two or three cows stood among the rotting garbage that lay a foot deep on the ground, grazing on whatever they could find.

I was pleased that we had someone to guide us through the area because I never could have found my way through that maze of alleys, and I definitely would have turned back, rather than walk through the filth that lay before us.

A few minutes later we reached a quieter, yet equally dusty, part of the village. The home of Kathy's landlord was at the end of a cul-de-sac. We walked through a pretty wrought-iron gate, and into the courtyard of a nice-looking house. A few rooms opened onto the courtyard, and, up the single flight of cement stairs, several more doors opened onto a wrap-around balcony.

"Sai Ram," called Kathy, through the partially open door of the owner's apartment.

"Sai Ram. Sai Ram," came the friendly voice of the owner. He smiled broadly at seeing Kathy.

"Do you have a room for my friends?" Kathy asked.

"No accommodation tonight," he said apologetically. "Tomorrow people leave. You like, you get room after 11 AM?"

We weren't able to go into the room because it was still occupied, but we decided to reserve it based upon Kathy's recommendation, and the little bit we could see through the window.

"We'll come back tomorrow after eleven. Do you need us to write down our names or pay you now?" I asked.

"No necessary. After darshan you come back tomorrow."

After a series of farewell "Sai Rams", we left, pleased with having found a nice little place to stay.

"This still leaves the issue of tonight. Do you want to stay around here or in Bangalore?" I asked John.

"I will take you to see a couple more places. See if you can find a place for one night," suggested Kathy.

We inspected a few more rooms. We mostly did it to appease the wrinkled old women who sat perched at the side of the path on their chairs. They called out in shrill crackling voices, "Rooms! Sai Ram. Rooms to rent...," as we walked by.

Those rooms were mostly dark, and more like prison cells than holiday rentals, so we headed for the only hotel in the area, called Sai Towers.

After inspecting the room, we decided that we would collect our baggage from Bangalore and move in there for the night. The rooms were very basic but clean, had big open windows, and boasted hot water on tap!

Having helped us secure accommodation, Kathy went to find her family. We thanked her appreciatively, and she disappeared back into the street.

"She showed up like an angel to find us a room," said John.

"She does have an angelic quality about her. I actually like this better than Bangalore, and there will be no more daily taxi rides," I said.

John agreed. So it was settled. We were moving to Whitefield.

We decided to go back to the Chancery to shower and retrieve our luggage.

For that particular ride, we selected a driver named Hari. Hari was friendly and talkative. He took us back to the hotel and agreed to wait for us for a couple of hours. I still couldn't get used to how willing drivers were to spend their time waiting for people to finish their chores, no matter how long it took.

We tried to get by reception as unobtrusively as possible. I imagined a warning sounding in the hotel lobby: "Look out!

Room 309 is back."

I had a quick shower and packed my bags. John was hungry, so we decided to order lunch in the room. The menu was filled with delicious sounding vegetarian delights, and I couldn't decide which entree to choose. In the end, I decided to order them all.

"Will you call room-service?" I asked John.

He called and gave them the list of food we wanted. (It probably would have been quicker to tell them what food we didn't want!)

A few moments later the phone rang. Surprised, I picked up. It was room-service. The woman wanted to tell me that one of the dishes was unavailable.

After a short while, there was a knock on the door. A waiter stood in the doorway with an enormous tray balanced carefully between his shoulder and his upturned palm. He set down the overladen tray on the coffee table and began to unload the covered silver serving dishes. There was so much food. It was a veritable banquet. With the delicious smells of mingling spices filling the air, I was suddenly ravenous. I realized that I hadn't eaten since the day before. I removed all the lids. The platters were filled with different kinds of rices, okra, brinjal, sag paneer, alu gobi, garlic nan, dal, mango lassies, and several other dishes. We ate hungrily, hardly speaking as we savoured the delectable flavours.

The phone rang again. "I get more calls here than at home," I said, getting up to answer it.

"Is food good?" asked the voice on the phone.

"Yes," I answered, my mouth still half full, "it's excellent. Thank you."

I sat down again and continued eating.

There was a knock on the door. John went to open it. The waiter walked in and handed us the bill.

"Thanks," said John showing him out again.

Within minutes there was another knock on the door.

"What is going on? Is everyone here bored?" I wondered as I went to open the door.

This time the waiter wanted money. I asked him to add our lunch to the room bill, but he just smiled at us, in no hurry to leave. I realized that he wanted his tip separate from the bill, and that he was not going to leave until he got it. So I gave him a tip and he left smiling.

The phone rang again.

"Maybe it would have been more relaxing to eat in the restaurant," I said, jumping up again.

It was room-service letting me know that Hari was downstairs. I asked them to tell him that we would be down shortly. I sat down to eat again, and, incredibly, there was yet another knock on the door.

John and I could hardly eat because we were laughing so hard about the routine that had developed over the course of lunch. A different waiter was standing in the doorway, this time with an empty tray.

"I clear away food," he declared, walking into the room.

"We aren't finished yet," I said.

"Let him take it," said John, deciding that it wasn't worth trying to finish the meal.

Our next task was to break the news to reception that we were checking out three days early. John thought it would be better if we went down with our bags, instead of calling first.

We settled the bill and exchanged some American money for wads of rupees. It took an inordinate amount of time to perform that very simple transaction.

Hari, who was still waiting patiently outside, loaded up our luggage and drove us back to the ashram.

Δ

By the time we got to the outskirts of Whitefield, it was very close to darshan. I was relieved that it was the last of the daily taxi rides. As we approached the vicinity of the ashram, there was a loud noise from the horn of an oncoming train. The old rusty gates at the intersection made their way down again, and the traffic immediately started to build up on either side. I knew from experience how long it could take.

"Is quick you walk," said Hari, knowing that we wanted to get to darshan.

"But our luggage is all in the car," I said.

"I wait. After darshan I drive back of village find you hotel," suggested Hari.

We jumped out the car, trusting Hari with our stuff.

These days I can tell who's trustworthy and who's not. I wasn't able to do that in the past. I used to only see someone's potential or higher Self, and I confused that with their human self. Inevitably, I got hurt or disappointed because so few people actually live their potential.

"Here! Take this for sit on," Hari yelled out the window, as we ran across the tracks. He was holding a small, foam cushion.

"Thanks Hari. What a treat!" I called, running back to get it.

The sound of the train was getting closer as we began to half run, half walk, along the dusty crowded road. The hottest time of day was between two and five o'clock, and we were right in the middle of the heat as we entered the ashram gates. Everyone had already filed into the main hall, so, luckily, lining up on the courtyard's cement floor was unnecessary. The cushion was really a blessing. Despite its thin size, it made sitting on the stone floor so much more bearable.

I wasn't seated long before the electrical current began to flow through the hall. Necks craned as chants and mantras began to be repeated in earnest. Bhajans began, and I spotted Baba's graceful body coming towards the hall. Unlike morning darshan, Baba walked straight onto the stage without walking through the crowd first. You could hear a pin drop in the hall, despite the thousands of people who packed the space. Thousands of eyes were locked on the man in the orange robe, and the energy in the room was noticeably different than it had been only minutes earlier.

Baba remained standing for a while, smiling at the people seated before him. The music seemed to ebb and flow in accordance with the slightest gesture of his hand. Most people sang along, knowing the words of each tune as well as I might know the lyrics from the Beatles' greatest hits. After Baba sat on the red velvet throne, he continued moving his hands in small circular motions along with the music. It was as though he was conducting the music, or conducting the energy, or both. It felt warm and peaceful to sit and soak up the sounds of the Indian instruments and voices.

I had nowhere to go, nothing to do, no appointments, no phone calls, nor any meetings. My only assignment was to BE. It is so difficult for us humans to understand the concept of *being* as opposed to *doing*. We are conditioned to believe that we need to achieve and accomplish in each moment. We have become so disconnected from the natural world and from our Souls that we have forgotten who we truly are. We have forgotten the greatness of our true Essence. We have forgotten that we are Divine beings who are a direct part of God. Instead, we misidentify who we are, believing that the person we see in the mirror with blonde hair and green eyes, or black hair and blue eyes, is who we are. We mistakenly believe that the person staring back at us who we describe as a loving mother, a successful doctor, a derelict alcoholic, or an aggressive salesman is the essence of who we truly are. The personality descriptions we offer in answer to the question "Who are you?" are disguises that our egos have tricked us into believing are our real selves.

We measure reality by its tangibility, and by its accessibility to our five senses. How ironic that the material world is the least real of anything. Actually, the only *real* things are those which cannot be experienced through our five senses. We have learnt to identify with our human self, which is mortal, rather than with our Soul Self, which is immortal. We search for meaning in the physical world, identifying closely with our jobs, chasing after a career, a relationship, or any number of material objectives, believing that they will produce the happiness we seek.

We have been intellectualizing God, reading about God, and going to seminars and workshops to learn about God (or Spirit or The Source or whatever it is we want to call the Supreme Energy that permeates every level of our Universe and beyond). Now, though, it is time to end the mental pursuit and to begin the experiential pursuit.

When I think about the lectures I've given over the past few months, I'm astounded by how deeply affected people are after I finish speaking. I know that the positive experience audience members describe comes not merely from the words I speak, but from the Divine Loving Presence who moves through me, filling the room and the hearts of the people who come to the lecture to connect with their Souls.

I can feel it begin just before I start speaking. My body starts to tingle and fill with incredible warmth, and then words pour out. I never keep to a pre-written speech; instead I allow the energy in the room to guide what needs to be said. Rather than having an intellectual experience of God, most people are brought into the experiential realm where they can feel God's presence. They can then experience a connection with their own Godliness. This experience is powerful beyond description.

I could recite the telephone book to an audience (an exercise we used to do in drama school years ago), and it wouldn't matter, so long as my intention in speaking was to convey the vibration of LOVE which resonates with the vibration of GOD.

Scientists have named the unseen force that we feel Energy. The religious have named it God. In both cases there is no explanation for what It is. It is an unseen presence that both separates us and glues us together. Our egos keep us separate from our Souls, from each other, and from God, as we argue about what It is. We argue about whether It even exists, what Its name is, and which of us It likes best.

To our Souls, It is the very energy that unites us. It is what holds us together, not only our physical bodies and the entire universe, but our Essence as well. The Essence of love, the Essence of truth, the Essence of who we really are.

God is like electricity.

Thomas Edison was once asked, "What is electricity?"

His simple reply was, "I don't know, but it's there, so let's use it."

Electricity is there, but it cannot be seen. It can be used to power and generate many things like air conditioners, lights, microwaves, and life-support machines. Or it can be used to shock and kill.

Electricity itself is not good or bad. There is no duality or judgment about it. The duality and judgment exists only when we make our choice about how we are going to use the electricity. Similarly, God isn't good or bad. GOD IS. The qualifying judgment and duality that we attribute to it only exists within the human experience. *We* make the choice to plug into God's Energy for good, or we make the choice to plug into God's Energy for bad.

We have entered into a time in our evolution when we need to stop blaming any external source, be it our spouse, our parents, our children, our boss, or God, for our circumstances. We make our choices in each moment. The constant flow of Divine love and support is available to us at all times. How, or if, we use it is our individual choice.

The Kaballah is a book of Jewish mystical teachings. The word "Kaballah" is derived from the Hebrew verb "to receive" (le'kabbell). It speaks of how happiness, love, joy, and God are always available to us. We need only choose to be open enough to receive it. Once we do open up and receive it, our Soul's voice will become clear and strong. Our ego's voice will no longer create a distraction from our connection with God.

Δ

I saw Baba stand up and leave through the back door of the stage. Just as before, it magically opened for him to the sound of ringing bells and high-paced bhajans. I sat still, waiting for people to make their way out. It felt good to be still and feel the powerful quiet that was within me.

John had handed me a small piece of paper on our first day in Bangalore. It was a copy of a simple suggestion written by Baba. It said that, in order to receive the greatest benefit from darshan, it was important to be still and not move afterwards. It said that engaging in conversation immediately after darshan dispelled the energy. Instead of it staying with the person, the energy went back to Baba.

Only a small percentage of the people did remain seated

afterwards with their eyes closed and their bodies in meditative positions. I didn't stay too long, either, because I knew that Hari was waiting for us. We easily found him amongst the row of drivers. I told him that I was happy to walk to the hotel, but he insisted on driving us there.

We gave Hari a generous tip and swore loyalty to him. We promised that we would use only him for the balance of our stay. In particular, we told him, we were planning a trip to one of Sai Baba's orphanages, which was several hours away, near Mysore.

John had unexpectedly stumbled upon the orphanage during a previous trip to India. The stories he told me about it sounded fascinating. I was excited about visiting it, even though it meant driving all day through the nightmarish streets of India. Hari was visibly elated at the idea of a full day's job, and he immediately launched into price negotiations with us.

We told him that we definitely wanted a car with A/C, padded seats, and shock absorbers. He would have agreed to just about anything.

"Friday would be a good day for the trip," said John.

"I very nice car for you. Very nice car ready for you Friday. I here find you," Hari readily promised.

"Hari," I said, not wanting to put out his fire, but also not wanting him to show up unnecessarily, "we aren't sure yet which day we'll do it. Also, we won't leave until after darshan, so maybe we should meet at the ashram."

"I give you my name," he said, writing "Hari" on a scrap of paper. "You make sure find me."

It was funny that he thought we needed a piece of paper with his name on it, because we had been calling him by his name all day. Putting it in writing, however, seemed to give him a sense of cementing our verbal deal. It felt as concrete as if we had just signed a ten page contract obligating us "...To find Hari, and use his taxi services, as long as we both shall live...."

I assured him that we would seek him out, and that he would definitely be the man to drive us to the orphanage.

Ecstatic with the deal, and with the tip we'd given him for his having gone above and beyond that day, he tried one last sales technique before leaving. He led me to the back of the car and opened the boot. It was filled with bolts of beautiful silks.

"Material for sari, Madame," he said. "You buy from me, I give very good price."

"They are very lovely, Hari," I assured him, "but I am not going to buy anything right now."

"What colour you like? Green? Blue? What colour you like? Very good price. I give you special price. All silk," he said, running his hand luxuriously over the finely woven fabrics.

"I really don't want any. They are beautiful, but I'm not interested," I told him again.

They were beautiful. Some of the richly coloured silks boasted elaborate gold patterns running down their sides, while others were woven with simple yet attractive designs. I could imagine a great Emperor or Sultan selecting his wardrobe from among the fine silks. I had no interest in shopping, though. I was looking forward to having my third shower of the day and just relaxing.

Hari decided not to risk losing his big fare on Friday by being too tenacious. "Okay. You look tomorrow. Very good price. Any colour. You choose tomorrow," he said, shutting the boot.

We checked into the Sai Towers and prepaid for the night. Then we climbed the three flights of stairs to our room. In tow was the porter with our bags. Another tip, another grateful smile, and we were left alone.

Δ

Later that evening, I tried to find the Internet cafe I'd seen earlier. I wasn't sure if I'd be able to find it again, because I had spotted it during the walk through the maze-like alleyways when we were searching for a hotel that morning.

I felt pretty brave venturing out into the streets alone at night because, once out, I would become fair game for all the merchants and beggars alike. I walked around trying not to let my eyes land on any particular item. Showing the slightest interest in any merchandise meant at least fifteen minutes of repartee that ranged anywhere from the usual "Very good price...how much you want pay?" to "Looking free...come inside...you drink tea? Come inside...just look...no buy...."

I did spot some beautiful things, but looking didn't seem worth the aggressive negotiations that would follow. Also, stopping for any amount of time, even if it was just to take a photograph, meant that five or six beggars would instantly appear, pulling on me to ask for money and food.

On both sides of the dusty path, women lay on the ground in their tattered, faded saris. Babies slept against their chests, and young children played alongside them. I tried to walk fast, stop as seldom as possible, and look as though I knew where I was going.

"Please, Auntie, milk for the baby," the mother would whimper as she tugged on my sleeve, sneezing and coughing all over me. It was pathetic to see a newborn baby covered in snot and flies, lying in its mother's begging arms.

I spotted a rusty sign hanging over the entrance of a rather dilapidated building. The sign said, "Ayurvedic Massage". Laughing, I thought I ought to tell John about the place. I wasn't ready for another Indian-style massage.

John got an Ayurvedic massage in Mumbai before I arrived. He was shown into a sparsely furnished room and was told that Patrick would be with him soon. With a name like Patrick, John formed the mental image of a skinny blond Irishman. He couldn't have been more mistaken! A six-foot-five black man with rippling chest muscles and bulging biceps walked into the room.

Without a word of greeting the man said, "Strip!"

John stripped.

Patrick led him into an adjoining room which was totally bare except for a wooden bucket and a huge stainless-steel pot that looked like an industrial-size pressure cooker. Patrick opened the pot's lid and steam gushed out, filling the room.

"Turn," came the next command.

Patrick pulled a large paintbrush out of the bucket and began basting John's back with hot aromatic oils.

"Climb in," said Patrick, after he finished painting the oils on John's naked body.

John wondered nervously if he was being marinated to cook in the steaming pot. What if Ayurvedic massage was actually a throwback to the days of human sacrifice?

Dutifully, though, he climbed into the seething pot. Patrick lifted the giant lid and placed it back on the pot, leaving only John's neck and head sticking out. Patrick screwed down the lid tighter and tighter until John couldn't move at all. Then he silently left the room, and John, unable to move even his head, was left to simmer in the pot.

He remained in there for ages, calling out to Patrick, who seemed to have disappeared. John was so hot that he felt his skin melt against the wooden slats which lined the inside of the pot. He became more and more lightheaded, until he thought he would pass out altogether. Finally, he gave up on the idea of getting out of the pot alive.

At some point (this part was hazy, given his delirious state) Patrick must have taken pity on John, because he answered the calls for help by unscrewing the lid of the cooker. For many days afterwards, John had stripes across his body from the wooden slats being branded into his skin.

I pulled myself out of the amusing reverie, realizing how fortunate I was that John had set me up with Pakua, not Patrick, when I was in Bombay.

I headed in the general direction of the market area and saw a sign with an arrow saying, "Sai-berspace Internet Cafe". I smiled at the clever play on words as I followed the arrow deeper into the maze, trying to find the cafe. I was amused by the paradox in this Third World country village. Plumbing and electricity were considered a privilege, but the technology to connect instantly to anyone, anywhere in the world, was readily available.

I had a vision of a world where even the Internet would be passe. We humans would send messages to each other without any machinery. A thought would form in our minds, and we would need only visualize it being sent. As long as the recipient was "on-line" telepathically, she would receive the message clearly and instantly.

"Soon," I thought, "we will look back and laugh at how, back in the year 2001, we actually needed a machine to send a message!" But, for this time and space, I was very impressed with the Sai-berspace Cafe.

Right now, computers and the Internet are demonstrating to us that what we thought impossible only a few years ago is now the norm. Similarly, I know that the vision I have for communicating with each other seems impossible but will soon also be the norm.

Clay and I stayed in contact with our friends, family and

work from these types of Internet cafes as we traveled around the Southern Hemisphere. These cafes are everywhere these days. Walking into one of them was like walking into an international convention. People of every nationality, race, colour, creed and religion sit in front of their rented computer screens, typing a mile a minute in every conceivable language. I still don't understand how Chinese characters appear from a computer that uses an English keyboard, but, as I demonstrated earlier, I am computer illiterate. I have a much clearer grasp on how it will work once we start utilizing other dimensions to communicate.

A friendly, handsome Indian man directed me to a computer, and I logged on. The keyboard was grubby, and the pads stuck periodically from the accumulation of dust and grime. I decided to send Clay a shortened version of the letter that had disappeared into cyberspace the night before. This time I left out the descriptions of the maniacal cab rides. I thought that they might be the most disturbing part given that they were an ongoing daily occurrence.

Although it took about twenty minutes to connect, the magic happened the first time I pressed "send". Minutes later, my family back home would read all about my adventures. Similarly, I could read about their adventures in the snow back home. Being reminded of North America's icy winters, I appreciated being where I was even more.

I paid the owner and left, hoping to retrace my steps.

Δ

A man emerged from the dark shadows. As he got closer to me, I saw that he had hand-carved drums hanging from every part of his body. The drums were two sided, with hide on either end. Ordinary household string crisscrossed the drums through little rusty metal rings around the outside. I loved the sound of his drumming. It was so evocative and, as only music can do, it set an instantaneous mood that distinctly and totally reflected the mystique of India.

"You like drum?" he called out from the shadows of the dark path. "You see drum in morning. Good price only 750 rupee."

I must have kept my eyes on the drums for only a few seconds earlier that morning when the salesmen walked the streets playing their instruments. Obviously it was long enough to cue the vendor that there was potential interest. I couldn't believe that he remembered me; thousands of people pass through the market each day.

"750 very good price. You take two, I give you 1200 rupee price."

"I don't need two. Actually, I don't even need one," I said, continuing to walk.

He followed after me, drumming louder with each step. The sounds coming from the drum were really lovely.

After a while, the vendor started running his finger along the hide to create a sound that was otherworldly. I knew that the salesman knew that I was going to buy a drum. I also knew that he was going to make sure it happened as soon as possible.

"Okay. Special price. I give you 600 rupee," he said.

"No thank you," I answered.

He quickened his step until he was walking alongside me.

"Okay! Best price. 550 rupee."

I stopped under a street light, which threw a weird yellow glow over both of us. I noticed his shabby green punjabi pants, with the crotch hanging to his knees. His ill-matching tan shirt hung down over his thighs. His black hair was cropped short, and his smile revealed a crooked row of rotting orange teeth. I looked down at his hands as he drummed enthusiastically for my benefit. I noticed that his skin was cracked, and his fingernails were black.

"I will give you 200 rupees for this drum," I said, pointing to the one he was playing.

It was his turn for indignation.

"Impossible," he retorted. "500 rupee last price."

"No. I won't pay more than 400 for it," I said, aware that I had just doubled my initial offer. "You do play very well, though," I said, walking off again.

The drumming continued behind me.

"Look this drum," he said, running in front of me. "This different drum. Two sides different size. Take this one 500 rupee."

He was showing me a drum that had one small end and one larger end. I stopped walking again and asked him to let me try to get sound out of them. He eagerly detached one from around his neck and handed it to me. I tried hitting it with my fingers, but it sounded nothing like the sound he was making. Not even close! I sounded like I was hitting a rubber tyre on an old car.

"Need loose," he said, grabbing my hands to show me that I needed to loosen my fingers as I struck the hide. I tried that, but to no avail.

Just then another drummer boy came up to us. He was intrigued by the lesson that was going on. My drum teacher angrily hissed something at him in an Indian dialect. I couldn't understand the words, but I could tell that he was warning the newcomer against infringing on his sales territory.

"Let me try that one," I said, wondering if I might have better luck getting a sound out of the other one.

He immediately unwrapped the strings of a different drum

from around his neck and handed it to me. I tried to do the loose finger technique, but that only produced a marginally better sound. He tuned the drum by adjusting the string and the rings. I still couldn't get my drum to sound like it even originated from the same instrument family.

"I'm no good at this," I said resolutely. "I'll try again tomorrow."

I started walking off again. Now, two men were following me, beating their drums as they tried to keep up.

"500 rupee," came the plaintive call of the salesman.

"No. I'll pay 450, and that's it. That's my final price."

I kept walking with the two drummers in hot pursuit, the drums sending harmonious tones into the night.

I could no longer remember how to get back to the hotel. The streets looked very different at night. The market shops were each lit with a single dangling bulb. The gloriously coloured silks, piles of unpolished rubies, Tibetan bells, and silver knickknacks looked as beautiful by night as they did by day.

I saw a familiar building and realized that it was the Saiberspace Internet Cafe. I laughed as I realized that I had walked in a full circle. The two men were still tailing me closely, the drumming never stopping for a moment.

Even though I didn't have a clue how to get back, I wasn't nervous. I just stayed present, enjoying the humour of the situation. I felt as though I was walking through the set of an overproduced Indian movie. My troubadours seemed unfazed that we had returned to the exact spot where the deal had first begun.

"I will look at these drums tomorrow. I am going back to my hotel now," I told them, wondering if I would ever be able to shake them off.

"Okay...you take it...450 rupee," he called out, emphasizing the closure of the deal with an elaborate roll of the drums.

"Okay," I said, turning back to them.

Next, I had to decide which drum to take. I asked them to choose the best one.

The lead drummer suggested that I take the one he had first played. The second drummer agreed. So, with two musical experts in agreement, I paid the 450 rupees and took possession of my drum.

"Thanks," I said, pleased that the deal was over, and that I was free to continue my search for the Sai Towers.

The name is somewhat misleading because it isn't really a tower; it is just a three-story building standing in the middle of an empty dusty lot. It only qualified as a tower in comparison to the other, primarily single-storied buildings in the village. I turned right, recognizing the turn by the hanging laundry, and the cows grazing on the garbage below. I headed towards another alley. From the darkness, I heard the familiar sound of drumming behind me.

"Why are they still following me?" I wondered, turning in the direction of the sound. I saw the second drummer a few steps behind me, beating on one of his drums. He was alone.

"You buy drum from me?" he called out.

"Are you joking? I'm finished buying drums for tonight. I don't want another one."

"You no buy good drum. I sell good quality drum. You no buy good quality."

"I'm very happy with the quality of my drum. I won't buy another one."

He kept following behind me, accompanying my walk with his drumming. I finally reached the hotel, and, grateful for the quiet refuge, I ran up the three flights of stairs, excited to show John my new purchase. John had just returned from a shopping spree himself. He was the proud owner of a giant box of export-quality Nag Champeer, Sai Baba's official brand of incense.

"Look what I bought," I said, holding up my purchase.

A drum beat sounded as though on cue.

"How does it do that?" asked John jokingly.

"I can't believe it! It plays by itself. It must be a magic drum," I said, laughing too.

Beneath our open window, the sustained beat got louder and softer as if going through different movements of a symphony. I looked out, and, sure enough, my friend was serenading me from the ground below.

"I feel like Juliette," I said to John. "I just need a balcony! I think this is the first time I have ever been serenaded."

I told John how it came to pass that we had a man beating a drum patiently below our hotel room window.

We decided not to leave the hotel again that night. We were still sated from our late lunch banquet, we had both had our fill of shopping, I'd had success with the Internet, and we didn't feel like being followed by a tenacious drum salesman. I thought that, if I stayed inside, he would get the message that I wasn't going to buy another instrument. I hoped that by morning he'd be gone.

I had another quick shower, even though showering in India provides a somewhat false sense of cleanliness. Unless you're in a luxury hotel, the shower water is not actually clean. You have to be quite vigilant about preventing any of the water from entering your mouth. I opted for the false sense of cleanliness. We were both tired, and, given our early morning darshan schedule, we decided to call it a day.

I lay on my narrow bed watching the thin white curtains move gently in the cool night breeze. After only a few minutes, relaxed beneath the cool cotton sheet and lulled by the sound of the drumming below, I fell asleep.

February 2

f

A rooster crowing in the distance woke me up. It was still dark outside and, other than the noisy rooster, remarkably quiet. John woke too, and checked his watch. It was around 4 AM, so there was no point trying to go back to sleep for half an hour.

I lay in bed, remembering back a couple of months to my time in Hawaii with Clay and our daughters, Nadi and Anna. We had rented a little wooden cabin on the beach, which was tucked away in its own little Garden of Eden, an hour east of Honolulu.

We were exhausted the night we arrived, but very excited to finally be in the land of magical rainbows and warm tropical breezes. We ate some take-out dinner and prepared to have a nice long sleep to overcome the jet lag we were all feeling.

Shortly after falling asleep, a rooster, who we discovered live permanently beneath our cottage, began to crow. I woke up wondering how it could already be dawn. The clock said midnight, so I realized the rooster must have made a mistake.

I went back to sleep, and not an hour passed by before he started crowing again. I couldn't believe it. It wasn't a distant call; it was more like a shriek which pierced right through the thin plywood that served as the floor of our cabin. After he settled down, I fell back to sleep out of sheer exhaustion.

On the stroke of two, that brilliant little bird started to crow again. This time he attracted some friends, so three or four of them crowed back and forth swapping stories for at least fifteen minutes.

I heard the girls laughing in the adjoining room, and I knew that we were up for the night. Clay decided to get dressed.

"That rooster must know that it's dawn in Boston," I said.

Clay laughed.

"Actually, the rooster has been crowing on the hour since midnight. I think he crows every time the sun rises somewhere in the world," I said, laughing too.

With that, the bird started to crow once again, and we knew that California would be next to experience the miracle of sunrise.

Clay decided to take the girls for a walk along the beach. It was a real adventure because it was pitch dark but for the light of the full moon, which popped out from behind the clouds every now and then.

I felt like I was in paradise as I watched the three of them with their flashlights, making their way along the white sand beach. I sat on the porch watching the moonlight dance rhythmically on the huge surf that crashed up against the shore.

Back in my room in Whitefield, India, I smiled, thinking that at that moment a proud rooster was puffing up his chest halfway around the globe, announcing to the sleeping residents of Hawaii that dawn was about to break over Sai Baba's ashram.

John decided to leave a little earlier than me so that he could get breakfast at the ashram canteen. I decided to skip breakfast because I didn't feel like standing in line to get food and then sitting in line for darshan.

After a while, I pulled on my white cotton draw-string pants, slipped the long matching shirt over my head, and wrapped my shoulders in the purple silk scarf. The soft, natural fibres felt good against my skin. I took one of the Australian Granny-smith apples out of the bag and set off into the cool night air.

Despite the early hour, young children were already hard at work begging. Some of the more enterprising little girls were carrying large baskets filled with multicoloured roses. They ran up to the passersby and tried to get a few rupees for the single flower they held up to the customer's face. After the third or fourth child had approached me, a sweet little girl with long black braids ran up to me.

"Auntie, rose? Please, rose, Auntie?" she begged.

I explained to her that I didn't have any more small change to buy her roses. She pointed to the apple that I had just bitten into, and acted out a little charade that made me think she wanted to swap a flower for the apple.

"You want the apple?" I asked her.

"Yes, Auntie," she answered.

I held out the apple for her saying, "Here, you can have this. You don't need to give me a flower."

"No that apple!" she said indignantly, "New apple."

"I don't have any others with me, but you can have this one if you want," I said.

She declined the offer, running off instead to greet two new prospects who were walking down the dusty street.

I walked past the market stalls, which were not yet fully open. The merchants, not wanting to lose any potential business, were already setting up tables and hanging out garments. There seemed to be some sort of unwritten commandment that said, "...Thou shalt not harass devotees on their way to morning darshan." The bylaw, however, must read

"...Thou shalt pay attention to what merchandise catches the devotees' eyes and sell it to them on their way back."

I reached the dusty, dilapidated bridge that Kathy had described as "the bad part" the day before. I held my breath and sprinted the ten metres to the other side. I couldn't stand to breathe in the foul smell, especially that early in the morning.

I continued through one more covered alleyway and found myself in the main market area, across the street from the ashram. Crossing that busy road in the dark was perilous, not only because of the fumes, but also because of the taxis, rickshaws, and trucks weaving around without headlights. I felt a wave of appreciation that I had been able to walk to darshan that morning at my own pace, free from the crazy taxi experience.

The rows had already started filling up on the women's side, although the men's area was quite empty. I thought that it would be a good idea to allow the women more than half the space in the hall, given that they seemed to be consistently providing more than half the occupants.

The seva dals ordered me to join a particular row with the familiar, "Sai Ram. Sai Ram." I sat down on the pillow I had borrowed from the hotel, infinitely grateful for the padding. The woman who was squeezed in next to me was writing frantically in her blank-paged journal. I could easily read the rows and rows – in fact pages – of the words "Om Sai Ram". I hadn't seen anything like that since I'd had to write out pages of "I will not chew gum in class" many years before.

I looked over in a different direction and saw another little journal, formatted the same way, with the same words written over and over again.

"Om" refers to the all-encompassing sound of the Universe. It is said to be the first syllable of creation – the sound of the Universe before anything existed. "Ram" means God, and "Sai" means Divine Mother; "Baba" means Divine Father. Sai is also said to represent truth, awareness, and ecstasy. The ecstasy is the bliss of being.

I thought about a woman I had met in New Zealand, who had come to the ashram a few years earlier. She had been granted an interview with Baba. She asked him what she ought to do with her life, and he answered, "Just be happy." It sounded really simplistic, and most people would probably think (correctly), "I don't need to travel to India to be told 'Be happy'."

It would, however, be quite a shift for us Westerners to routinely live in a state of happiness. To be guided to action by what brings us happiness is to be guided by what makes our Soul sing, by how our heart feels, and not by what our head thinks.

Our Soul's natural state is to always be happy – a true, connected, peaceful, and profound happiness that fills our physical being with waves of warmth. This is not the kind of happiness we have come to settle for, which is the happiness emanating from the temporary satiation of the ego.

In other words, when our happiness comes from an external source, like a new romance, a job promotion, or a new house, it only provides an illusion of happiness and connection. It will be a temporary, hollow happiness. The true lasting happiness that we all seek is found in Waking Up.

When we Wake Up, we realize that none of the reality that we have created is real. When we Wake Up, we realize that the only lasting happiness is found in knowing that we are part of the greater whole – knowing, not just believing, that we are a beautiful, integral part of God. It is that simple.

When we know this, with an *Awakened knowing*, a sense of peace fills us. Suddenly the Universe becomes a supportive, loving environment, not a cold, tough, lonely place. When we

Wake Up, we realize that we are not victims of our circumstances, but rather the co-creators of our reality. We are the artists drawing whatever designs we choose on our canvas of life. We realize that our ego needs results and bottom-line answers, but our Soul loves the process.

Even the concept of co-creator, however, implies a level of duality. In other words, there is "God" and there is "me" – two separate beings creating one reality together. What I call "The New Wave of Being" takes this to a level beyond co-creator. It's the place where we become witnesses or beholders of God's Love. We surrender to the Mystical Marriage, which is our conscious union with God. Then we just open and allow God's energy to flow through us. The New Wave of Being brings us a blueprint of a new way of living in time and space. Within this New Wave we become true mystics. We simply behold God's presence taking form in the earth realm.

The great Chinese Sage, Confucius, was once asked if he was a Saint or a God. He answered, "Neither, I am just awake." Similarly, the name "Buddha" means "The Awakened One". Being Awake reminds the Soul of its greatness, of its true Divinity. Once we begin to identify with that expanded vision of ourselves, we discover tremendous love for ourselves. For the first time in our human experience, we begin to love ourselves. This leads to huge love and compassion for others. That connection brings ecstasy, happiness, and pulsating as one with the entire Universe.

Amazingly, once this happens, the people who come into our lives begin to reflect the lighter, more awakened state of our being. Even if we only catch a glimpse of our awakened state for a few moments, it is impossible to go back to the sleepwalking state we were in before.

The topic of the talks I gave around the world was "Choosing the Voice of the Soul". I wanted to share that message in particular because, once we choose to listen to the voice of the Soul rather than the voice of the ego, our awakening begins and happiness starts to flow.

Δ

My line was called. I stood up, quite stiff from sitting for so long. I made my way through the metal detector and into the main hall. I managed to sit about halfway from the front, and a little nearer to the centre aisle. I realized that, with each darshan, I was getting a little closer.

Baba came out earlier than usual. I was pleased to hear the music suddenly start, see the crystal chandeliers light up, and feel the excited current of energy shoot through the room. I watched men and women doing strange little movements with their hands as Baba approached from his living quarters. In any Western country, these movements, along with the repetitive writing and mumblings, would probably be labeled Obsessive-Compulsive Disorder.

A few years back, I interviewed some people on my TV show who were diagnosed with OCD. What they described seemed minimal compared to what I was witnessing at the ashram. I wondered if there was a diagnosis called D.D.D. "Daily Darshan Disorder".

The hand movements had a distinct pattern. Both hands were brought to the forehead with the fingertips touching the Third Eye. Then the hands were thrown forward in a straight line until the arms were almost fully extended. (It looked as if they were plucking hairs from their eyebrows very quickly.) The hands were then abruptly brought back down towards the chest, and back up to the Third Eye. Then the whole routine started up again and was repeated over and over with a mesmerizing rhythm.

Some people were holding their hands in a prayer position, repeating "Sai Ram, Sai Ram, Sai Ram" over and over again. Others held their hands above their heads with their palms towards Baba. Whenever someone did raise their hands above their heads, they got bopped on the shoulder by the person behind them or by a seva dal for blocking the view.

Baba selectively gathered letters as he slowly made his way down the aisle. Suddenly he stopped in front of a young boy who appeared to be in his late teens. Baba started to move his hand around in a slight circular motion just in front of the boy's face. Then, for the first time, I witnessed the white Vibhuthi fall from Baba's fingers.

Vibhuthi is a white powder that Baba manifests out of thin air. It is said to have wonderful healing properties, so it is both eaten and put on the forehead over the third eye. It also helps purify the mind.

Vibhuthi is actually ash, the end product, or, what all · physical matter ultimately becomes. It symbolizes the ultimate surrender or detachment from the material world. Devotees say that to eat Vibhuthi directly from Baba's hand during darshan is to receive a direct charge of purification and divinity.

Watching Baba materialize Vibhuthi is an opportunity to witness the creation of form from the formless. It is witnessing the manifested emerge from the unmanifested. For me, it is a message that we can all reach into space and take hold of our dreams, of our visions, and make them manifest in a form we can experience on the Earth. It reminds us to allow our own divinity to flow from our fingertips.

When we allow The New Wave of Being energy to flow through us, and we express and extend our divinity – thereby bringing our creations into physical form – it is as though we are manifesting our own Vibhuthi.

The boy looked like he was going to faint from the ecstasy of the moment. He kneeled adoringly as Baba placed some of the white powder on his forehead. The love and devotion on the faces of the men sitting next to the boy was evident, even from a distance.

Baba moved on. He took a few letters from the women's side and then turned back again to the men. He went behind the back row of men and walked up their side aisle. Baba spent much more time chatting with the men than with the women. He weaved in and out of their seating area, so that almost all the men could get a close view of him regardless of where they sat.

The D.D.D. continued unceasingly on both sides of the hall. Whenever Baba stopped to chat with someone, the energy in the hall became more intense. There was a collective thrill when Baba gave any person his direct attention.

Suddenly, a young woman sitting three rows in front of me jumped up and waved her triangular white scarf in the air. She twirled in ecstatic circles, her shoulder-length blonde hair flowing behind her.

A seva dal ran up to her.

"Interview!" I heard the young woman say excitedly.

The magic words having been spoken, she was whisked off like royalty. I couldn't understand how, from across the room, the woman knew that Baba wanted to see her. I had been told that, in rare instances, a seva dal would show up at someone's hotel or restaurant table to inform her that she'd had been granted an interview by Baba. That seemed unbelievable, but, at least in that situation, the seva dal actually notified the interviewee. How did this woman deduce that an interview had been granted?

The room was quietly abuzz with everyone whispering "interview" to the person next to them. I asked the woman beside me the question on my mind. She pointed to the men's side and whispered, "Swami picked a man. Maybe she is from the same family."

Later, I saw another man stand up and get whisked off by the male seva dals. I had noticed that particular man earlier in the morning because, when his line was called to enter the hall, he began waving and smiling at a woman on the other side of the courtyard. He was balding, and his extended belly pushed through his white punjabi. His suspenders were hooked onto the pants under his shirt, and their red colour showed through the thin cotton.

Baba climbed onto the stage and then sat for a while, moving his hands to the music. The bell rang, and the closing ceremony began. Two young men prostrated themselves at Baba's feet. Then came the flame ceremony and a blessing, and Baba disappeared into the magical garden.

The final "Om Shanti" was chanted, signifying the end of darshan. I continued sitting in my spot. I noticed some men pushing against the flow of people filing out. The men were trying to get back up the stairs into the women's side. They had an urgency in their expressions. Then I saw the round balding head of the man who had been granted the interview earlier, surrounded by male seva dals. He was pointing and gesturing so wildly that he could hardly focus on whatever he was doing.

I realized that the man had come back to try and locate his wife. She must not have seen him get whisked off for the interview, so she hadn't followed him. He was panicking because, if he didn't find his wife quickly, he would lose his precious time with Baba.

I tried to imagine how the man would break the news to his wife that he'd had an interview, a once-in-a-lifetime dream come true, without her. I considered offering to be a witness that he really had come back to find her; their marriage could depend upon it.

He finally gave up the search and, together with the seva dals, ran back through the tall wrought-iron gates towards Baba's house.

Δ

As I reached the courtyard statue, I saw Kathy and John talking. Kathy said that they were going to Bangalore because Chilita wanted to shop. We told invited them to come with us to the orphanage. Kathy was very excited about joining us, but only if we could go on Saturday.

"Saturday's fine. It doesn't make any difference to us," I said. "We'll try to get a big car so that we can all fit in."

I told her about Hari, and she was pleased that we would arrange it all.

"Let's meet here tomorrow after darshan," I suggested.

"Okay. Sounds good. Adios," they called, walking off.

John and I went to line up outside a little canteen window. The women queued up in one line, and the men in another. The two people behind the counter were serving samoosa-like savoury cakes filled with vegetables and soya. John had bought me one the day before, and it was delicious. The only other item for sale was coffee.

The pastries were served in little bowls that were handmade from leaves. I decided to save them for Nadi and Anna. They reminded me of the little bowls that the girls used to make when they were younger. They had created bowls using leaves and flower stems. They filled them with food and water droplets and left them for the fairies under the forsythia bush at the bottom of our garden.

John bought a cup of coffee, and I bought a couple of little pastries. We decided to go back to our room to rest for a while.

As soon as we left the ashram gates, I spotted Hari. He hurried up to us and told us that he had a car, complete with air-conditioning, which was ready to go to the orphanage.

"We aren't going to do that today, Hari," I said. "We have some friends coming with us, and they can't do it until tomorrow. Can you take us tomorrow?"

"Tomorrow?" he said suspiciously. I could tell he was trying to determine whether we really wanted to go the following day, or if we had contracted with someone else despite our sworn loyalty to him.

"Yes, tomorrow. Can you still take us?" I asked again.

"Okay," he said, happy that we were remaining loyal.

"We will meet you right here tomorrow after darshan, but we need a car big enough for five or six people. Do you have a big enough car?" I asked.

"Yes. Very good car. Big enough for six," he assured us.

"Can you show us which car it is?" asked John, hip to the bait and switch routine.

"Very good car. Big car for six people," he repeated.

I knew by then that salesmen were hiding something when they simply repeated what was just said without answering the actual question.

"Can you show us which car it will be?" John asked again. Hari started walking towards the taxis which were lined up against the exterior wall of the ashram. He stopped next to a small white four-seater.

"This car for you," he said.

"Hari, this car isn't nearly big enough," said John.

"Very nice car. You want air condition? This car air-condition."

I realized that he was doing it again. He was not

answering the question at hand, which was about the size of the vehicle, not the air conditioning.

"This car will be too small for all of us. Do you have a bigger car, Hari?" I asked.

"I have big car, but this car very good. Four people in back and two next to driver," said Hari.

John and I started to laugh as we pictured ourselves squeezed tightly into that little car, like devotees at darshan. Ten minutes in that car would be uncomfortable; seven hours would be torture.

Just then a young boy came over and asked me if I wanted to buy a fan from him. I saw dozens of beautiful round fans gripped in his hands. Each fan was made entirely from brilliant peacock feathers, and each was a work of art.

I was pleased because, just before she returned to Boston, Nadi said, "Mom, if you see a pretty fan in India, will you buy it for me?"

Nadi collects fans from all around the world, and I knew that this one would be the most beautiful, exotic one in her collection. I was touched by the simple little present she had requested, and I was so pleased to have found her exactly what she wanted.

"200 rupees," said the boy, bringing me out of my daydream.

"After I'm finished with the taxi, I will talk to you," I said.

"How much you want pay?" asked the boy, trying to close the deal.

"I'm in the middle of something. I will find you later," I told him, knowing that I wouldn't need to find him – he would find me, even if I went into hiding.

"100 rupees," he said, ignoring my attempt to delay.

"Okay. I'll pay one hundred rupees, but not now. I'll buy it after I'm done with the taxi."

The boy left, but I knew we'd be seeing each other again very soon.

I focused again on Hari and John, as John said, "Perhaps we will find a bigger car from someone else."

At that suggestion, Hari realized he was not going to convince us to squeeze into the little sedan, so he told us he'd have a bigger car waiting the following day.

"No," said John. "Show us the car now. We want to see it first."

Reluctantly, Hari told us to follow him. We walked past the long line of taxis, crossed the street, walked through a little market area, and arrived at a vacant lot near the Ayurvedic massage parlour. The lot was empty except for piles of garbage, several cows, a few beggars, and three cars.

Hari pointed to one of the cars. It was slightly bigger than the previous one, but still not nearly big enough for all of us to spend the day together and still be friends at the end of it.

I spotted another car on the lot, which was decent by any standards. It was a pale green Toyota Land Cruiser. I have no interest in cars; I rarely even notice them. But I could tell from looking at that one that it would be big enough. It probably also had padded seats and shock absorbers. It boasted an extra pair of headlights above the front bumper, large enough to light up a football stadium, although I doubted they had ever been turned on.

"What about this car?" I asked Hari.

"Oh, this is a good car. Can we use this one?" asked John.

It was really quite funny that I spent more time selecting a suitable car for a one-day taxi ride than I'd spent buying the car that I own in Boston. Somehow, though, it seemed part of the fun to spend the day as a never-ending adventure. Each day was a period of time in which anything or nothing could happen.

I felt like I was more aware of each little dynamic. Every mundane incident had a humorous, fun element to it. We were so free of any time commitments or arrangements that we could just hang out and be present, whether it was a sublime darshan experience or a mundane shopping experience. It was being present and aware in each ordinary moment. Buddhists refer to this as mindfulness.

"You like this one, I give you this one," Hari said.

I sensed that he was a little uncomfortable with our choice in vehicles.

"Is it your car?" I asked him.

"I need fix car for tomorrow," he answered, begging the question.

"Fix what?" asked John.

"Air condition broke. Wait here. I go see I can fix before tomorrow," said Hari, running off.

"I think he's going to find the owner to see if he can sublet the car for the day," I said to John.

"Should we just wait here?" asked John.

"We should probably finish dealing with it now, so that we can leave straight after darshan tomorrow," I said.

We stood in the hot, dusty, shadeless lot, waiting for Hari to return.

While we were waiting, a very thin beggar-woman came up to us. She was carrying a basket very similar to the ones the little girls with the roses had carried earlier that morning. The basket had a lid on it, so I couldn't see her flowers.

She started begging for money. We told her "no" and moved away from her.

She followed us.

We said "no" again, but she continued to follow us. Wherever we went, she followed, all the time asking for money in a plaintive half-moan.

She finally stood just inches from us. Suddenly she opened the lid of her basket and a huge cobra, which had been coiled up inside, quickly lifted its head and poised to strike with a resounding "hsssssss".

I don't know what happened after that, but I do remember John screaming and running around the Land Cruiser, a look of complete terror on his face, as the woman chased after him with the killer cobra.

I started laughing so hard that I could barely stand upright. After he put several feet between himself and the snake, John discovered the humour in the situation too, and he joined me in a fit of unbridled laughter.

Not sharing our amusement, the woman stepped aside, leaving us doubled over from laughter.

Barely able to speak, I spluttered, "Is this the way they mug people in India?"

"It might work if the fright of it didn't send you running for your life in the opposite direction," said John, still laughing hysterically.

"American Tourist Survives Assault With Dangerous Snake," I said, imagining the newspaper headline.

I looked over and saw the woman approach another unsuspecting couple. I watched to see how it was going to play out.

The female of the couple was in a Sari, and her husband was in his punjabi. The beggar removed the basket lid again. Instead of terror, however, the woman in the sari cooed as though looking at a newborn puppy. Within minutes, she had the long, thick snake coiled around her neck. She and her husband spoke lovingly to it, stroking it as if it were an adorable house pet.

"Doesn't that illustrate how cultures are socialized into one belief system or another?" I said. "Something that is repulsive and frightening in one culture is accepted, even pleasurable, in another."

We were so absorbed in watching the cobra (from a distance) that we didn't notice Hari return. It seemed there was a bit of a problem with the green Toyota Land Cruiser. Hari couldn't explain exactly what the problem was, but he wanted us to choose a different car. We told him that we had seen similar, although much older white cars in the row of taxis.

"Those car more expensive," he said.

"It doesn't matter," I said. "Can you get us one of the white ones that look like this green one?" The sun was getting hotter and hotter, and I had begun to lose interest in the process.

"Yes. I waiting outside ashram after darshan," said Hari.

We left Hari to figure out how he was going to convince the car's owner to let him borrow the vehicle for the day.

We started getting sleepy as we walked back to the hotel. We had both noticed that a peaceful exhaustion flooded over us after darshan. Even though I wasn't having any remarkable experiences during darshan, I needed to do nothing but relax afterwards; my preference was to sleep.

"You ready now?" called a voice behind me. I turned around to see the gleaming smile of the boy with his fans.

"Yes," I said, amazed that he had kept such careful track of my whereabouts. "One hundred rupees, right?"

"Two hundred," he said.

"A few minutes ago you said one hundred – that's what I'll pay," I said, starting to laugh.

He held out a fan for me, seeing the humour in it, too. I paid him, and we continued walking.

My new fan was beautiful. As the sun shone on the feathers, the iridescent greens and royal blue "eyes" in the middle of each feather glowed exquisitely.

"I think I am going to buy Anna one as well," I said to

John. "Later, though. I need to shower and relax first."

As we were about to turn the corner leading to the hotel, I heard it again: the familiar sound of rhythmic drumming.

"Oh no...he's back!" I didn't want to turn around to look at him, in case it would encourage him to keep following me.

"Why don't you just tell him you're not interested in buying another one?" said John.

"Do you really think that will work?" I asked.

John laughed, recognizing how futile it is to say, "I don't want to buy that," in India.

The drumming was getting closer. "You buy drum from me? Drum you buy no good."

John decided to try his strategy anyway. "She doesn't want to buy another drum. Leave us alone. Please go away."

As expected, it was a useless gesture.

"You buy no good drum. This drum very better. This drum mango wood – is real wood. You drum cardboard – no good."

Now, he had my attention.

"I bought a cardboard drum?"

"Yes Madame – you need buy mango wood drum. 500 rupees very cheap price."

"Did you hear that?" I asked John. "He's telling me that I bought a cardboard drum."

"He'd tell you anything to make you buy from him. Yours isn't cardboard," scoffed John.

"If I bought a drum that is no good," I said, stopping to speak to the drum salesman, "why didn't you tell me that before I bought it? You were standing next to the man I bought it from. I asked you which was the best drum, and you pointed to the one I bought. Now you tell me it's no good."

He looked down for a moment, not sure how to answer. Then he formulated his response.

"If I say drum no good, other man very angry," he offered in explanation.

"Well anyway, I like the drum I bought, even if it is no good. I'm not going to buy another one."

"You need buy today. Tomorrow I go Bombay; then you can no buy. Today last chance you buy mango wood drum from me."

Several different vendors had told me that they were going to Bombay the following day to expedite a sale.

At that moment, I wished he would go to Bombay.

I really couldn't get over the tenacity of the salespeople. I suppose that, when people are starving, selling their wares takes on a sense of urgency. There are close to one billion people in India, most of whom, it seems, are starving. The country is very small geographically compared to China, which has a population of just over a billion people, so the Indian cities, towns and villages are densely packed with hungry mouths and no money to feed them.

Our drumming companion followed us the whole way to the hotel. Back in the cool, breezy room, we could still hear him playing the drums outside our window.

I showered and hand washed my clothes. I ran up the last flight of stairs to hang them up on the hot flat roof. Afterwards, I lay down on my bed.

"I like it here," said John. "It's more fun being in the middle of it all, rather than being isolated in some hotel in the city."

"I agree. It's much more interesting here. Besides, I'm sure that the Chancery staff are relieved to be rid of Room 309."

The drumming, mingling with the muted sounds from the bustle outside, continued to drift through our open windows.

"It's a never-ending process to buy something here," I thought to myself. "Even after you buy the item, it isn't over."

I decided that I would only buy one more fan, and that would be it.

Clean, cool, and relaxed, I drifted off to sleep.

Δ

We must have slept for about half an hour.

John asked me if I was interested in going to a lecture. Each weekday morning someone gives a lecture at the ashram.

"We've probably missed most of it, but we could catch the last forty minutes," he said.

Neither of us had much interest in moving, but we decided to go anyway.

I saw the drummer sitting patiently in the shade of a cement wall as we walked out of the hotel.

"Look, he's still there," I said.

"Please don't start talking to him," replied John. "Just ignore him, and maybe he'll leave us alone."

"Okay," I promised. I knew that John had completely lost his patience with the drumming saga.

The man immediately jumped up as we walked by. I didn't turn around, although I wanted to suggest that there had to be some other tourists in town who were more likely to buy from him than I was, and that camping outside our hotel wouldn't work. But I didn't say anything.

"Exchange. Only 400 rupees extra....exchange drum," he called after us.

"What does he mean by that?" I asked John curiously.

"It doesn't matter what he means. I don't want him to keep following us."

So we kept walking, and he kept following, all the way to

the ashram. Luckily, beggars and salespeople are not allowed inside. So once we walked through the gates, I knew that we would have some respite from the mania.

We found the building that housed the lectures, removed our shoes, and entered through our separate doors. Although it was hot in the sun, there was no humidity in the winter in Whitefield, so the temperature was lovely as soon as you entered a room or stood in the shade of a tree. I sat on a plastic chair at the back of the women's side. A man was giving a talk in a language I didn't recognize, and a young woman was doing simultaneous translation into Spanish.

After listening for a while, I realized that the man was speaking in English. The combination of his thick Indian accent, together with the woman's Spanish, made the talk extremely hard to follow. I really had to concentrate to understand anything at all.

The lecturer was explaining the meaning of a "yantra". I started feeling very sleepy. (I wondered if a Hindu Yantra and a Jewish Yenta would produce curried matzah-ball soup.)

As though in a trance, I moved to sit on the floor. Before long I lay on the cold, hard floor. The lecturer was full of his own importance, and he droned on monotonously. We had come in quite late and had already been sitting there for at least an hour, so I was sure that it would end soon.

After about twenty more minutes, he started taking questions from the audience. The few poor souls who did venture a question were shot down with an unloving, condescending answer.

An older man seated on the floor near the front asked, "If I want to recite the mantra you taught us, how would I begin it?"

"You would begin it at the beginning. How else *could* you begin it?" replied the lecturer.

I wondered if he was trying to be cruel, or if he genuinely

didn't understand that the questioner was simply asking for the beginning words of the mantra.

I was relieved when the lecturer finally said that people were free to leave, although he was quick to reassure everyone that they could stay to ask him questions if they wished.

I left. John was already outside putting on his shoes. He was talking to a man who held a large piece of white paper in his hands. I had seen the papers being handed out earlier.

"This is the description of a yantra," he explained. "You can get one inside. He has them in both Sanskrit and English."

It looked interesting, almost like a mandala filled with words, so I went back to see if I could get myself a copy. I enjoy reading short explanations of different philosophies and beliefs, and I was hoping that it might help decode the talk that I had just heard.

The lecturer was still pontificating in front of those people left in the room. I waited for a while, but he ignored me. As I was about to leave he said, "Yes?"

"Could I please get a copy of the papers you were handing out?" I asked.

He stared at me blankly for a while, finally saying, "What is name of paper you asking for?"

"I think it's called a yantra. You were handing them out earlier from that blue plastic bag," I said.

"To receive yantra, you need ask for yantra – not just stand there!" his voice boomed at me.

"Okay," I thought, "he wants to play a power game. Still, I'm already here, so I might as well get the handout."

Aloud, I said, "Can I please have a copy of the yantra you were handing out?"

"In which language you want yantra?" he asked.

I wondered if this was a trick. Perhaps asking for one in English would mean that I wasn't dedicated enough to the authentic study of yantra. Perhaps, to prove my dedication, I was supposed to ask for one in Sanskrit. But if I did that, I wouldn't understand it. So, in the end, I just stood and looked at him, not saying anything.

"Well? What language you want yantra?" he asked, enjoying every moment of this.

"English," I said.

"I no have more in English. If you want find out more about yantra, you buy my books. Is three volumes in book shop. Go to book shop and request my books. This they look like," he said, holding up a copy of his book.

Amazed by his arrogance, I turned around and left.

"Why didn't you get one?" John asked, looking at my empty hands.

"He wouldn't give me one," I said and proceeded to tell John what had just transpired.

"I got that feeling from him as well after a few minutes of listening to him. I only stayed because I thought you might be enjoying it. I thought that maybe it was beyond me, and that I just wasn't getting it," said John, pleased that his reality was being validated.

"I only stayed because I thought you were enjoying it. It's hard to believe that someone who professes to teach on behalf of Baba, within the confines of the ashram, can use such shaming methods in relating to people."

There was no love in that room at all. It was pure ego. Even though both John and I understand the difference between ego and love, we each doubted our perceptions of the experience. Just because the speaker was calling himself a teacher and was lecturing at the ashram, we assumed that he must know something worth learning.

I thought about how many teachers, gurus, and self-proclaimed Avatars use this kind of intimidation to gain power.

It is absolutely antithetical to The New Wave of Being. The only way to truly teach is through love. Many people claiming to be spiritual and religious leaders have opted for the ego method because seeing someone squirm at their feet seems to fill these leaders with a quick, albeit false, sense of power. The result is that, rather than being empowered, the student is demeaned and disempowered.

Any true teacher working within The New Wave of Being paradigm will help every student recognize his or her own Divinity. A true teacher will help the student recognize that the only difference between the teacher and the student is the degree to which they are Awake. He will help the student recognize that the world we have created as our reality is only an illusion or maya. When leaders adopt this method of teaching through love, the old ego-based system of teaching through fear will crumble.

There is only one language in this entire Universe, and that is the language of the Soul. The language of the Soul is LOVE. Anything that makes one feel inadequate, scared, or insecure comes from the ego.

Most traditional religious doctrine teaches that God is outside of us and that we must prove ourselves worthy of God's love. We are taught to believe that we are sinners, not good enough, or lacking in some way. These shaming, disempowering belief systems run through many religions in one form or another and are the sentiments of the ego.

But this code no longer resonates as Divine Truth. God is not external but is within each one of us. We do not need to earn God's love. Each one of us *is* God's Love. We can all experience joy and happiness; we need never be shamed or harmed by another, even by one who professes his divinity. We need never accept anything as gospel unless it resonates with our own Soul's Song.

We each have our own Soul Song. It is as unique and beautiful as a snowflake. When we find our Soul's Song, and we begin to sing that song, we feel the peace, the love, and the Oneness of God.

I was pleased to have had that experience with the lecturer. When I experience the shaming and humiliating of students, it reinforces my responsibility to open up and allow love to flow through me.

I have met spiritual and religious leaders who justify their demeaning, fear-based methods by saying that they are breaking down the students' egos. But just as you cannot teach kindness through punishment, you cannot elevate a Soul through humiliation. There is no other way to teach love than with love. When you fill yourself with love, there is no room left for the ego.

One day Vicki asked me a wonderful rhetorical question.

"Where does the darkness go when you turn on a light?"

Darkness instantly dissipates when the light shines. If a light is bright enough, no amount of darkness can put it out – but total darkness can be dissipated by a single candle.

Similarly, when Love is the primary force that underscores our teachings, the darkness and fear that is the ego will disappear. No amount of beating on the ego can ignite love or light.

I assume that the lecturer thought he was teaching about love, but, because it came through in an unloving, egotistical way, his lecture served only to spread shame, fear, and darkness. If we learn to differentiate between love and fear, the Soul and the ego, we will always be able to hold onto our power and remain centered.

In The New Wave of Being, no true teachers will invite devotion to themselves. The goal of teaching through Love and of listening to the Voice of the Soul, is that everyone will ultimately stand peacefully and confidently in his or her own truth, filled with Love. What any other person thinks, be it a spouse, boss, parent, or teacher, will matter no longer. It won't matter because we will truly *know* our own Essence and Truth. When we only speak our innermost Soul's Truth and fill only with the highest vibration of Love, no one will be able to shake us off our foundation.

We recognize when our Soul is speaking to us by simple things, like a warm feeling of expansion in our chest when making a decision. It is the feeling that we are loved, happy, and never alone. It is knowing that we can gather all our teachings through love, joy, kindness, and gentleness. It is about deciding to fully embrace life as a joyous gift. It is about experiencing our Divinity right here on the Earth in linear time. It is about following Spirit's direction, even if we have no idea why. It is trusting that the only way to find our wings and fly is to step off into the void.

When the ego is expressing through us, we feel a tightness, a contraction of energy. We hear a little voice in our heads telling us that we are not good enough to get the job, not pretty enough to get a boyfriend, not clever enough to get the promotion, not rich enough to buy the house.

The ego can also show up in much more subtle ways. False humility is a very common ego trick. It keeps us from shining our light. We might hear the voice tell us that we are bragging or that we're too full of ourselves. We ask, "Who am I to get..? Who am I to be...?"

Ego can show up in the form of flattery, like when we feel better about ourselves because someone compliments us.

In all these ways our egos are searching for an exterior source of validation. This is a completely useless yardstick to measure anything about ourselves. Any time we invest in the outcome of a situation, wanting it to resolve one way or another, we are allowing our ego to manipulate us. We need to release the ego's desire to be the martyr, to suffer, and to be in control.

The Soul has no attachment to an outcome, because the Soul resides in the place of total trust. The Soul knows and understands the perfection of the greater plan.

Δ

John and I were moving to our next abode, so we went back to the Sai Towers to check out. I decided to have another shower because the new place only had hot water for two hours in the early morning each day. We packed our stuff and checked out at the front desk. The receptionist told us to wait while someone did a quick room check.

"What could we have taken?" John asked me. "There was nothing in the room other than two small beds."

We waited to be given the green light.

Happy with the condition of the room, they released us. I smiled, thinking that the next occupants of our room were going to be serenaded by dulcet drumming all night and wouldn't even know why.

I should have known better than to think that our whereabouts weren't being carefully monitored! From behind the corner of a building appeared an unfamiliar young man laden with drums.

He walked up to me and said, "Yesterday night you buy no good drum, 450 rupees. I exchange for mango-wood drum, 500 rupees."

"Wait a minute!" I said to John. "This man, who I have never seen before, knows where, when, and how much I paid for my drum! These guys should be working for the C.I.A."

We continued walking, while the young man persisted with his calls to exchange. I told John to walk ahead because I knew that it could get messy if the guy didn't stop pestering us, and my friendship with John did not extend to visiting him in some rancid jail cell in Bangalore.

I was also getting irritated, but a part of me was intrigued by it all. I recognized it as just another colourful piece of the India experience. John walked on, and I stayed behind to find out, once and for all, why my new drum was being branded a total dud.

"Show me the drum you want me to exchange," I said to the man.

He handed me one of the mango wood drums. I looked it over. I could hear John's voice in my head telling me, "You aren't ever going to play it. It will be just another souvenir in your house, so buy the one you like the look of, not the one with the best musical capabilities."

When I travel, I always try to find one thing in each country that will not only remind me of the country itself, but that will bring back the whole experience of having been there. This drum was definitely shaping up to be the Indian relic that would serve that purpose.

I hit my fingers on the good drum and then on the bad drum. I really couldn't hear the difference – probably because of my lack of skill. So I looked at them both side by side and decided that I really was fond of the one I had initially chosen. It had more interesting carvings than the other ones, and I liked the lighter wood, or cardboard, or whatever it was.

"Okay. This is really it this time," I told the anxious man. "I will not be exchanging drums. I like my drum. I understand it is no good, but I like it."

"450 rupees exchange, Madame," he implored. "Tomorrow I go Bombay..."

"I am keeping my drum. I'm not buying another one, and I'm not exchanging. Now please go and tell all the other drum sellers in Whitefield that no amount of following me around will change my mind. No exchange is going to happen."

I walked to our new house. John was already settled in.

"That's it. I tried out both of them, and I like mine the best. In any event, I'm sure we won't be hearing from them again because they're all attending a huge drummers' convention in Bombay tomorrow. The drum saga is over!"

As disappointed as the drum salesmen were, so relieved was John.

Δ

It was time for darshan. I dressed in my newly washed punjabi, which had dried nicely on the roof earlier that day. It only took a few minutes to dry clothes in that hot, dry sun. It looked very wrinkled though, because it was pure cotton. I didn't really mind. I preferred that it be clean than pressed. John suggested we take our washed clothes to the young woman who lived in a banana-leaf structure very near our apartment. It really was nothing more than a permanent lean-to. She stood ironing in the shade of the braided leaves all day. The iron was a large, old-fashioned kind that was heated by burning coal in the body of the iron. The woman had a long ironing table which was piled high with beautiful, pressed clothing. Other than the table, there was nothing but a cot which served as her bed.

I noticed her asleep there in the early morning. Clearly, she worked out of home. I thought it would be a good idea to ask her to iron for me, but there wasn't time because darshan was about to begin.

People were already filing into the hall when we arrived at the ashram courtyard. I slipped off my sandals and went to sit in line. Luckily, it wasn't long before I was sent into the hall. It wasn't too crowded that afternoon, which was a nice change. I sat on my pillow and closed my eyes.

I sensed Baba entering the hall. When I finally opened my eyes, he was standing on the stage. I was starting to learn some of the words of the bhajans, so I sang along quietly.

I noticed the young blonde "twirling woman", who had been granted an interview that morning, sitting serenely with her eyes closed. I wondered what it would feel like to get an interview with Baba. Would it be a life-changing experience?

Baba makes an interesting analogy. When a dog eats a dry bone, the thrill he gets from eating it is mostly derived from the blood that accompanies the eating experience. What the dog doesn't realize is that the blood is coming from his own gums, not from the bone.

I wondered if, after spending time alone with Baba, people realize that what they are searching for is actually coming from within themselves, and not from any outside source. All the incredible qualities that we attribute to others have resided in us from the beginning. What an exciting revelation.

After Baba left the stage, I closed my eyes again and waited for the hall to clear. I didn't feel like moving. I just wanted to enjoy the serenity I was feeling before heading back into the crowded courtyard.

I saw Kathy outside with Bernado, John, and Chilita. We chatted for a while. Kathy had seva duty in the kitchen, so she needed to eat dinner early. I told them briefly about our morning adventure with Hari, and that we were pretty sure a spacious, air-conditioned car would be waiting for us the following day.

Δ

Later that evening John and I decided to have supper at Pacals, a little restaurant that was hidden behind the street market. It looked clean, and there was a sign hanging outside that read: "We use filtered water for cooking". We were still enjoying the novelty of having such an abundance of vegetarian Indian delicacies.

As always, we ordered a wide variety of dishes and began the meal with a freshly squeezed mix of papaya, pineapple, and mango juice. It was delicious and so thick that the rich pulp held the straw upright.

We ate slowly, enjoying the luxury of just BEING. I was constantly aware of how good it felt to just BE. We sat talking in the restaurant for a long while.

"What happens here when Baba's in Puttaparthi?" I asked.

"It's incredible," he said. "When Baba leaves, the entire village shuts down. No one knows when he is going to leave until the last minute, and then the rush to get to Puttaparthi is unbelievable. The only people left are the local residents. You probably can't even get a restaurant meal here once Baba goes. Even the beggars go to Puttaparthi."

"A whole industry built around a Holy Man! Imagine that!" I said. "The Indian government must love him. He probably attracts more tourists to India each year than any other single person. This village wouldn't have any financial viability if it wasn't for Baba. It's no wonder that the words 'Sai Ram' are in every greeting and virtually every sentence that is spoken."

"Baba might leave while we are here," said John. "He has stayed a long time. Usually he spends very little time in

Whitefield, but now, because of the enormous new hospital he's built, he comes back more often and stays longer."

We passed by the hospital every time we drove to or from the ashram. The gleaming whitewashed building is very impressive and, even from the outside, looks state of the art and very clean. It is unlike any building I had seen in India.

"Doctors from all around the world, especially cardiologists, work there," John explained. "Baba meets with them every night and tells them in precise detail the diagnosis and prognosis of each of the patients. On some of my previous visits, I spoke with a few of the doctors. They were all in complete awe of Baba's accuracy and knowledge of medicine."

"John, what's the difference between God and a doctor?"

"What?" said John.

"God knows he's not a doctor," I answered.

It was funny to think of Sai Baba hanging out with a group of doctors who were all trying to figure out which of them was God.

The waiter cleared our plates and surprised us with a bill for four dollars, even though we had ordered several entrees and two large fresh fruit drinks.

We left and walked around the village shopping for CD's. A friend of John's had requested a tape of Baba singing bhajans, and John also wanted some to take back home. The selection was enormous. Almost every cover included a photo of Baba, whether or not he was actually singing on that particular CD.

I enjoyed looking at the piles of unpolished rubies and the different varieties of Tibetan bells. I was very cautious, though, not to let my eyes linger. I was definitely perfecting what could become a very useful technique – seeing, without actually looking.

After buying two CD's, we walked back to our little apartment. It was more difficult to fall asleep that night because an animated group of Italians were sitting in the courtyard below our window, chattering loudly. Across the street, a group of devotees were gathered at someone's apartment singing bhajans. I had noticed that gathering to sing bhajans into the night was a common pastime.

So, between listening to Hindi songs and Italian chatter, I drifted off to sleep, longing for the quieter beat of the drum. I wondered if it was possible that it was still the same day that had begun with a crow from the proud village rooster.

February 3

f

We were woken early by a strange rumbling sound in the distance.

"Is that the train?" asked John, still half asleep.

"It sounds like it, but it isn't getting any closer."

"It sounds like someone's moaning in agony over a megaphone."

"Oh...I know what it is," I said. "It's the Moslems calling people to prayer."

"But it's the middle of the night," he grumbled.

The droning sounds coming through the amplifier were getting louder, and there was no point trying to go back to sleep. But for the droning, I would have slept a little later than usual that morning. Arriving early at the ashram didn't make a difference to where I ultimately sat because the lines were called randomly; the first person to show up could easily be the last one seated in the hall.

After John left for breakfast, I showered and dressed at a very leisurely pace. I put an apple in my pocket in case I came across the little girl with the roses. I made sure it was a "new apple" this time.

I had noticed that every house, in fact almost every building in the village, had a pretty design (a "sacred geometry" design) on the cement threshold of its gate. These designs were all drawn in white chalk and were occasionally accented with various other coloured chalks. They were lovely, ranging from very simple to rather elaborate. I thought they had to be newly drawn each day, because they never looked faded or washed out. I had no idea how they got there. I had never seen anyone actually drawing them. It was as though a little artist fairy lived in the village and came out at night to draw the little designs.

I found out that morning that I wasn't too far wrong. As I opened the gate to leave, I saw a frail young woman squatting on the cement, clutching a little handful of chalk in her right hand. She dropped the white powder through her pinched fingers, and the chalk, as though by magic, fell in perfect little circles and waves. In moments, flowers within flowers were created, and petals formed faster than I could move my eyes. The lines and contours formed with perfect symmetry as if created by a machine.

As soon as the artist was done, she seemed to float over to the next house. She squatted again, pinched a little chalk between her fingers, and quickly began to create a new intricate design on the threshold.

I kept an eye out for the little rose girl, but I couldn't find her. I did see all the old women with their flower baskets. They looked as if they'd spent the night right where they were sitting. They were making flower garlands for people to wear in their hair or to hang around their necks. The sweet fragrances from the flowers were intoxicating. The orange, white, purple, yellow, and pink petals were softly heaped on top of each other in enormous handwoven baskets, waiting to be delicately threaded onto a string. The contrast between the beauty of those little flowers and the dirt all around them was stark.

The women only stopped the quick threading movements they made with their fingers long enough to hold up the completed garlands for the passing crowd to see, and hopefully buy.

At darshan, several of the women sitting in line had the garlands tied in their hair, wrapped around their heads, or hanging around their necks. The delicate flowers looked and smelled so beautiful.

Like music, smells transport us back in time very quickly. Entire scenes replay in our minds from the slightest whiff of a scent. Sitting in line with my eyes closed, I caught the scent of a delicate white flower that I thought was probably Frangipani.

Instantly, I was back in Hawaii.

Honolulu was the first stop on my lecture tour. When I arrived at the centre where I gave my talk, the coordinator told me that they had prepared a little ceremony for me and my family. In the true spirit of Aloha, they presented us with exquisite leis (as the garlands are called in Hawaii). They looked like prized pieces of jewelry. The intricate work that went into making them was evident.

The lei they gave me hung around my neck elegantly and graciously, giving off a most delicate fragrance that probably best resembles the scent in Heaven. Nadi's lei was a soft light orange and the most fragrant of all. Anna's was made from the perfect little petals of a purple orchid, which also smelled sweet. Clay's was more masculine-looking, made from exotic hard red berries intertwined with a dark green leaf.

Standing at the podium that night, I felt like a Polynesian princess.

Back in the ashram courtyard, I thought how this world tour had begun with those beautiful leis in a place that is often referred to as Paradise. Now, almost three months later, I was sitting on a cold cement floor in a dusty hot village in the heart of India – a country that some refer to as hell.

It became clear to me, however, that once we integrate heaven into our beings, hell cannot exist. Hawaii is not heaven, and India is not hell. Neither heaven nor hell actually exists. Nothing exists outside of ourselves. What does exist is our mind's perception of the experience. It doesn't matter where we are physically, so long as we carry the Essence of heaven with us at all times.

I didn't visit any places on my tour with the expectation that they would provide me with a feeling of heaven. I felt as if my trip was arranged, with perfection, by an all-knowing, invisible spiritual travel agent. My friend Vicki calls this travel agent "Grace".

Grace first arranged for me to visit and experience heaven. I had the opportunity to be in that frequency, and to fully integrate it, until I became it. Only after I integrated heaven did Grace send me to India. Then could I walk through the poverty, the dust, and the filth and continue to hold a vision of Heaven on Earth.

We must each establish a strong foundation for ourselves. Our spiritual bodies have to be so fully integrated with our physical selves that we're able to go anywhere and do anything, while continuing to carry that scent of heaven.

We need to continue to carry the sound of Om. We need to always walk in beauty, surrounded by light, no matter where on the Earth we find ourselves.

It is exciting to be alive right now. Amongst others, the Central American Maya and Aztecs, the Ancient Egyptians, and the Jewish Kabbalists predicted a massive spiritual transition during this time. Astrologically, it is the beginning of the Aquarian Age. Sai Baba calls it the Golden Age, and John and I think of it as the Third Wave.

We are now able to choose whether we want to live in

heaven or to continue living in hell. We are being given the information and the tools, right now, to help us make that shift. This shift is not apocalyptic; it is simply a personal choice to live under Universal laws or to continue living under man's laws, to be led by the Soul or to be led by the ego.

This is a time for us to live our dharma. When we follow our unique Soul purpose, everything happens easily and effortlessly. When we come up against obstacles, or our work seems a struggle, we know that our ego is manipulating the situation. We get back on the mark by releasing any of our own goals.

We can measure how aligned our work is with our dharma by how passionately we approach our work, and by how easily all the different aspects of our work flow together. If it's an effort to get up each morning, and we hate our jobs, our Soul is telling us to move on.

Our egos will argue that we can't possibly leave a job because it pays the bills and feeds the family. This is the type of fearful ego talk that keeps us from following the Voice of our Soul.

We need to follow our passion rather than remain stuck in our obligations. When we feel excitement and enthusiasm flow through us, we are really feeling the infusion of God's energy moving through us. When we feel listless and duty-bound, we are experiencing a separation from God.

The New Wave of Being only supports our doing that which fills us with passion and joy. The age of martyrdom is over. The age of divine expression, creation, and extension has begun.

A couple of weeks before I arrived in India, about seventy million gurus, swamis, saints, sages, and spiritual seekers descended on the Ganges to immerse in the river for a holy celebration called Maha Kumbh Mela. Although this festival happens every few years, it was especially significant this year because it coincided with a rare and powerful planetary alignment that occurs only once every 144 years. It was predicted that this huge event would result in dramatic changes for humanity. Within two weeks, India experienced one of the most destructive earthquakes the world has ever known.

All around the world, we are noticing significant changes in our weather patterns. Volcanoes, hurricanes, flooding, and sun flares occur with greater frequency. Gaia, our Earth, is mirroring our internal upheaval. These massive external events simply reflect our huge internal shifts and changes. As above, so below. As within, so without. The microcosm and the macrocosm. There is no need for fear or panic. We are simply evolving from our physical bodies into our spiritual bodies, and the Earth is expressing herself in much the same way.

Δ

On my way through seva dal security, I got caught. The woman pulled me aside, and pointed to the apple she found in my pocket.

"What is this?" she asked, like a school teacher out of a Dickens novel.

I knew that she knew what it was, but, in deference to the the long line of people behind me, I said, "It's an apple."

"No apple," she said curtly.

"I'm not going to eat it, it's for after darshan," I said, not wanting to get into the whole explanation of the little girl who wanted a new apple.

"No apple in darshan," she repeated, taking it from me. "Leave it here – return after darshan."

As she grabbed it, the apple rolled out of my hand and fell

to the floor. I decided not to come back for it after darshan. It didn't count as a "new apple" anymore.

I sat nearer the aisle that particular morning. Although I was still almost at the back, I was getting a better view each time. At that rate, I knew that I would be right up front by the time I left.

Bhajans, D.D.D., pushing, cramping, and meditating – it all flowed together once again as we waited for Baba. It was truly a blend of the mystical and the mundane. The paradox that is India is clearly mirrored in the hall each morning. I knew we weren't going to be back in time for darshan that afternoon, so I sunk into the stone floor and enjoyed the morning's blessing.

Δ

Even though we had plans for the day, I sat quietly with my eyes closed after Baba left. I really understood why he tells people to be still after darshan. We tend to use words as an escape from *being*. We are so uncomfortable being still and journeying within, that we chatter non-stop about anything and everything. We get nervous if there's a pause in a conversation. We often interpret a friend's silence as moodiness or rejection and wonder if we have done something to upset her. An unintegrated person may use silence to sulk and manipulate another's energy. In the book, *The Celestine Prophecy*, this is called a "control drama".

In The New Wave of Being, the highest experience we can share with a friend is the silence between us – being present in each other's energy without any apology, shame, mistrust, need, or embarrassment.

In this new paradigm, friendships which cannot reach that

level of love will fall away. We will only be attracted to those friendships which raise our vibration. Friendships will be based on total equality, a joining together for a synthesis of Souls.

We have very little understanding of Soul connections, past lives, or energy. In fact, we have little understanding of earthly relationships at all. When we meet a member of the opposite sex who feels familiar to our Soul, our ego tricks us into thinking it's a sexual attraction. But Soul intimacy need not be sexual.

When we are connected to our Souls, we understand the difference between mere sexual attraction and attraction for a higher purpose.

When we meet someone and instantly feel an excitement, or sense that we have known the person all our lives, our ego may persuade us that we should be romantically and sexually involved with each other. Our ego ecstatically announces to the world, "This is it!! I have met my soul mate."

On one level the ego may be right. The other person may well be a soul mate – but we will encounter many soul mates during each lifetime. People enter our lives for a reason, a season or a lifetime; we need to learn to differentiate between them.

If we are awake, we may hear our Soul warn us that, in a past life, the other person was an abusive husband, a negligent mother, or an unloving partner. The purpose for meeting again in this lifetime is to heal that old wound and to facilitate the release of the cellular memory of fear and pain that has been blocking us from being in healthy, loving relationships during this lifetime. The purpose for meeting is not to re-create a physical union during this incarnation.

In accordance with the adage, "When the student is ready, the teacher will appear," our soul mates show up when we are ready to break the cycle of dysfunction which we carry from this and prior lifetimes.

If we are not Awake, we may only hear our ego's voice.

We may fall in love with, and perhaps even marry, the person who appeared in our life merely to heal prior wounds. We feel so familiar with each other's energy that we feel as if we have known them our whole life. We feel as if we have finally "come home".

Inevitably, though, the old patterns start to emerge, and the same unhealthy relationships begin to play out again. We wonder where the fiery passion went, and we ask why empty loneliness is once again our companion. Before we are conscious of it, we are a part of the fifty-percent divorce statistics.

How can we avoid this outcome? How can this scenario play out for the highest expression of our Soul?

First, we must feel a strong, unwavering, loving connection to *ourselves*. If we are looking to any other person to fill our needs, to allay our fears of getting old, to provide companionship or financial security, we can be certain that it's a meeting for further healing and is not the ultimate oneness we seek. We are then using the relationship to distract ourselves from learning to first love ourselves.

When we feel the excitement of meeting someone with whom we have a Soul connection, we are being handed the gift of healing wounded parts of ourselves. We must be careful not to label the relationship or get attached to the outcome of it. That immediately limits its potential.

Soul connections have little to do with how much we have in common, how much we enjoy the same types of activities, or even how much we think alike. These types of distinctions are often ego based and create a fertile arena for the ego to step into denial.

"With all we share, how could it be anything but true love?" the ego asks rhetorically, hoping the Soul won't answer.

The Soul may simply be asking that we forgive each other, so that we can continue to evolve. Only forgiveness can set us free of our wounds. Forgiveness allows us to let go of the cellular pain we have been carrying for so many lifetimes. When we jump into relationships without acting on forgiveness, we end up creating even more pain.

The Soul whispers, "I just wanted you to forgive each other; I didn't want you to act out the whole sorry story again. The attraction between you had to be strong enough to motivate you to attempt the healing! Stop being fooled by its appearance, and recognize this simple teaching."

Suddenly, by shifting our focus, a painful breakup needn't be experienced as an ending or as a traumatic event. It becomes a wonderful step forward in our healing that can lead us to even greater happiness.

The ego, resisting change, labels the experience bad and frightening. Immersed in the fear, it becomes even more difficult for us to step back and see the higher Soul picture. This higher Soul picture would show us that we have actually been set free.

Souls say good-bye to relationships with the sentiment, "Thank you for what you have taught me. Thank you for what our time together has allowed me to release and remember about myself."

When we approach relationships in this way, we're set free from addictive relationships with people, substances, behaviours, thought forms, or beliefs. Instead of lashing out in fear, feeling victimized, or trying to hurt the other person, we see the experience as our Soul's opportunity for growth. Ultimately, we can only ever hurt *ourselves*, change *ourselves*, and heal ourselves.

The reason is that on a much higher plane none of these karmic relationships, nor these experiences of reincarnation, really exist. The New Wave of Being ushers in the understanding that karma and reincarnation only exist in our human perception.

Both karma and reincarnation support the ego's belief in separation. These notions perpetuate a false reality and an illusion of our own making. The illusion is that God, and every other human, is outside of us. The New Wave of Being releases us from endless karmic cycles and from the need for reincarnation. It dissolves the whole illusion of our separation from Source. It is this separation that has been keeping our Soul's voice quiet and our ego's voice booming.

The way we have perpetuated and played out the karmic ties in the human realm is through projection and denial. Every person we attract into our lives is brought in to perfectly mirror where we are blocked and wounded. That person will mirror the most deeply hidden parts of ourselves, those aspects that are hidden so deeply that we don't even know they're a part of us. So we get angry with, and begin to hate, the qualities we see in the other person, because deep down we know it to be a reflection of the part of ourselves that we have tried to deny for so long.

The Soul doesn't care that we are trying to hide these pieces of ourselves, because the Soul doesn't feel shame, sadness, humiliation, or guilt. The Soul merely invites in another person to act as the perfect mirror. At that point, our ego gets enraged and turns the healing opportunity into a painful experience of external projection. The extent of our anger or irritation towards the other person is directly proportional to the depth of our hidden shadow self. It is easier to hate an outside source than to hate ourselves. In the end, though, it is all only self-hatred.

Similarly, because we hide our light and our greatness, we think that those qualities we respect and admire in others belong to them only. But we would not even recognize or notice those wonderful qualities in others if we didn't possess them ourselves. It is easier to love an external source than to love ourselves. In this way we avoid ever needing to meet and love our own Soul's Essence. Without truly loving ourselves, it is impossible to fully love another, or to fully receive the love of another.

My friendship with John is a good example of how male/female relationships can work in The New Wave of Being. We feel love for each other, spend time together, and travel together, even though I am married. We can express our Souls' recognition of each other in a joining of true brotherhood and respect. Deeply bonded friendships need not be sexual.

By women limiting themselves to deep friendships with women only, and men with men only, we do ourselves a great disservice. We all carry male and female energy, we have all been both sexes before, and, in truth, we are really only energy, spirit, and light.

If we allow conventional rules and etiquette to control us, we are deprived of the gift inherent in two Souls meeting for a higher purpose. We are ultimately poorer for that restriction.

We need not reside in the lower chakras' unhealthy manifestations of fear and lust. We can rather elevate ourselves to those same chakras' higher manifestations, which express as love and joining. In The New Wave of Being, we expand our hearts to include everyone who is drawn to us by our Souls, regardless of their gender.

Δ

John and I walked back to our room to shower and change for the orphanage excursion. The young boy who sold me the fan the day before ran up to greet me.

"Buy more fan?" he asked eagerly.

"I thought you were going to Bombay today," I said, teasing him a little.

"Tomorrow I go Bombay," he said, laughing.

Much to his surprise and delight I said, "Okay, I'll buy another one."

Thrilled, he held out a fan for me. "150 rupees."

"Why did the price go up so much since yesterday?" I asked him.

"How much you pay yesterday?" he inquired.

"100 rupees," I said. "I will give you 100 rupees for another fan today."

"You buy two fan, I give price 200 rupees," he said.

I only wanted one, but I decided to buy both of them anyway. I caught up with John, who, fearing another drum-sale experience, had walked on ahead.

We quickly showered, changed into non-ashram clothes, threw some muesli bars, fruit, and a bottle of water into a bag, and headed back to meet everyone.

Hari was waiting for us just outside the gates.

"Ready?" he asked expectantly.

"Yes. We're meeting our friends here. Do you have the car ready?" I asked.

"Car ready. Very good car," he said

"Is it the big car we asked for with A/C?" John asked.

"Very nice car," came the equivocating reply, which made me wonder what Hari was up to.

Just then Kathy, Bernado and Chilita arrived. After I introduced them to Hari, we set off to find the mystery car. Hari stopped next to an old white Land Cruiser.

"Here is car," he said proudly.

"Wow! He actually got us what we asked for," said John.

We got in, and Hari said, "I go find driver."

"Aren't you driving us?" I asked.

"No. No today. I get very nice driver," he answered.

We waited to see who our driver was, hoping it wouldn't be a driver from one of our Bangalore odysseys. Hari returned with a young man. He assured us that our new driver would take care of us, stop for breaks, lunch, or shopping, and would drive carefully.

Bernado sat in the front with the driver. Kathy, Chilita, and I sat in the middle row, and John was alone on a bench in the back. We laughed, trying to imagine how we all would have fitted into the car Hari had tried to pawn off on us.

Our first stop, as was customary, began with the petrol station. The driver asked for money. He had no petrol in the car, and no money to fill up.

We had to drive through Bangalore to get to Mysore. The fumes in the city were starting to get bad, so I closed my window and asked the driver if he would turn on the A/C.

"A/C no work this car," he said, turning the button marked A/C to the "on" position to demonstrate his point.

"We asked for A/C, but we didn't specify that it had to be working!" I said amused that, after all we went through the day before, we still managed to get stuck in a non-airconditioned car, about to suck black fumes for the next seven hours.

Within minutes, though, the A/C seemed less important as the near-death experiences began to happen fast and furious.

Kathy brought along a portable CD player and some of her favorite bhajans to listen to on the ride.

She told us stories about life on the ashram. She and her husband and their three-year-old daughter had been living there since November. They recently came for six months after their five-year-old daughter died from cancer. With much love in her voice, Kathy explained how her daughter had loved Baba. Her daughter used to sing herself to sleep at night with bhajans and comforted Kathy all the way through her own illness. She told Kathy not to worry because she knew that Baba would take care of her.

Kathy and Bernado's devotion to Baba was truly whole and complete. Kathy prayed to Baba to take away her daughter's pain. It was a painful form of bone cancer, but the child never needed any painkillers. She kept singing right until the end – happy and pain free. The child continued comforting her parents with insights into life and death, and the role that Sai Baba had in her acceptance of it.

Kathy explained, "Baba says that the person still needs to experience the karma, but he can take away the physical pain."

John asked Kathy why she thought people flocked to see Baba.

"Nostalgia," she answered.

"What do you mean?" asked John, wondering if the word she was using had a different meaning in Spanish.

"Nostalgia for what the Soul remembers its true state to be. It's a memory that can be re-experienced when you are in Swami's presence," Kathy answered.

I agreed that we all have a deeply hidden memory of being connected to our God-Self. We need to fill our emptiness with vitality and passion. The fullness and excitement of who we truly are can then be experienced in each moment.

Nostalgia is also that deep yearning for, and remembrance of, being "Home". When we seek a peaceful, happy home on the Earth, we are nostalgically trying to mirror our spiritual non-Earth home. Receiving glimpses of that non-Earth home through meditating, dreaming, or being in the presence of an Avatar can motivate us to Wake Up and bring its energy into the Earth realm.

Every now and then Chilita grabbed my hand and said

something in very rapid Spanish. I had no idea what she was saying, but, judging by the terrified look on her face, I assumed it was a prayer. It always happened when a truck was approaching us at full speed on our side of the road. Several times, scooters appeared out of nowhere, and cows crossed the median strip, forcing our car into a ditch. It seemed like we were constantly about to kill someone or be killed ourselves. A few times, Chilita landed right on top of me as the car swung around and came to a stop on the dusty soft shoulder. We avoided hitting little children, and an assortment of animals, by inches. The windows had to be kept open because of the heat, which allowed the thick black smoke to blow into our car.

Then there was the incessant hooting. Whether we approached a vehicle from behind or headed towards an oncoming one, our driver (joined by all the other drivers on the road) announced his presence by blowing the horn. The result was a non-stop tuneless symphony in A-flat horn.

We eventually stopped outside a little restaurant to use their toilets. We had to walk through the kitchen to get to them. Several men leaned over a brick oven, which was filled with black smoke and orange flames. It was like a sauna in the kitchen. The walls were all painted dark blue, and the stone floor was thick with years of food droppings. I didn't see a refrigerator anywhere, and all the water seemed to be drawn out of an enormous old barrel that sat in the middle of the floor. Dirty plates were piled up to be washed, and "clean" plates were sitting ready to be filled with the food that was cooking in the wood-fired oven. My eyes began to sting from all the smoke and humidity, so I quickly headed in the direction of the toilets. I wondered how many people would have eaten there if they had the opportunity to walk through the kitchen first.

We bought a few litres of water for the drive and got back in the car.

The scenery on the second half of the journey was prettier, although the driving was equally as treacherous. The towns soon became villages, and the villages became open countryside. Sugar cane grew in huge fields. There were prehistoric-looking mounds and hills covered with unusual rock formations. The mounds appeared out of nowhere and were completely incongruous with the surrounding landscape. They looked as though they had just landed there from another planet.

"Have you ever been to the orphanage before?" John asked Bernado.

"No," he answered, "but I've heard a lot about it."

"I brought along some little glass bottles to collect the Amrith," John continued.

Amrith is a sweet liquid, considered by Baba's devotees to be the nectar of God. I'd tasted it a few years before at John's house.

"Do you think that they will let us take any Amrith home?" Kathy asked.

"Last time they did. They put a little metal button in your palm," John explained, "and the Amrith flows from the button. Last time I was there, enough of it flowed from my palm to fill a small canister."

After a CD battery change, a few apples, bananas, muesli bars, and water, we finally arrived at the orphanage. It was a square two-story building just off the main street. We noticed a few pairs of shoes sitting at the door, so we knew that there were other visitors. We entered a large empty hall that was filled with pictures of Sai Baba and Shirdi Sai Baba, his predecessor. Shirdi looked completely different from Baba. Shirdi was from Northern India, and he had a friendly, thin face and little hair, compared to Baba's full face and halo-like hairstyle.

We followed John into the adjoining room, which looked like a little chapel. There were carpets on the floor with a centre aisle to separate men and women. At the front of the room was a little fence which closed off the altar area. Statues, photographs, and flowers were placed all around. Directly behind the little half-gate that opened into the altar area was a strange-looking glass picture-frame. The photo beneath was almost completely obscured by a thick layer of fine greyish-white powder.

John pointed to it and whispered, "There's a photo of Sai Baba underneath all that Vibhuthi."

I looked more closely, seeing how the Vibhuthi, growing on the photo under the glass, fell off onto the table below.

I'd heard that photos of Baba grow Vibhuthi if they're hung in devotees' houses, but I'd never seen it myself. This was a very impressive example of it.

The other barefoot devotees were seated on the floor, talking to a plump old man.

"He's the priest. He takes care of the place," said John.

The priest motioned us to sit down. I sat and looked around the room. There were more pictures of Shirdi, Baba, and other Indian gods and goddesses.

"Baba has already told his devotees that he will die in another twenty years," said John. "Then there'll be an eight-year period before Sai Baba reincarnates as Prema Sai Baba in the town of Mysore – ironically, this town."

The other group gathered up their belongings and silently left the room. The priest walked over to the Vibhuthi-covered photograph and scooped up some of the white powder from the table below. He poured it into little origami-like containers which he deftly crafted out of scraps of paper.

He filled up five little packets and waddled over to us. He handed one packet of Vibhuthi to each of us. Kathy was almost in tears as she held the precious little packet. It had a very powerful smell. I had smelled Vibhuthi purchased at the ashram, but it smelled quite different. The smell was like nothing else I could describe. It wasn't sweet, spicy or fragrant – it was strong and unusual.

Then the priest went back to the altar area. He was dressed in thin white punjabi pants, the kind that hung down low around the knees, and a shirt covered by a shawl. His large, protruding belly, which I suspected was the root cause of the wheezing, made it difficult for him to get around.

He sat on the floor next to me first. I was excited to see what would happen. He motioned to me to open my hand. Using a teaspoon, he lifted a little metal button out of a container filled with golden syrupy liquid. The button had a photo of Baba on it. He placed the button at the top of my open palm. A little syrup started to run from the button. I couldn't really tell whether the liquid was flowing from the button, or whether it had come from the spoon.

After about thirty seconds, the old priest took his teaspoon and scooped up the nectar that was running down my hand. He motioned me to open my other hand. I did, and he poured the spoonful into my empty palm. Then a little more started running down my right palm, so he scooped that up, too, and poured it into my left palm.

This happened about five times. I was hoping he would let the button sit long enough to convince me that the nectar was, in fact, coming from the button.

He didn't. The priest finished with me and motioned to me to lick the nectar off my hands and rub some on my forehead. Then he moved over to Kathy.

I licked the sweet golden liquid. I was happy to eat it, but I didn't like the idea of licking my hands given all the surfaces I'd been touching. John handed me a wet-wipe to clean off the sticky residue. I could tell that the old priest wasn't pleased. He clearly thought it sacrilege to wipe off God's nectar with a wet-wipe.

The taste of the Amrith, like the Vibhuthi, does not resemble anything I have ever eaten before. It is definitely the sweetest substance I have ever tasted. It doesn't, however, taste or smell like syrup, honey, sugar, or molasses. John told me that some Western scientists tried to disprove the authenticity of this nectar. They analyzed it in a laboratory but apparently could not determine its composition.

After each of us had a turn with the Amrith, we sat quietly on the carpet. The old priest picked up a large blue ledger and pushed it towards us. He pointed to a big container sitting just outside the altar area, which had a sign on top saying "donations". He opened the ledger and handed Bernado a pen. We were to write down our names, addresses, and the amount of our donations. The priest checked each entry before handing the ledger to the next person. Not a single word had passed between us and the priest. Everything was communicated using body language and the travelers' version of sign language.

I wrote down my information and made a donation, but the implied quid pro quo didn't feel right. Sharing and giving needs to come freely and unconditionally. Any time there is a giving with any expectation of getting something in return, the gift is compromised, and so is the energy exchange. That kind of giving is man's law rather than Universal law. When the giver has no expectation of getting anything back, the heart of the recipient is so filled with the flow of love that the recipient wants to give back openly and willingly. The flow of unconditional giving is contagious, and the ripple effect of it enormous. Interestingly, we were about to experience that exact unconditional flow of love and giving the following day.

An even higher understanding of this concept is that there is no giver and no recipient. To distinguish between the person who gives and the person who receives is to remain in the human perception of how the world works. It is to retain the illusion that we are all separate from each other, and separate from God.

In The New Wave of Being, we begin to understand that in God's world (which will become our world) we are all connected, and Spirit is the Giver. What is passed from one person to the next doesn't *belong* to anyone. Through Grace everything is given, and through Grace everything is received. We simply share in the energy of it.

We asked the priest for some Amrith to share with friends back home. The priest filled a little bottle for each of us to take.

A new couple arrived and sat down on the carpet. The woman had on a lovely brown sari, and her husband was wearing a white punjabi and a navy blue turban. Like many Indians they each had a red dot over their Third Eye. I watched them interacting with the priest. They both had tears in their eyes as they watched the Amrith flow from their palms. Delightedly, they licked it up and spread the residue all over their hands. They even rubbed drops of it onto their faces. There was no sign of the sacrilegious wet-wipe.

I quietly left the room, and headed back into the blinding midday sun. We had one more thing to do before leaving.

A stone gazebo-like structure stood at the bottom of a path which led to a lake. Inside the gazebo, on top of a pedestal, stood a nondescript wooden box with the word "Baba" scrawled on the lid in fading black marker. John explained that, when Baba opened the orphanage, he placed a bronze mold of his feet on the pedestal, and he said that it would symbolize his ever-present energy watching over the place. Baba told them that the statue would always smell like Jasmine flowers. Jasmine is the flower that carries the essence of Baba.

I lifted the lid of the box, and the sweet smell of jasmine wafted up. It is said that whatever you rub on the feet will hold the scent of the jasmine forever.

A little boy approached me and watched carefully to see what I was doing. He was sweet, with a broad smile. I assumed that he lived at the orphanage.

The Peruvians rubbed different objects on Baba's feet. John and I watched them for a while, and we started laughing.

"I'm going back to the car to get my silk scarf," I said. "I want to see if it will really retain the scent."

"People back home would think we've lost all connection with reality," laughed John.

"If we ever made a movie of our nightmarish taxi rides, cobras striking out of baskets, eating white powder from the fingertips of a God-man, licking the Nectar of God as it manifests on the palms of our hands, and rubbing clothing on a statue to get the smell of jasmine to immortalize in cloth," I said, "who would believe it's true?"

Soon we were all laughing. We laughed partly from the humour of the situation, and partly from the beauty of joining together in absolute brotherhood. Although we were all born in different corners of the earth, we were meeting in India, with no goals other than to experience our own divinity.

Millions of people flock to Churches, Temples, or Mosques each day because they fear the wrath of God. They're afraid that something bad will happen if they miss a service, so a sense of guilt or fear motivates the action of going to the service. Contrast that with the millions of people from all around the world who willingly and excitedly flock to the ashram.

We hadn't come to the ashram because we feared the consequences of not doing so. We were there because we were tuning into a call from our Souls. When we listen to that call, our Souls sing and dance with joy. Our Souls get washed with a wave of Love that is the higher vibrational frequency of The New Wave of Being. Any time we are motivated out of a sense of guilt or fear, we cannot carry that higher frequency.

We all stood there laughing together in celebration of having answered that call from our Souls. We were following Baba's instruction to be happy because we chose to, not because we would be punished if we didn't.

Living this way can extend to every aspect of our lives. Another principle of The New Wave of Being is experiencing love and happiness as the only motivating forces behind our actions.

I rubbed the silk shawl on Baba's scented feet and put the soft silk over my face to breathe in the beautiful fragrance. Another teenager arrived to chat with the young boy who had been attending us. He asked me if I would take a photograph of him. I knew the lighting was completely wrong to take the photo, but I did it anyway. I enjoyed being in the company of a teenager who still found joy in having his photo taken with a regular instamatic camera.

Finally we were ready to leave. We climbed into the hot car, and headed off in the direction of Whitefield. Kathy asked the driver to take us to a department store nearby that sold everything from incense to CD's very inexpensively. I wasn't sure how anything could cost less than it did in the markets, but apparently that store had such a reputation. The driver assured her that he was familiar with the shop.

After about thirty minutes, Bernado asked the driver, "Why are we driving in the opposite direction of the shop?"

Instantly, the driver's English became non-existent. Incredibly, he could no longer understand or speak enough English to converse with Bernado. He just kept telling Bernado not to worry by flapping his hand up and down in a gesture that meant "Relax!"

I knew then that we would not be going to the store Kathy had requested, but rather to a store of the driver's choice.

And so it was. He pulled into a dusty parking area with a

medium-sized, unpretentious cement building at the back.

"Here is shop," he said, his English coming back temporarily.

"Is this the famous department store that sells the CD's and incense?" asked Kathy, somewhat skeptically.

"Yes. This very good shop. Everything sell here. This is shop you ask," he said, his English back in full swing.

We walked in. It was the tackiest selection of tourist junk ever accumulated in one spot. "Garish" was the word that came to mind. Nothing was authentic, and there wasn't a whiff of incense or a single note of music. After about three minutes, Kathy told the driver that it couldn't possibly be the place.

"Very nice shop. Good prices," he said.

"This isn't the shop we told you about," said Kathy again.

"Other shop far. You want I take you? Come I take you," he said indignantly.

"No, it doesn't matter. Just take us back to Whitefield," said Kathy irritatedly.

I had no interest in shopping, so I was pleased to head straight back. After about ninety more minutes in the car, the driver pulled up in front of a little cafe. He told us that we could find clean toilets there.

Everything is relative!

While everyone else was buying chocolate ice cream, I went to pee. I entered a tiny metal cell-like room, with a hole in the ground that served as the toilet. There was no toilet paper. Feces were smeared on the walls, and urine lay in puddles on the dirt floor. The most disgusting part of the experience, however, was standing in a most bizarre pose to take down my long pants while my feet got wet from the unidentified substances on the floor, seeping through the slits in my sandals. I felt sick to my stomach.

I had watched children using the side of the road for a

toilet. At that moment, the roadside would definitely have been a preferable alternative. I wondered what the places were like that the driver had passed up along the the way, if this was his first choice in clean toilets.

I wanted to shower. Right there, in that little courtyard, I wanted to strip down and have a long, hot shower. Unfortunately that wasn't an option. In fact, even washing hands wasn't an option, because the dirty exterior sink looked like it used recycled toilet water. I thought I would do more damage by washing my hands than by leaving them unwashed. After that I didn't want to eat anything. I suspected dysentery would be inevitable if anything touched my mouth before I had a good scrub.

Back in the car, the driver unfortunately decided to try a new road that would bypass Bangalore's rush hour traffic. It was one of those good-in-theory-terrible-in-practice ideas.

We drove past the same buildings over and over again. The driver kept stopping to call out to rickshaws and taxis for directions. We were sent all over the place, but each time we arrived back at the same spot. The driver was getting irritated, and his driving mirrored his mood. I longed to see the dirty little marketplace outside our Whitefield apartment.

A while later, I noticed some neighbourhoods with enormous mansions that looked more like hotels and casinos than houses. They were all single family homes, though. They belonged to the elite of the social caste system who were on the opposite end of the spectrum from the untouchables. The contrast was massive. It was an abyss that could never be bridged by the lower castes during their lifetimes. Wealthy Indians live like royalty, using the castes beneath them as servants in their homes.

In America, the 1990s began an age of opulence that showed itself in part with the construction of enormous houses.

They are often referred to as "McMansions". Entire forests were cleared away for these soulless, cookie-cutter mansions, each containing five or six bedrooms, as many bathrooms (with jacuzzis), great rooms, and three-car garages. They are mostly inhabited by young couples with one or two kids. These McMansions pale in comparison with the lavish houses that we were passing in India. In India, however, they are all the more remarkable because of the stark contrast with the banana-leaf huts which are erected in very close proximity on the sides of the road.

The Peruvians ate the sandwiches and chips they'd brought with them. They offered me some of their picnic, but I'd lost my appetite after our last stop. After a while, the second set of batteries in the CD player ran flat, so we all settled into a quiet half-sleep, hoping that the driver would find his way back to Whitefield before we would need the headlights.

Δ

It was close to six o'clock when we finally pulled up to the ashram. We paid the balance of the taxi fare and practically rolled out of the car.

I headed straight for the shower. I had forgotten that the water was only hot for two hours in the morning, and I wasn't in the mood for a cold shower. If anything, I wanted to have a scalding hot shower to melt the grime off my skin and then luxuriate in a hot, candle-lit bubble bath for an hour. Instead, I stood under a tepid flow of not-very-clean shower water.

Compared with the earlier toilet experience, though, everything felt extremely clean – sanitized even! Despite the water's cool temperature, I stayed under it for ages, scrubbing my skin with soap and lathering my scalp with shampoo.

I felt much better afterwards. I lay down on my bed and waited for John to take his turn to disinfect.

The only drainage in the bathroom was a small hole in the far corner of the room, so whoever took the second shower had to wade around in several inches of water and soapy residue from the first shower. After washing your hands in the tiny sink, you had to jump out the way to avoid the rush of water from the sink's drain, which was securely connected to nothing at all. Once the water hit the tiled floor, it snaked its way over to the corner hole. The result was that the bathroom floor was wet and soapy most of the time.

Having eaten very little all day, we were both hungry. We decided to go back to Pacals restaurant.

We ordered all the same dishes again. The only deviation was a mango lassie instead of the pureed fruit drink. I liked the yogurt mixed with the fruit, especially when eating spicy curry dishes.

"You know how dreams are so real to us while we're asleep, but they seem weird or impossible when we wake up. That's what each day here is like," I said.

"It's weirder here than in a dream," said John. "For the past few nights, I haven't even remembered my dreams."

"I haven't either, but I do love dreaming. It's such an easy way to access other realms. The timing and confirmation for this around-the-world trip came to me in a dream."

"What was it?" asked John.

"One night, I dreamt that I was on the side of a mountain just north of Aukland, New Zealand. I hadn't ever had a desire to go there before, maybe a mild curiosity, but not a burning desire. In the dream, I was told that I needed to be there on New Year's Eve. The next morning, I looked on a map to see exactly where Aukland was."

"Really? So that's why you went there?" John asked.

"Well, it became clear to me that my Soul was trying to send me a message through the dream. I made the commitment to go there without having any clue why I needed to do it. The incredible thing was that, as soon as I made the commitment to trust the dream, I started getting invitations from people all around the world. The invitations ranged from meeting for dinner, to giving lectures."

"Did you meet all the people who contacted you?"

"Yes, and so many more," I said. "Everyone was incredibly warm and hospitable. It was really The New Wave of Being in action. It was perfect validation for me that, when we follow our dreams, the potential for happiness and growth is unlimited."

I slowly sipped my delicious mango lassie, thinking about how freely our Souls can express during dreamtime. We do not have a Soul just because we have a body; we have a body to experience our Souls. During our waking hours, our Souls are constrained by our bodies and are restricted to experiencing life through our five senses. Once we enter the Alpha state of dreamtime, daydreaming, and meditation, however, our Souls soar freely.

Dreams are not a "New Age" concept, although there seems to be a resurgence of interest in pondering our dream state. People have analysed their dreams throughout history. Dream Temples, set up by the ancient Greeks, were the first known hospitals. They recognized the importance dreams played in diagnosing the root cause of a person's illness. The Bible has numerous references to the important role dreams play in guiding us through our daily lives. The Talmud says, "A dream forgotten is like a letter unopened."

The ancient Egyptians, the Senoi, the Aborigines, the Native Americans, and so many others through the ages have respected and honoured the dream state.

When we're asleep, our Souls exit our physical bodies and journey in the etheric world. Once there, we experience a reality that is different from, but just as real as, our awake state. When we interact on an etheric level, the Soul is not restricted by our egos, our physical selves, or our five human senses. The dream state is the closest we can get to experiencing the unlimited potential of our Souls, while still being in human form. It is a place of limitless opportunity for self-growth, evolution, and revelation. It is a realm where all is possible.

Our physical bodies are mortal, needing rest and sustenance to regenerate. Our Souls are immortal and need no sleep because our Souls do not know time and are not constrained by space.

A wonderful way to start getting in touch with our highest Self is to write down our dreams every morning. Phenomenal worlds open up from that simple process. Dream recollection works just like a muscle. The more we use it, the stronger it gets. Many people say they don't dream, but everyone does dream; not everyone *remembers* their dreams. My friend Karen calls dreaming "free therapy".

There are so many different ways of looking at dreams. As with an artichoke, we can peel away each layer, getting closer and closer to the heart.

A dream can be symbolic, or it can reveal hidden parts of ourselves. Those hidden parts can show up as another person who enters the dream. A dream can recall a past life experience or show us future events. Sometimes we can move through dimensions and soul travel or astral project while asleep.

When we are visited by another person in a vivid dream, that interaction does actually take place on some level. Even if it is only registered and comprehended energetically, the healing from it can still be powerful. Some dreams can bring us beautiful messages directly from our Source.

With practice we learn to differentiate between the various types of dreams and to appreciate them on all their different levels. In much the same way as a musician learns to easily tell the difference between the chords A minor and G7, so can we easily learn to tell the difference between a mundane dream and a dream that reveals information from our Souls.

Δ

Back at the apartment I fell asleep easily, looking forward to my nightly dream movie.

February 4

f

I was getting into the rhythm of life in Whitefield. The early morning walk to the ashram, the lines, the waiting, the pushing, the people watching, the meditating, and, of course, the seva dals.

That Sunday morning, I sat quietly in the ashram's courtyard with my eyes closed. I was able to shut out the commotion.

I began to hear a simple mantra form in my head. I felt the words move through my whole body. I sat perfectly still, allowing the words to fill me. My mind filled with the same simple, yet powerful words that began to form their own rhythm and frequency. I could feel it beginning to happen. I sensed each of my cells as holographic representations of my whole body. Then my body began to feel like a hologram of the entire Universe. I wasn't saying anything aloud, but I could feel the words moving through me.

I stayed like that, without opening my eyes, until I felt the women around me stand up. As though in a trance, I moved towards the metal detector. I passed through and went into the hall. It was already full, and I thought I'd be in the back again.

From somewhere, though, a seva dal appeared and called me over. I followed her as she motioned me to sit near the aisle, well forward of the others from my line.

I sat down and closed my eyes again. The words continued to vibrate through me over and over again. When the bhajans started, I felt the rhythm of the music, but still the same words kept moving through me. I was very still.

I knew that I would get a good view of Baba for the first time. I liked the pattern of getting a better spot each day without pushing and shoving.

Then it was time for Baba to come in. Spines elongated, hands flew up, palms opened, and the crowd was ready.

Baba walked down the aisle towards me. He stopped to talk to a young man across the aisle. It was my first good look at Baba. Although he was several rows away from me, I could easily see his full, clean-shaven, dark face with the distinctive mole on his left cheek. His mouth was wide and full, and his nose quite flat. His eyes were dark brown, and his whole face ringed by his characteristic black halo hairstyle. His face was large in proportion to his tiny body.

He stopped briefly to touch the head of a woman on the aisle and to take letters from some of the other women. It felt very different to be so close to Baba. A lovely warmth filled my body.

The sun rose. I was seated directly in the path of its rays and bathed in the soft early morning light.

It is an extraordinary experience to be seated in a room with thousands of people who believe with all their hearts that the man walking around the room in an orange robe was God. Not a representative of God, not even the son of God, but God Himself – the Creator of the entire Universe. I supposed that this was how it would feel to be in a room with thousands of devout Christians witnessing Jesus turn water into wine. Being in a room with that intensity of pure devotion and love is incredible. Whether or not I believe it to be true is irrelevant, because immersing in that energy of total belief is so powerful.

Many people have criticized Sai Baba for his practice of manifestations and materializations. They disparagingly call him a magician or a charlatan.

People ask, "If he's really God, why does he have to perform these little tricks?" Ironically, those same people would never accept his Divinity *unless* he performed godly acts. They would skeptically say, "Prove your Divinity to me!"

In truth, we need never prove anything to anyone. We need not even try to convince anyone to believe what we believe. We need only offer our experiences as a sharing of our truth. We cannot allow ourselves to be invested in whether others believe as we do. Those that resonate with the same higher truth will naturally be drawn together. Only our egos care if someone agrees with us or not.

Baba doesn't advertise his ideas, nor does he recruit his devotees. There's no charge for being in the ashram; only sleeping and eating there incurs a minimal fee. Baba's beauty lies in the simplicity of his message and the generosity of his love. This, and not the "magic", is what really attracts people to him from all over the world.

When witnessing a miracle, a healing, or even Baba's manifestation of Vibhuthi, our brain shifts into a different gear. Witnessing a miracle dislodges our egos enough for us to admit that there might be something beyond the tangible, temporal world we know.

Δ

Darshan followed its usual pattern, and, after the bell ringing, Baba left.

I didn't move, although there was a sudden mad rush towards the front of the room. Women grabbed their pillows and pushed forward to claim the places of women who stood up to leave. I didn't understand what was going on, but I felt so peaceful and relaxed that I didn't care what the race was about.

I later learned that on Sundays the bhajans continued all day without a break until afternoon darshan was over. You could secure your seat until you returned by leaving your pillow in place. Without the pillow, your seat became the property of the first person to reach it. There were no lines for Sunday afternoon darshan; it was a free-for-all.

Sitting on the floor all day didn't appeal to me, but I felt so relaxed that I thought I'd stay for part of the day meditating and listening to the music. I sat in place for a long time. About a quarter of the crowd stayed on to sing. I didn't know how long I would stay, but I had no interest in the craziness outside. I really wanted to enjoy the energy I was feeling.

Finally, leaving my pillow in place, I went to get something to drink and stretch my cramped muscles. I felt like I was floating above the ground. I walked down the back stairs of the hall, squinting across the courtyard in the bright morning sunshine.

John and I had an arrangement with our Peruvian friends to meet a little later in the morning. Kathy had told us about an old man named Dorairaj, who lived behind the ashram. Baba's sister used to live in his house before she died several years earlier. After she died, Baba gave Dorairaj and his wife the house. In gratitude, they opened their home to anyone who wanted to come and visit. Kathy promised to take us there, but not until eleven o' clock, so I decided to bliss out in the energy I was feeling and do nothing.

It's funny how things turn out, though. This was the first time since arriving in India that I was really deep in an awake meditative state. I wanted to be totally alone without speaking to anyone.

All of a sudden I heard, "Ilana, hi! I've been looking for you. How are you?"

I looked over in the direction of the voice, but I couldn't quite make out who it was. The voices dragged me back to earth, and I realized it was some of John's friends from Boston. They had decided to overlap their trip to India with part of our time there.

"You got here," was all I could think to say.

"Yes," said Pat. "We all arrived yesterday afternoon. We're staying in Bangalore. Let me introduce you to Susan and Kate."

I said hello, hardly able to form the word. I suppose some people might have thought I was drugged at that moment, because it was so hard for me to interact. Even simple words took a while to form.

"You look great," continued Pat. "So relaxed."

"Thanks. I feel really good," I said.

"Where did you get that great punjabi? We need to get punjabis, too."

It was getting harder and harder for me to stand out in the sun talking about punjabis, but I didn't want to be rude. I knew it wasn't anything they were doing wrong; it just wasn't the vibration I wanted to be in right then. It is so rare in our chaotic lives to experience a place of total connection and bliss. When we do experience it, throwing it away with chatter is like flushing gold down the toilet.

I noticed them looking at me, waiting expectantly for an answer to the question.

"Oh...You can buy them across the street. There's a vendor

there," I said.

Just then John walked up. "You found her," he said.

I realized that they must have already met up.

"Where is the rest of your group?" John asked.

"The others are sleeping. They didn't wake up in time," said Pat.

"Really?" John asked incredulously. "They flew all the way to India to see Sai Baba for a few days, and they're sleeping through darshan?"

The three women really wanted to buy punjabis, so John offered to take them to the market. I went back into the cool shade of the hall. I sat on my pillow, relieved to be able to close my eyes again, listen to the bhajans, and be silent.

I wondered why I'd chosen, on some level, to be brought back into the mundane world when I was feeling so blissful and peaceful. Perhaps it was a reminder to me to hold my centre, even when the surrounding energy was not congruent with mine. We need to learn how to carry that energy of Paradise, whether we're in an American supermarket, on an African mountain-top, or at an Indian ashram. Spiritual maturity comes from being able to consistently hold our centre and not get blown off our course.

I might also have attracted the chatter because it is so overwhelming to carry the true connection we feel with God for any extended period so our egos bring in outside distractions. A well known quote speaks to this: "Our greatest fear is not that we are inadequate, our greatest fear is that we are powerful beyond measure. It is our light, not our darkness that frightens us most."

In other words, we fabricate daily dramas to distract ourselves from connecting with the huge, magnificent light of our Souls. We play small in an attempt to hide our light because we are terrified of surrendering to God and to our higher Selves.

In The New Wave of Being, we step into our greatest vision of our Selves, and we no longer fear our union with God; we welcome the union as our natural state of being.

When we make a true inner connection, it feels like we are sitting with God. It is a peaceful place of total surrender. In this place, we realize that conflict only appears in our lives when we are living according to our ego's agenda.

When we surrender to our Soul's agenda, we feel God's presence in everything. Surrendering to our Soul's agenda means accepting that we don't know what is ultimately in our best interests. When we accept that we don't know, we are able to more easily detach from the outcome of each situation that presents itself. We can more easily trust that the outcome, whatever it may be, is for our highest and best.

When waking up and sitting with God becomes our only goal, everything else falls into place. Wholeness and peacefulness become our constant state. Life begins to flow with an ease that could never be accomplished using our usual controlling ego methods.

Δ

At eleven o'clock, we met Kathy, Bernado, Chilita, and a young German man, Reiner, who had befriended Kathy. We walked through the gates and around the back of the ashram wall. I had never been to that part of the village. It was really filthy. It smelled and looked worse than "the bad part". The ground was strewn with feces that looked more human than animal. Then we turned right onto a dirt road, and a different village appeared before us. It had its own personality, with little shops and houses.

We followed Kathy down a few more roads until she stopped in front of a small, single-story cement house. She knocked on a tall wrought-iron gate. An older woman in a bright purple sari smiled warmly as she opened the gate. Kathy asked her if we could all come inside.

The elderly woman nodded her head in a uniquely Indian way. It is not an up-and-down nod. Instead, the neck turns to rubber as it undulates from side to side.

There are three variations on this sideways nod. There is a right side only undulation, a left side only, and then the full side to side. They each have a different meaning. I never did figure out the exact differences, but it seemed that a right nod meant "okay" while to the left implied, "I don't really like the sound of your suggestion, but okay anyway". And the full undulation meant, "Yes, please, that would be very nice".

Come to think of it, I don't think there is a head movement for "no".

We followed her inside, putting our hands together with a "Sai Ram" in answer to her "Sai Ram" as we each walked by. The interior walls were painted bright green, and all the floors were cement. The ceiling was made from a blue tarpaulin that hung down quite low. There was a little kitchen across from the room where her husband was talking to a group of devotees. They were all crowded together on the floor.

A single electric bulb dangled at the end of a bare wire in the middle of the tarpaulin ceiling. That room was the only one with any light. One wall was bare, and one was covered in frames, photographs, and paper-thin bronze etchings.

We stood in the narrow hallway waiting for the group on the floor to leave. Judging by their accents, I concluded that they were Italian. After a few minutes they got up, and we squeezed into the room as they squeezed into the hallway.

We all sat on the floor. The six of us, almost touching

shoulders, filled the little space. It was stuffy and hot in the windowless room.

Dorairaj introduced himself with a big sweet smile and an undulation of the head. His thick glasses made his brown eyes seem even larger than they were. He lit a new stick of incense and told us the story of how he got the house from Baba.

"Swami bless this house – now everyone welcome come here, get blessing from Swami," he explained.

He walked over to the frames hanging on the wall. I knew from the orphanage that they were probably photographs covered in white Vibhuthi. One of them was red, though, and its red powder was falling out from beneath the glass, dusting a statue below.

"This photo Sathya Sai Baba," he said pointing to one of the frames.

Each of the frames was large – at least a couple of feet wide. He pointed to the next Vibhuthi covered frame saying, "This one Jesus, and this, Shirdi Sai Baba."

Shirdi was covered in the red powder.

"This red...kum kum," he explained. "Vibhuthi for eat. Kum kum no for eat. Only put here for frighten bad spirit away." He put his finger on his forehead to illustrate where one would place the fingerful of kum kum.

His head moved around as though on its own spring, as he smiled continuously. The soft bhajans played on a portable tape recorder, and we settled into the warm, loving feeling in the old man's home. He showed us photographs of himself with Baba, as well as other photos that showed what was obscured beneath the powder and glass.

"My wife wipe this, show photo under," he said, as we looked at the faces of Baba, Shirdi, and Jesus showing through a small cleared circle on the glass.

The photograph of Jesus was black and white. Baba

apparently manifested it after being asked by a devotee what Jesus really looked like. It was a beautiful photo of a man with dark hair, parted in the middle, falling down to his shoulders. He had a dark brown beard and moustache, which was trimmed close to his face. His large, dark Jewish eyes stared out from beneath his narrow eyebrows.

"Baba say no more wipe photo," said Dorairaj.

He sat on the floor in front of us, and took off the huge diamond ring he was wearing. He held it out towards me and said, "This ring present from Swami."

It was a beautiful piece of jewelry. I was hesitant to touch it, though, because most of the people I'd met who'd received jewelry materializations from Baba didn't want anyone touching their gifts.

"You hold," said the old man sweetly.

I took the ring from his hand and held it between my palms. It felt so good to be immersed in the same loving energy that had begun my day. He let everyone have a turn holding his ring, and he sat with us, answering our many questions about Baba.

After a while, he took a few plastic packets of white Vibhuthi and red kum kum off the table and handed us each a little bag. He also gave everyone a bookmark with a photo of Baba on it.

"Can you feel the love in this room right now?" Reiner asked rhetorically

The love in the room was palpable. We all felt it.

Dorairaj asked if we would visit again.

"Would it be okay if we come back to meditate in this room?" I asked.

"Very good," he answered, with the full side-to-side nod. "You come tonight six o'clock very good. Only six people, very small room."

We thanked him and left.

John and I decided to have lunch at a devotees' apartment complex which served Indian food in its canteen. It was by far the hottest day since we'd arrived, and the walk along the main dusty road was uncomfortable.

We separated at the entrance because men and women weren't allowed to eat together. It was difficult to stand in the hot sun outside the coupon office. I was thirsty and hungry, and my cotton clothes were soaked from the sweat pouring down my back. Standing still in the queue, my skin felt like it does after an aerobics class. The old women in front of me seemed to take forever counting out the change for their lunch coupons. I finally reached the cashier.

"Can I please have the complete meal?" I asked.

"Eight rupees," she responded.

I thought she must have misunderstood me. It seemed impossible to be handed change from twenty cents for a complete meal.

So I said again, "I would like the *complete* meal, please."

"Eight rupees," she repeated.

I went in and stood in line to be served. Huge stainless-steel containers were filled with rice, lentils, vegetable curries, and milk curd. The women behind the serving table gave me a little of everything, and I went to sit down. The food was tasty. I didn't eat the curd, even though it was the protein in the meal.

A young Indian woman in a light blue sari asked if she could sit with me. She told me that she was an intern at Sai Baba's hospital. It was interesting to listen to her stories and to hear her speak lovingly of Baba.

The canteen was closing, so I went outside. The young medical student followed me wherever I went. I didn't mind; I just wasn't sure why she wanted to hang out with me. I saw John speaking to someone in the courtyard.

"Ilana, this is Kryshna. We met last time I was in India," said John. "Kryshna lives here."

I said hello, and introduced them to the young woman, although I couldn't remember how to pronounce her name.

After a few minutes of her telling them about the hospital, she gently tugged on my arm like a spouse at a boring party and said, "Can we leave now?"

"Where do you want to go?" I asked her.

"Maybe back to the hospital," she said.

"You want me to go with you?" I asked.

She answered with a broad smile, and the full side-to-side undulation.

Realizing that I wasn't going to go wherever it was she wanted to take me, however, she said goodbye and left.

I turned back to the two men. Kryshna had a lovely glowing energy.

"Ilana!" he said. "That's my daughter's name."

I could tell that Kryshna was American. "Where is your daughter?" I asked him.

"She's here, too. She's sixteen," he said smiling. "She has been such a gift to me. Baba says there are four categories of children. Some come in to teach the parents. Some come in to learn from the parents. Some are just a gift from God. The fourth category are those who are Avatars, but that's not very common."

I thought about my two girls and knew immediately which category they fit. Thinking about them in that way made me smile.

"That's beautiful," I said. "It can also help parents figure out parenting dilemmas if they accept which category each of their children fit into."

I liked Kryshna straight away.

"Have you been to India before?" Kryshna asked.

"No, this is my first time," I answered. "Have you had an interview with Baba?"

"I've had several interviews, but my daughter has had nine already."

"Ilana does a radio show in Boston," John said. " It's a spiritual show. Every week she has on different guests."

"What type of guests?" he asked curiously.

"She interviews spiritual authors, healers, musicians..." said John.

"I know someone you'd enjoy meeting," said Kryshna. "His name is Michael. He knows Baba well. He's been coming here for a few months each year since the early '70s. I will introduce you to him. He'd be a good guest for your show."

John went on to tell Kryshna all about the show and its purpose. John sounded so proud as he spoke about what I've been doing. It's always funny for me to hear someone describe what I do, because I don't ever think about it as a big deal. When I hear it being talked about to a third person, however, I suddenly think, "Wow! That's me he's talking about." I really don't take the credit for what I do. I feel like I'm just being sent places, and, although it sounds like a cliche, I feel like an instrument for a Higher Source. That's why it always catches me off guard to hear someone describe my work.

I suddenly felt compelled to tell Kryshna about a dream I'd had about Sai Baba. It isn't accurate to call it a dream, because it was so much more than that. I didn't know at the time whether I was awake or asleep. It was, without doubt, one of the most beautiful, loving experiences I have ever had – it was a total connection with Divinity. It was pure LOVE. I was so affected by it that I couldn't speak for a long time afterwards. The intense feeling of warmth and love stayed with me for a couple of days.

When I had that experience one year earlier, I knew almost

nothing about Sai Baba other than the bits and pieces John had shared with me.

I immediately wrote the "dream" down. It was so precious that I felt the energy and intensity of it would dissipate if I spoke about it. Suddenly, though, I found myself telling all the details to Kryshna, even though I'd only just met him. For some reason I felt like I was meant to tell him.

"That is unbelievable," Kryshna said after I finished recalling it. "That is really incredible. What a rare and beautiful experience. Baba says that, anytime he appears to someone in a dream, it is real. He is actually there."

I could tell from Kryshna's voice and the look on his face that he understood how sacred it was. He asked if we would like to meet up with him and Michael after darshan. We arranged to meet them later that afternoon at a place that served delicious fresh-fruit smoothies.

John and I walked back to our apartment, and I had my third shower of the day. Given the heat that day, I didn't mind the lack of hot water.

"I heard that Baba is leaving for Puttaparthi tomorrow," said John.

"Really? Do you want to go, too?" I asked.

"I don't feel like moving again, especially given that we're leaving India on Wednesday," he said.

"I know. I don't feel like getting back into a taxi cab either, and this is such a nice little place we found."

"Puttaparthi is really different, though. You would probably enjoy seeing it. Puttaparthi is Baba's real home, so it's huge with museums and meditation areas. The ashram is enormous and beautiful compared to this one," John said, weighing the pros and cons of leaving.

"Do you think Baba's definitely leaving tomorrow?"

"No one ever knows for sure," he said, "but word usually

starts in the kitchen because they need to know whether to cook for the next day. Once Baba leaves, this village will empty out immediately. You won't recognize it."

"A great day for the cab drivers, and a sad day for the landlords," I said. "All of a sudden their income becomes non-existent. The taxi drivers, on the other hand, will be in their full glory. Can you imagine how chaotic it will be? Maybe we should try and find Hari. That will make his day!"

"It's a long drive to get there, and everyone takes a cab or a bus," he said.

Rather than deciding if we'd go to Puttaparthi, we decided to wait and see how the day would unfold. We only relaxed for a few minutes before it was time to go to darshan again. I realized that I hadn't gone back for bhajans, but it didn't matter because I really enjoyed the people we'd met during the day.

On the way back through the market, I spotted a familiar face. He spotted me, too, and started walking towards me, flashing his orange-toothed smile.

"Oh no," I said.

"Exchange drum," he called, beginning the routine. "Drum you buy no good. Better exchange for mango-tree drum."

He kept smiling as he beat on the mango-wood drum, running his fingers on the hide to illustrate the unusual sounds that could emanate from a *good* drum.

"You sold me the other drum!" I said. "I asked your opinion, and you told me that the cardboard one was best. You said it was a very good drum. Now you want me to give you more money to exchange it because it's no good."

I got the neck swing to the left only, and he disappeared into the crowd as quickly as possible.

"What's with the orange teeth?" I asked John, who was relieved that the showdown had gone so smoothly and quickly.

"They chew on something called a betel seed. It turns their

teeth orange like that," he explained.

"It's funny that the same guy who sold me the 'bad' drum tried to do the exchange routine," I said.

Laughing, we walked through the gates of the ashram. Everyone was already seated and singing. I crouched down and began searching for the pillow I'd left earlier that morning. The hall had filled up so much that I had no idea where it was. I squeezed into a row. Many people had been sitting there singing since early morning, so the energy in the hall had built up in intensity.

Baba appeared on the stage smiling. He wiped the white handkerchief across his face and sat down. Another darshan began.

Δ

We met Kryshna at the ashram gate. John invited his American friends to come with us, so we all walked over to the restaurant together.

I ordered my favourite combination of mango, pineapple, and papaya juice. Some of the others ordered veggie burgers, but I wasn't hungry. Kryshna, who was sitting next to me, introduced me to Michael. Michael was a large man with a thick crop of hair, glasses, and a friendly smile. Everyone had questions for him about Baba, and what it was like to hang out in Baba's house. He answered everyone's questions kindly and patiently.

"Devotees often ask Baba, 'Is it true that you know what's written in every letter?'" Michael explained. "Baba will smile and tell them to pick one out of the pile. He then tells them what is contained in the letter. Afterwards he has one of his assistants open the envelope and read the message. He will do it two or three times to prove the point.

"He can be very stern with people, too," Michael continued. "He knows exactly what you've done and every thought you've ever had, and he'll call you on it. A lot of people are terrified of meeting with him."

Someone asked Michael if he had ever been on the receiving end of Baba's wrath.

"Oh yes!" he said, smiling openly. "Several times he has scolded me for choices I made. He said I was too wild in my life. He nicknamed me 'Rowdy'."

Someone else asked how he knew Baba so well.

"I started coming here thirty years ago. Back then there were very few people coming to the ashram, especially from the West. We used to hang out in Swami's house. I've been coming here every year since then. It's incredible how many more people are here these days."

Michael turned to me and said, "Kryshna said you had an amazing dream with Baba. Can you tell me about it?"

I was quiet for a moment, not sure how to respond.

"Perhaps another time. I really haven't told many people."

"Oh, I'm sorry," said Michael. "I didn't realize it was that type of thing."

"It's not a big deal," I assured him. "I will tell you about it later."

I did feel all right about telling Michael because, after all the stories he'd shared with us, I knew he'd understand the sacredness of the dream. The problem was that I didn't know a lot of the people sitting at the table, and I had no interest in my dream becoming the centre of attention.

After a while, we had to leave to meet our meditation

buddies. When I awoke that morning, I did not have a single plan, yet the entire day had filled with beautiful people, synchronicities, and happenings. It's the type of thing we miss when we refuse to surrender to the greater plan and over-schedule our lives in an attempt to feel as if we're in control.

There's a saying, "If you want to make God laugh, make plans". It's so true. Although our egos try to make us feel like we are in charge, nothing could be further from the truth. When we surrender to the flow of the Universe, the most unimaginable, wonder-filled adventure begins.

Δ

We found Kathy and Bernado at the ashram, and we all made our way back to the little house. We were once again greeted warmly at the gate and shown in. Reiner was already waiting for us on the floor.

We sat quietly and meditated. The room was hot and stuffy, and a mosquito buzzed around continually. In spite of all that, it was lovely to be in the warmth and love of that humble home. The energy felt qualitatively different than at the orphanage. It carried a purity that is hard to find.

We asked Dorairaj if we could give him a donation for the Vibhuthi, the cards, and the kum kum.

"No money. I serve Swami," he said, moving his head from side to side. "Swami give me this house – all devotee who want, come here. Only give me photo of Baba for hang on wall, or electric bulb."

It was such a simple request.

"Only take money," he continued, "when buy yantra."

He got up and walked over to the bronze etchings hanging

on the wall. They each had a design with a few words etched into the bronze and some red kum kum sprinkled over them.

"This is yantra," said Dorairaj.

"Here we go with the yantra again," I thought, noticing how different his energy was when discussing the yantra.

"If doctor want heal patient quickly, he hang yantra on wall in office – he say special mantra, is write on here, one hundred eight time."

John's interest was piqued. "You say that is for doctors?"

"Yes, only doctor say this mantra," answered the old man.

"I'm a doctor," said John. "If I hang that yantra up, will my my patients heal quickly?"

"You doctor?" asked Dorairaj, his head going side to side.

"Yes. I would like to buy one of those to hang in my office."

"Oh, very much money," said the old man.

"How much does it cost?" John asked.

"Two hundred, American, " Dorairaj responded.

His style was so different. He had no interest in making the sale. He had only brought it up in explanation of what he was teaching us.

John decided that he would buy the yantra and a little talisman that went along with it. The silver and gold talisman, which looked like a little tube, was to be worn around his neck. It contained a special healing mantra. The square bronze etching was to hang in his office.

The old man told John to come back the following day to pick it up.

"Anything you want from India, you tell me. I send it," he said. "This I do all devotee. My wife she do astrology for devotee. No money for this. We love Baba and we do this."

He was so gracious and kind that we wanted to keep sitting in his presence. It was unusual to be with someone who was filled with the type of joy that only comes from giving and sharing unconditionally.

"What you work?" Dorairaj asked me.

"I do a radio talk show," I answered.

"What you talk?"

"It's a spiritual show, " I explained.

"Very good. I make you cassette all mantras – you teach mantra on radio."

"That's a good idea, I'll do that," I told him.

"Tomorrow you come get yantra and talisman with Dr. John. I give you cassette me read mantra."

We left smiling and happy. We all decided to go out for supper together. Feeling a definite need for protein, we gave the Indian food a miss for the night and went instead to a restaurant that served omelettes.

"It's lucky you and Kathy met," John said as we sat waiting for our food.

"We were upset about the way the Argentinean woman was behaving the day we met," I said. "On one level the woman's behaviour was rude and hurtful, but it was a great example of being able to look beyond the ego. Now we can see how it was perfectly orchestrated on a higher level. If the Argentinean hadn't been so insulting, Kathy wouldn't have asked me if she could move into my line. Her request gave me an opportunity to extend a kindness, and I was rewarded with Kathy's help and friendship."

I saw how important it is to stop judging every situation in our usual myopic way. It's always useful to wait for the big picture to be revealed, trusting that each situation is for our highest and best. When we get out of our own way, we don't have half the anxieties and dramas that we create for ourselves each day.

"Swami always knows best," said Kathy, her devotion to Sai Baba never floundering.

"You found us our apartment and introduced us to Dorairaj," said John.

"His wife is so sweet, too. She does Vedic astrology for all devotees," said Kathy.

"Do you believe in astrology?" Bernado asked me.

"I do, but astrology, past-life regressions, numerology, and all that are really only signposts for us during our lives," I answered. "I think that all these modalities are like stage directions. They're tools to help us understand our part and our role in the play of Life. All these teachings are extremely helpful in our character development and in showing us where and how to move around the stage. But that's it. In the greater scheme of things, we only have one direction. That is to Wake Up, and understand that our life is a play."

"Did Ilana tell you about the 'Third Wave' concept?" asked John. "It's a time that we're coming into when we will understand that we are all just a vibration of Love. It's really *feeling* the Presence of God. Understanding of the Third Wave is just beginning to come into human consciousness."

"Astrology, psychic readings, and all those other modalities are part of the 'Second Wave'," I continued. "In other words, those teachings have expanded our awareness of other dimensions, and they help us understand our roles during this and past lifetimes. But it isn't the final act. The Second Wave is more of an intellectualization of God. The Third Wave will be an *experiential knowing* of God. It will be living it."

"So is there a First Wave?" asked Bernado.

"Yes," I said. "The First Wave is when we experience life only through the five senses. It's when we're guided by our egos, and we think that God is external or non-existent."

"What do you think about aromatherapies and crystals?" asked Kathy.

"It's the same thing," I answered. "It can all work and be

helpful, but we do ourselves a disservice by thinking that any of it is an end in itself. It can help us during this lifetime and make our lives more comfortable or pleasurable, but it can also be a distraction to the only simple truth there is. The simple Truth is that anything that is not Love is false. We're all just a vibration of that Love, and we need to Wake Up to our Divinity. Our fear of Waking Up can keep us distracted by holistic things too. Using homeopathy or acupuncture to cure an illness carries a higher vibration than using antibiotics or other traditional medicines and surgeries. It's important, however, to understand that illness is just the manifested symptom of our separation from our Souls and from our Source. Addressing it at that cause level is how true healing happens. Healing begins with recognizing our wholeness and our perfection. That is the place where miracles are found."

"So do you think people should only use alternative remedies?" asked Kathy.

"No, but as often as possible," I said. "We can't ignore or denying the physical illness, but it's always best to address it right at the source. Physical illness only happens when there's a void in the emotional or the spiritual body. The last place for the void to manifest is in the physical body. If we catch it when it's still in the emotional or spiritual realm, it won't need to become a physical ailment.

"It's incredible how people continue overworking, arguing, and getting stressed until they get ill. Only then will they make changes in their lives. We think it's okay to nurture our physical selves if we are sick, but we don't take time to nurture our spiritual and emotional selves. Whether it's conscious or not, we distract ourselves with activities like shopping, watching TV, or even going to endless self-help workshops and seminars."

"We're so busy seeking spirituality and looking so hard to find God that we miss God completely," said John. "When we decide to be still, we find God in every moment, and in every ordinary incident."

"We also take ourselves and spirituality much too seriously," I added. "We experience God directly when we find the humour and the fun in each moment."

It occurred to me that, since its inception, my radio show has progressed through the "Waves". It started as a political talk show, moved into the psychic realm with readers and astrologers, and has emerged into a show which offers the opportunity to tune into the frequency of Oneness. When I stopped inviting psychics to do readings on the air, I got letters complaining that the show was boring. But a whole new group of people started writing about how stimulating the show had become.

Our work is just a mirror and an expression of our own Soul's evolution. Every aspect of our daily lives reflects our growth on the Soul's journey. We can't compartmentalize our lives, growing in one area but remaining stuck in another.

Just then Reiner arrived, so we invited him to sit with us. He had an Italian friend with him, so we pulled up another table and all sat together. It was fun sitting at dinner, once again following Baba's command to be happy with new friends from all over the world.

A few young children stared hungrily into the restaurant from outside the gate. I saw the hunger in their eyes as we sat at our table laden with food. It brought the teachings of The New Wave of Being from the intellectual into the experiential realm. I realized that the only way I could make sense of India's street culture, with its poverty and rampant disease, was from the perspective of the Three Waves.

As with everything, we need to follow our intuition. Perhaps we might feel guided to hand money to every beggar who approaches us. Perhaps we might say, "I'm not giving beggars anything; I don't know why, but I'm not moved to right now." There need be no judgment about either response so long as it expresses our truth.

From the perspective of the First Wave, we cannot understand the poverty; it's overwhelming to our human selves. We can throw some guilt-money at the problem, because it makes us feel like kind, generous humanitarians. That, however, is gratuitous giving, and is only a temporary solution to the poverty. It is also only a temporary solution to dealing with our shadow-self shame and guilt. We need to fully embrace our shadows, not get a quick ego fix while suppressing the deeper issues.

I recently read a book about Bali, Indonesia. The huge influx of tourists has not only damaged their delicate eco-system, but also their delicate eco-nomical system. When tourists give porters, cab drivers, or beggars on the street western-world size tips, they hurt the whole economy. Suddenly, the uneducated beggar or porter earns in one tip what a school teacher earns in one week. Why spend years studying at university? Why spend your days in white collar employment when the spoils on the street are so much more lucrative?

Also, a huge underground economy develops. In the case of Bali, the money is being funneled out of the country and not helping support the infrastructure of the island at all.

How arrogant to think that we can save the beggars of the world from their misery, and then leave, feeling like heroes from a Hollywood movie. We can't pretend to fix any of it. We give a few rupees and run away feeling better superficially, but that bankrupts us spiritually and perpetuates the belief in a false reality.

The Second Wave often explains poverty and suffering from the perspective of karma. Reincarnation and karma are integral to the Hindu religion. Incarnating as a beggar or a wealthy businessman in any particular lifetime seems to be passively accepted as being one's karma.

According to the laws of karma, everything is governed by cause and effect. What you do in one lifetime directly affects a future lifetime: "As you reap so shall you sow"; "What goes around comes around".

Perhaps the beggars are living a life of abject poverty because they want to "burn off" many future mediocre existences in one foul swoop. In that case, do we try to alter a person's karma?

What happens when we know that a merchant or a taxi driver is not being honest in his dealings with us? Do we excuse his dishonesty because he's poor? Do we dismiss the mendacity because we have money and he doesn't? If we do, are we actually helping anyone?

The question of karma leads to another question: is the poor street person necessarily worse off than the stressed-out, overweight, alcoholic CEO of a multi-million dollar corporation? Whichever side of the economic spectrum these two people are on, if they have lost their Godly spark, they are poor. If they are not connected to their Souls, they are impoverished. Karma and reincarnation, however, are still Second Wave energy; they imply that we need to suffer, or that we are anything less than whole and perfect at all times.

The Third Wave shows us the difference between dissociating from a problem, or denying its existence, and not engaging in its appearance. We cannot fix or solve the problem of global starvation from this human realm. We can only share the *spirit* of wealth and the *spirit* of abundance, and try to energetically anchor in that consciousness, wherever we are.

Giving money only creates a temporal change. We may do it when our hearts feel guided, but we shouldn't do it because we feel guilty, want to save the world, or feel better about ourselves. That only sets up a co-dependent relationship which enables the situation to continue.

We also cannot judge appearances in this physical, dualistic world. Everything in physical form is merely a mask for a greater energy. First we create dramatic situations, then we enable them, and then we perpetuate these situations by buying into their reality. So we end up identifying with the false reality that our egos created in the first place.

On the human level it may seem cruel, hard-hearted, or condescending to walk by a beggar, or demand honesty from a hungry merchant. It isn't at all.

On the Soul level, by not engaging in the dualistic world, we are ultimately benefiting the world more. When a friend is upset about what her co-workers are doing to her, or what her husband is or isn't doing to her, we don't help her by buying into her story and pouring pity onto the drama. We help by reminding her of her divinity and wholeness. We help her by seeing through the illusion she holds that she is a victim trapped by her circumstances. We empower people by helping them step up to their highest Soul vision of themselves.

What we see in a beggar's face – like everything we see – is only a projection of our own mind. What we see mirrored back will differ depending on what our own particular shadow-self is hiding. We could be hiding guilt, repulsion, sadness, inspiration, inferiority, superiority or any number of emotions. What surfaces emotionally for us is a greater comment about ourselves than it is about the beggar.

In The New Wave of Being, we understand that the world we see is merely a screen for our projections. We also understand that we can shift our focus and begin to see everyone and everything as a projection of our divinity rather than as a projection of our ego. Seeing in this way is seeing with true Third Wave vision rather than with First Wave eyesight.

We don't need to judge a beggar as unhappy and pitiful. Pity resonates at the frequency of victimhood. Guilt resonates at the frequency of resentment.

We need simply recognize a beggar's divine spark which, in turn, allows him to see the divine spark in himself. We can instead greet him with the energy of Namaste. This Sanskrit greeting means "The divine in me honours the divine in you".

This is how the G-String Theory works. When we sound the G-string in a beggar's presence, he responds by sounding the G-string back. Everything outside of such an interaction is merely a disguise covering Truth and covering Love.

In The New Wave of Being, we keep our attention on the Soul's world. In that way we allow each person to experience his own divinity. God resides within every human and within every being, animate or inanimate. Every rock, every tree, every blade of grass carries God's essence, and it is all whole and perfect.

Deprivation, lack, starvation, and poverty are of our collective making; collectively we can wake up and shift out of it. This is true compassion. This is the Eternal Now. This is the *integration* of the Oneness we all seek.

Δ

I fell asleep that night wondering if it would be our last night in Whitefield.

February 5

f

I arrived at darshan early that morning. I sensed a very different feeling in the air from the moment I entered the gate. Although I arrived unusually early, people were already making their way into the hall. It was much less crowded than usual. I was told that a lot of people were skipping darshan that morning so that they could get to Puttaparthi early and settle in before the masses arrived.

As I approached the metal detector, people started calling out "Baba! Baba!" and running towards the driveway which ran between Baba's living quarters and the area where I was standing.

Within seconds, there was pandemonium. Chaos ruled supreme. The seva dals might as well have gone home because everyone on the grounds of the ashram suddenly knew that Baba was about to drive out of his house. He was not going to do morning darshan after all. He was leaving Whitefield.

I had, however, underestimated the organizational skills of the seva dals. They quickly regained control of the anarchy. They interlinked hands, creating a human barrier the whole length of the driveway, men on one side and women on the other. Baba was safe from the raging crowd.

Minutes later, a white truck with flashing orange lights drove through the waiting crowd, closely followed by Baba's gleaming deep red BMW. Bringing up the rear was a large white Mercedes. I hadn't seen luxury vehicles like that since leaving the States months earlier. Baba was in the back seat of his car, dressed as always in his orange robe. People waved adoringly as he drove by. It was still pitch dark, and I noticed that Baba's entourage deviated from the Indian custom by driving with their headlights on.

It was quite an experience to witness this exit scene and the craziness that followed. For the first time, no one had any interest in getting to the front of the hall. Everyone rushed around trying to get their belongings packed to make the move to Puttaparthi.

John and I hung around the ashram for a while and met his other American friends. We told them that we were going to Dorairaj's house to collect our purchases. They wanted to meet the old man, too, so we all walked over there together.

While we were walking, one of the women asked, "Do you feel the energy? I feel dizzy from it."

"It's more likely that the dizziness comes from breathing these diesel fumes," I said, as huge trucks spewed black smoke to illustrate my point.

Young children were washing clothes in the "stream" along the side of the road. There was very little water, and it looked like runoff from the building next to it. They were pounding the cotton garments against the rocks and then wringing out the water with their experienced little hands. I wondered if they ran the clothing over to the ironing lady afterwards to have her press it.

The brilliant orange ball of fiery sun was just peeking over the rooftops. I wasn't comfortable knocking at Dorairaj's door so early, but the rest of the group really wanted to meet the couple we had spoken so much about. Also, we were about to leave for Puttaparthi.

We woke the old man up. He was still in his pajamas and didn't have his glasses on. Despite the early hour, he told us to wait a few minutes and then warmly welcomed us in.

Back in the familiar little room, Dorairaj showed the others the photos and handed out Vibhuthi and kum kum again. He asked if John was sure that he wanted to buy the talisman and the yantra. John was sure, so the man handed him a beautiful piece of jewelry and the yantra to go with it.

Then he gave me the little cassette he'd made of himself reading the various mantras. The rest of the group decided to buy stuff, too. Suddenly currency was flying everywhere! They bought yantras specific to their different professions, and they all wanted cassettes of the mantras, too.

Dorairaj gave John a few more bags of Vibhuthi and told him to hand it out to his patients.

John turned to me and said, "This is the law of karma in action. Yesterday I gave my only bag of Vibhuthi to one of the women who was sick. I didn't really want to give it to her, but I did because she asked for it. Today, without my asking, he hands me four new bags! Isn't it great how it works! And these days it happens so much faster – the waiting period's very short."

"It's also interesting," I said, "that he didn't ask for money, and he didn't encourage anyone to buy anything from him. Yet he's collecting more money than the millions of merchants on the street who beg you to buy from them. He's also getting more than the old priest who made us give a donation yesterday."

Finally, after several good-byes, Sai Rams, exchanges of e-mail addresses, and promises to stay in touch, we left, laden with our plastic bags. John and I walked back to our apartment, and the others caught a cab back to Bangalore.

"So, I guess we are going to Puttaparthi," I said. We hadn't really voiced it, but it looked that way by our actions.

"Yeah. Let's do it – it will be fun being there," said John.

We packed our bags. I went downstairs to pay the landlord and to tell him we were leaving a night early.

The narrow alleyways were filled with taxis. People were squeezing huge suitcases into tiny boots. I couldn't figure out why there was such an urgency about getting to Puttaparthi. Most of the people would be spending long periods of time at the ashram, so the rush to get there first didn't make sense, unless they wanted to get the first choice of rooms.

The shopkeepers had no interest in stopping passersby. They were heading north as well, and there was no time to make a sale. Even my drum salesmen were nowhere in sight!

I carried the lighter bags, the water bottles, the drum, and the delicate fans. John carried the two heavier bags, and we set off down the dusty road, over the smelly bridge, through the alleyway, weaving in and out of the market stalls, and finally finding our way to the main street.

"Taxi? Please. Taxi?" came the cries from the delighted drivers as soon as they saw us with our luggage.

The bidding war began. Prices were yelled out ranging from 1200 to 2700 rupees. A/C or no A/C. One person in the car or five people in the car. Shock absorbers or no shock absorbers. These were all issues that needed to be taken into account for the big drive north. There was also the old familiar query, "One way or come back?"

In the middle of all this, Hari showed up smiling.

"You need taxi, Mr. John?"

"Yes, Hari. We're going to Puttaparthi and coming back to Bangalore tomorrow," John explained.

"Okay," said Hari. "I find you very good taxi."

I wondered if Hari actually drove a cab or if he was more like a taxi broker – just securing business for the regular drivers.

He returned after a few minutes, smiling. "I find bus. You only pay driver 400 rupees each. Very nice bus."

A bus seemed like a good idea. We thought it might be more comfortable than a car for the long ride.

"Okay," I said to Hari. "Where is the bus?"

He pointed to a large old bus across the street. He grabbed our luggage and started packing it into the overhead racks. We sat down. The seats were padded, and it seemed alright.

A little boy who looked no more than eight years old banged on the window where I was sitting. He was holding up a small round wooden box.

"What is it?" I asked him through the window.

He wasn't nearly tall enough to reach the window, so he just kept tapping the box against the window with his outstretched hand.

"Look!" he kept repeating, offering me to take it inside the bus.

I was curious to see what was in the little box. I reached out the window. It was a small hand-carved chess set. I liked it and thought perhaps I should buy it.

"What are you going to do with it?" asked the ever-practical John.

"I don't know. It's cute, though," I said. But then I thought about all the stuff I needed to carry, and that I really wanted to have less "stuff".

I handed it back to the little boy. He kept banging it against the window imploringly.

"When is this bus leaving?" John suddenly asked, looking at the beggars and vendors who were starting to attach themselves to the bus windows.

I realized that that was one piece of information Hari had neglected to tell us, and we had neglected to ask.

"Just a moment. Wait here," said John, getting up out of his seat.

He came back a few minutes later. "This bus isn't leaving for at least another hour. They're going to try to fill it first. Let's just take a taxi rather than sit here indefinitely."

I agreed. I didn't want to sit in a stationary bus when we could be sitting in a moving car, so we unloaded all our bags and went to find the taxi driver we had liked from the first few rounds of interviews. He was delighted to take us to Puttaparthi. No sooner was the price agreed upon than he had our bags in the car.

John sat in the front with the driver, and I sat in the back seat. Most of the taxis were so overloaded with people and luggage that I felt like royalty having the whole back seat to myself.

We set off in a different direction than usual. After about ten minutes came the customary stop for petrol. I got out the car to get the water bottle from the boot. Immediately I had two little children pulling my arm.

"Pen please, pen Auntie," they begged, their hands cupped in a receptive way.

"Pen?" I asked, not sure what they were saying.

"Pens," said John through the open window. "They want pens. Kids here often ask for them."

I looked through my purse and found a ballpoint. I handed it to the little boy, who was ecstatic with the present. I felt like I had just handed him a million dollars. The problem was that the other boy also wanted a pen, and I couldn't find another one. The first boy skipped off elated; the other stood in abject disappointment.

If I'd allowed the external to influence and shape my self-image, I would've gone from feeling like the world's most wonderful, generous human being to feeling like the world's most loathsome, selfish human being in one short minute.

I got back in the car, and we headed off down a very narrow, bumpy road. We drove on that road for a long time before John asked, "Is this the road to Puttaparthi?"

"Yes sir," said the driver.

"How come there are no other taxis on this road? Everyone was leaving at more or less the same time – where are all the others?" asked John.

"They take bad road," answered the driver.

"There's a worse road than this one?" asked John.

"Other road many buses, many cars," he explained. "This road small, no cars."

"Small" was an understatement. It was more like a path. It was also hard to tell whether the road was full of potholes, or if we were driving through a pothole that had some blacktop around it. The bouncing around made it difficult to sit upright and impossible to lie down in the back seat. On the positive side, because there were no other cars on the road, we could leave the windows open without inhaling black smoke, and there weren't any trucks approaching us on the wrong side of the road.

We bounced along through very pretty countryside. At one point we drove by some people who were gathered a few metres from the roadside. They were dressed in gorgeous silks, which looked entirely incongruous with the surroundings.

"What's going on?" I asked the driver, curious about the different rituals and ceremonies.

"Wedding. They wedding, Madame," he answered.

"Do they have a big feast afterwards?" I asked, my thoughts rarely straying too far from Indian curries.

"What is this mean?" he asked me.

"Oh," I said, "a feast is a big meal. Do they have a big party and eat a lot after they leave the field?"

"Yes! Very big eating after," he said.

We continued on. We couldn't drive fast at all because of the condition of the road. A short while later, we had to slow down to a crawl because the road was filled with piles of hay that had been spread out for quite a distance.

"What's this about?" I asked.

The driver told me that they spread sugar cane or hay on the road and let the cars run over it to crush it. In this way, private cars are used as involuntary farm vehicles.

After another hour, we stopped at a roadside cafe. I had no intention of trying out the toilets until we were safely in a hotel room, but we did buy another bottle of water. We stretched our legs for a few minutes and got back in the car as soon as the beggars started to surround us again.

After a while, the driver turned to me, "I drink."

"Excuse me?" I said.

"You give me water. I drink," he said stretching his arm back towards me.

I didn't know what to do. I didn't want to be rude and tell him I wouldn't give him our water, but I did not like the idea of sharing backwash with a complete stranger. Suddenly, I remembered that I had come to India without getting any immunizations. I wondered if hepatitis, which is rampant in India, could be caught by sharing a water bottle. I wanted to ask John if he knew, but with the taxi driver's outstretched arm off the steering wheel and in my face, there was no time to find out. I considered giving him the whole bottle, but I knew that I needed to keep drinking for the long ride, and cafes were few and far between on that road.

My Western etiquette started waging war with my gut sense of trepidation. Then, miraculously, an empty plastic bottle rolled out from under the driver's seat. I was delivered from my dilemma! I picked up the empty bottle, poured some of my water into it, and handed it to the driver. I was relieved that he'd have something to drink and get his hands back on the steering wheel.

Δ

After at least another hour we arrived in Puttaparthi. Flowers were strewn everywhere. The streets were filled with coloured chalk drawings and the words "Sai Ram – Welcome Home" were written all over. Palm leaves and flowers were tied to all the metal street posts. Clearly, Baba had received a very warm welcome back to his home town. As we passed under the official archway entrance into Puttaparthi, a policeman motioned our driver to turn around. He obeyed the order and drove back out.

"You get out here," he said.

"Can't you take us into the village?" I asked.

"No taxi allow inside," he said.

I was about to believe him, when I saw one taxi after another drive under the arch without being sent back.

"Why are they allowed in then?" I asked him.

"No license go in," he admitted. "You take rickshaw to hotel. What hotel you stay?"

"We don't know yet."

I really didn't feel like walking around with our luggage in the midday heat. Even though Puttaparthi was only about three or four hours away from Whitefield, it was much hotter and more humid.

There was nothing to do. Our taxi wasn't allowed in.

A little black rickshaw pulled up next to us. Our taxi driver started shoving our luggage into the rickshaw. We thought we were squashed when we drove around Bombay that first night! But this time, the two of us, the driver, and all our bags and packages, were squeezed into the tiny rickshaw. My drum was hanging out the side, held onto my knees by its string. The fans lay across my lap on top of my backpack, and the water bottle rolled around between my feet. I couldn't even see the rest of the luggage because I was doubled over, trying to fit under the low roof of the rickshaw.

We bid our driver farewell and drove back under the arches. While we were driving, a little boy who looked nine or ten years old jumped onto the seat beside the driver. It would be more accurate to say he jumped onto the driver's lap.

"Where you stay?" he asked us, trying to see our faces behind the bags.

"We don't know," I said.

"Okay," said the young entrepreneur, "I show you very nice hotel."

I was impressed with this little kid, and he actually had something we needed. I asked the driver to go wherever the boy suggested.

We turned left off the main road and came to a stop at the end of the street. I couldn't see where we were, but, by the sound of things, we had arrived. I tried to climb out of the rickshaw without inflicting too much damage. We were stopped in front of a clean, unpretentious-looking building. An older man appeared, and the young kid told him that we wanted to see a room. John ran up to take a look while I waited with our stuff.

"It seems okay," said John, returning a few minutes later. "Nothing fancy, but it's clean."

I really didn't care to spend the rest of the day in that

rickshaw looking for accommodation, and John had uttered the magic word, "clean".

"350 rupees. You want?" asked the older man, smiling broadly.

"Okay. We'll take it," I replied.

With those words, the little boy who had rickshaw-napped us, along with two other boys, pulled our luggage from the vehicle, and carried it upstairs.

The room was filled with the porters, the landlord, and us. I handed the little boy my last ten rupees. His face lit up like a light. He was so elated that he stuffed the money in his pocket and ran out of the room. I realized that I had no more money for the others, and John was completely out, too, having paid his last rupees to the taxi and the rickshaw.

"We'll get money and give you a tip later," I assured them, ushering them out of the room.

That just left the landlord standing there.

"You need pay first," he said.

"Okay, but we need to change money," answered John.

"You come down, I show you," he said and left the room.

The room was very simple, but clean and full of windows. There was no A/C, but there was a ceiling fan, which I turned on immediately to get a breeze blowing through the room.

"If this is the temperature in the middle of winter, what's it like here in the summer?" I asked.

"It gets really hot," said John. "That's why Baba goes to Whitefield during the very hot months. It stays cooler there."

I much prefer the heat to the cold. There's something very freeing and sensual about the heat, and something very restrictive and repressive about the cold. I find it a lot easier to cool down in the extreme heat of summer than to heat up when the chill of the cold North American winters settles into my bones.

I had a cool shower, and we went downstairs to change money and find a restaurant. We were both hungry, and, because darshan at Puttaparthi lasts a lot longer than in Whitefield, it would be a while before we'd be able to eat.

The landlord offered to walk us to the nearest bank. I wasn't sure if it was out of kindness or fear of not getting paid. As we walked by a little Internet cafe – that also sold toilet paper – the lone woman in the store called out to our landlord.

"She say she change you money," he translated for us.

We went in, and I handed her my travelers cheques. She looked at them and said something to the landlord.

"She say she no can change traveler cheque. She must need cash."

"I have some cash, but not enough," I replied. "I could just change these at the bank."

After the man translated what I said, the woman motioned us to sit down. She didn't want us to leave. She took my travelers cheques and walked up the little street at a very quick pace.

I eyed the boxes of toilet paper stacked up amongst the high tech computers, remembering how shops in less-developed countries put together the most extraordinary assortment of items for sale. I remembered a little shop in Istanbul that sold diapers and magic markers in a photo developing store. At the back of that Turkish store, an assortment of women's lingerie was displayed which made Victoria's Secret shops look dowdy.

It made a lasting impression on me because the majority of women in Turkey are Moslem. They're covered from head to toe in long, black, formless dresses and veils, leaving only their eyes peeking out. I wondered how much of a market there could be for G-strings and strapless bras, but I noticed more sexy lingerie shops in Istanbul than anywhere else in the world.

This illustrates what happens when we suppress or deny a

natural part of ourselves. It inevitably becomes extreme in the opposite direction. Orthodox women in many religions are forced to cover themselves up and look as asexual as possible so that the men won't feel tempted and distracted. In a matriarchal society, men would be encouraged to wear paper bags over their heads if they couldn't control their wandering eyes.

I glanced towards the back of the internet-and-toilet-paper shop in Puttaparthi to see if G-strings were perhaps the under-punjabi attire, but there were no such items to be found there.

The shopkeeper returned, a little out of breath, with a form for me to fill out.

"Wouldn't it be easier if I went to the bank myself, so that she didn't have to run up and down the street?" I asked our translator. "It would probably be quicker, too."

The woman wouldn't hear of it. She grabbed the form from me, had me sign it, and disappeared once again.

We waited a while longer, getting more and more hungry. We asked the hotel owner for a restaurant recommendation.

"Turn left, top main road. No many restaurant open now. Baba arrive surprise this morning."

The restaurant and hotel owners didn't get word of Baba's return until very late, so almost nothing in the village was ready for the huge influx of visitors.

The woman finally returned with an enormous wad of notes. I needed to count it out several times. Counting that many notes made it difficult to remember if I was up to 3645 or 3564. John and I finally succeeded at counting out the 4562 rupees. Feeling like a multi-millionaire, I peeled off a few notes for our landlord, and we set off to look for a restaurant.

The place we were sent to was a Chinese restaurant. It was a big open room with no decor, just a few plastic tables set up in the dark room. A Chinese family was eating at one of the tables, but, other than that, it was empty.

A young Chinese waitress handed us a menu. I really don't like Chinese food. I always wonder what types of animals cooked in MSG and corn syrup are hidden in the thick sauces. I ordered plain steamed rice and plain tofu. John, being a little more daring than me, ordered vegetable balls in sauce. It was listed under the vegetarian section, so he assumed it was safe.

We sipped our freshly-squeezed fruit juices while waiting for the food to arrive. I hardly ate because, even though I was hungry, the dark restaurant didn't feel right to me. It didn't seem worth getting dysentery from food that was completely forgettable. I decided that, if I was going to get dysentery, it would be from the best-tasting food I ever ate.

We paid and left, realizing that we couldn't hang out because it was time for darshan. We walked over to the ashram and entered the gates. This ashram was very different from the other one. I could already tell why people were urging me to come to Puttaparthi, if only for two days. The grounds are many times larger than Whitefield's. There are huge buildings spread around the large grounds and elaborate statues and temples built along lovely tree-lined paths. It had a much older, warmer, more inviting feel about it. The colour scheme was the same pink and light blue.

Several men had already started to file into the enormous main hall. John followed the men, and I went in search of the women's entrance.

It took a long time to walk around the building. I kept walking through doorways which led to passageways, which led to seva dals barring the entrance. Every time I asked one of them where the women were supposed to enter, I was sent in an arbitrary direction, without so much as a "Sai Ram".

I finally found a long line of women standing against a building, lining up for darshan. Everyone pushed up against the side of the building trying to get some shelter from the hot sun. We were supposed to take off our shoes, but, when I stood on the hot cement, I got a quick mental image of erupting blisters. I decided that, for the hour or so that I would be waiting outside, I needed to wear my sandals. The line got longer and longer behind me, until it looped around another corner, and I couldn't see the end of it anymore.

Three young women speaking Arabic suddenly slid along the already-cramped side of the wall. They were trying to get to the front by moving along the inside line, hoping to go unnoticed by the seva dals. Pushing and arguing broke out as the other women, who had been waiting for ages, became upset with the new group elbowing its way to the front. Had the gates not opened just then, the three women probably would have been sent to the back by the angry crowd. Everyone forgot about them, however, as the focus shifted to getting through the gates. The three women managed to sneak ahead, happily applauding each other's success in muted tones.

I followed the crowd, heading up a cement ramp towards a larger courtyard. I couldn't see much because of the mass of people around me. Balancing on one foot, I slipped off my sandals. Because of the crush, all I could do was throw them over the heads of the women around me, hoping that I'd be able to find them again after darshan.

I was getting tired of all the pushing and shoving. It seemed so antithetical to the whole darshan experience. In so many countries, religious institutions are trying to figure out how to get people through the doors. Here, people were beating down the doors and literally fighting to get in. I knew that I would not be able to go through that routine every day if I lived in India. I would enjoy going to darshan every day, but I could not endure the hours of sitting, pushing, and waiting day in and day out.

Pushed up the stairs by the people behind me, I found

myself in a large rectangular courtyard outside a massive hall. It looked to be several times the size of the hall in Whitefield. With the help of the seva dals, women were forming lines on the cement floor just outside the hall's locked gates. I sat down in a line that was partly shaded by a plastic roof. I recognized several faces from Whitefield. The place filled up very quickly as new lines began to form. We sat and waited a long time before the gates were finally unlocked.

Before I knew what was going on, my line was called. I couldn't believe it! I was in the first row to be called. I stood up, and followed the women in front of me into the hall. We went through the metal detector, which was set up on the threshold. Once inside, I looked around the vast room and wondered which of the many entrances Baba used.

I laughed, thinking, "I am finally called first, and I have no idea where to sit."

I quickly realized that if I followed in the direction of the other racing women, it would be a pretty good indication of where the prized seats were.

This hall had a completely different layout. Although it also had a stage area, there were aisles and entrances everywhere, and it was set up more like theatre-in-the-round.

I sat down one row from an aisle near the low stage. My seat was just about as good as it gets. I was excited because I knew that, when you get close to Baba, the energy is so much more electric. It isn't something you are necessarily aware of at the time. It is afterwards that a warm peacefulness washes over you. I realized, too, that for the first time I was actually close enough to hand Baba a letter or to talk to him.

I wondered what I would ask for in the letter; what would I say? If I could ask one question, what would it be?

Imagine that God is standing next to you, willing to grant you one wish or to answer one question. Where do you start?

It's overwhelming. I wouldn't want to blow it with something small. What if I held out a letter, and he didn't take it? Would that mean that my wish wouldn't be granted?

I hadn't even considered writing a letter before. So there I was with all of these thoughts and feelings; I could actually feel the electrons flowing through me.

Sitting and waiting for Sai Baba to walk by me, I thought back to the first time I met Vicki's father, Louie. He's a very unusual man. He's probably under five feet tall, and he weighs almost nothing. He moves between the sacred and the profane with an ease that is masterful.

He feels the presence of Mother Mary around him in a very palpable way. He sees her, talks to her, and is guided by her. He doesn't have too much interest in her son, but he does love Mary's energy. He instantly lets people know if he thinks they lack integrity and won't allow them in his house if they fail to reach his standard for authenticity.

Vicki once told me about an occasion when she had a group of friends over to meditate. Louie came in and instantly picked out the con-artist in the group. It's as though he sees a light around some people, and a darkness around others. He says that he follows Mary's guidance in everything he does.

I was at Vicki's house one day, and in walked eighty-six-year-old Louie. Vicki had warned me about him, so I was wondering if I would be acceptable. He was wearing thick glasses, and, despite his small stature and age, he was carrying the bags of groceries he'd just purchased.

"That son of a bitch! Do you know what he did?" exclaimed Louie, not noticing me in his tirade.

"Who, Daddy? Who are you talking about?" asked Vicki, winking at me.

"I have been filling up with gas at that place for over forty years, and that son of a bitch failed my car inspection. He wouldn't give me the sticker! Can you believe it?"

I realized that it probably wasn't the best moment to be meeting Louie for the first time, but there was no alternative.

"Daddy, this is Ilana," said Vicki.

"Who?" he asked, looking at me for the first time.

"Ilana," said Vicki, "she's a friend of mine."

Louie looked at me, quiet for a moment, and then he said, "Come over here!"

I did as I was told.

"Let me take a look at you," he continued.

A few seconds passed very slowly as I awaited the verdict.

"Vicki, I like this one!" he declared, much to my relief. "This girl is the real thing. Look at that! She has light radiating from inside her. Vicki, Mary sent this girl to me!"

I was hoping to merely pass the grade; I hadn't expected to be voted the shining star.

"I want to take you upstairs," said Louie. "I know the real thing when I see it, and you have Mary's light."

I looked over at Vicki, who just shrugged, a big smile filling her face.

"I want to show you something," he said, grabbing me by the arm in a vise-grip that belied his eighty-six years.

I went, or should I say I was pulled, up the stairs and into his bedroom. A TV sat at the foot of the two big single beds, and statues of Mary covered another small table.

"Do you see this?" asked Louie, pointing to a statue of Jesus on the cross with people gathered at his feet. It was made from porcelain and was only about two feet high.

"Do you see this statue?" he asked again.

"Yes, Louie, I see the statue," I said.

"I got this statue when Mary appeared to me the first time. Every one I've let hold this statue to make a wish, tells me that the wish came true. Do you understand what I'm saying?"

"Yes, I understand," I said, smiling at how emphatic his little body could be.

"Okay. You understand what I'm saying?"

"I think so," I replied, wondering if I was supposed to do something.

"Kid, put your hands on the statue, and ask for whatever you want. Whatever you want will be yours."

With that he pulled me towards him again and planted a big wet kiss on the crown of my head.

"You are so beautiful," he said. "What a light shines in you. It makes me want to cry."

I wasn't sure what to say, so I just stood there wondering what on earth I should ask for. This man, who Vicki tells me hasn't been wrong yet with regard to all this Mary stuff, was telling me to hold a statue of Jesus, and pray for whatever I most wanted. What pressure!

I was laughing inside at the irony of seeing myself, a young Jewish woman, clutching a statue of Jesus and praying after being told that I carry the light of Mary. What would my grandparents say? My grandmother's whole family was wiped out by Hitler, and here I was, a few decades later, clinging onto Jesus' bloody porcelain body.

"Go on," said Louie, moving over to another small statue of Mary. "Think careful, because it will come true. Take as long as you need. I'll wait here."

I focused my attention on my deepest wishes. It's like tossing a coin to make a decision. There is a split second, while the coin is spinning in the air, when you know intuitively how you want it to fall. In that millisecond, your heart knows what result you truly desire.

It is powerful to know, absolutely, that what we desire on a Soul level is ours to receive. We are only limited in what we receive, by our capacity to contain the energy coming through.

So I put my hands on the statue, closed my eyes and thought, "Okay, Ilana. This is no big deal. I mean, what are the chances that any of this is will come true anyway? This is all silly. You don't need a statue to reach God. You can access Him/Her directly, but go ahead and hold the statue anyway. You trust Vicki, and she swears by her father's gift, so don't blow it with all this mind chatter – just do it!"

I slowed down my breathing and allowed myself to go into a meditative, receptive state. I heard a very beautiful prayer start to form in me. I stood there for quite a while allowing it to flow through me, and wash over me. Then I slowly opened my eyes and looked over at Louie, who was beaming on the other side of the room.

We went back downstairs.

"Vicki," he said, "you stick around this girl. Honest to God, the hair on the back of my neck stood up when I first saw her. You know that don't happen often, Vicki. Tell her. I don't see this too often."

Before Vicki could confirm his observation, he swung around to me again.

"And you stick with Vicki, because she will help you, too. The two of you will work together. Mary sent you to me. Do you understand me? You ring a bell in my heart, you crazy kid," he said, his eyes tearing up.

"Yes, I understand. Thank you, Louie. You are very kind," I said, looking at his little smiling face.

Suddenly, he noticed his vehicle's failure report on the table, and he was back to cussing the S.O.B. who refused him a sticker after all those years.

Just before I left, Louie gave me a box of baklava and a little necklace which he wanted me to have. Every morning at four, Louie goes down to the kitchen and bakes several boxes of baklava. He gives each of his daughters a few boxes, instructing them to give the pastries to anyone they meet that day. He also drives around with a few boxes in his car and hands them to people he happens upon during his daily errands. Every day he bakes, and every day he gives it all away.

The following day, I was getting a shiatsu massage from a woman who also does energy work. I didn't say anything about my previous day's adventure. During the session she suddenly said to me, "Do you know that you have a new female energy around you? It feels to me like a higher vibration female, like Quan Yin or Mother Mary."

I didn't respond because I wanted to see if any other information was going to come through.

"I'm being told to rub rose oil on the soles of your feet," she said, just before finishing the session. "I know this sounds weird, so I didn't do it at first. But I keep hearing the message, so I am going to do it."

On the way home, I stopped at John's office to say hello. I told him where I had just been.

"I feel really relaxed," I said. "She rubbed rose oil on my feet at the end of the session."

"Oh," said John, "that's Mary's scent. Sai Baba's scent is jasmine and Mary's is the rose. They say that when you smell those flowers unexpectedly, you know that person's energy is around you. So maybe you have Mary hanging out with you these days."

I told him what had happened the day before with Louie.

Back in Puttaparthi in my own little world of jasmine and roses, I suddenly sensed the electrical current announcing Baba's presence.

The room had really filled up since I first sat down. In front of me was the plush red carpet, which was rolled out just for Baba. Across the aisle sat all the little girls who were studying at Baba's school and their teachers. Each girl had perfect little braids down her back. They all wore uniforms, and their faces were shining with excitement as they waited for Baba to walk by. It had been a long time since any of the Puttaparthi students or the locals had seen Baba, so they were thrilled to have him back home.

He entered through the large open door to my right. He had a big smile and clearly was happy to be back in Puttaparthi.

I was also getting excited as I watched him move closer. The women around me all had their letters ready. I thought that perhaps I should scribble a note on a piece of paper that I had in my purse. But, again, I didn't know what to ask.

I know that the answer to every single question is out there, and readily available. The key isn't really getting the right answer; it is asking the right question.

In truth, the ultimate answer to every single philosophical, psychological, and metaphysical question, no matter how complex, boils down to one word. Love. Actually, and more specifically, self-love. Upon self-love, everything else will build. From self-love, everything will flow. Without self-love, nothing makes sense, and happiness seems out of reach.

I knew then that I had no questions which needed answering. I could enjoy the presence and the energy of this Avatar without wanting or needing anything. I felt totally at peace as I sat and waited for him to walk by.

Baba moved towards me. When he was about three people away from me, he stopped and turned to a young girl. He held up his right hand and started making tiny circular movements. Sure enough, the white Vibhuthi started to flow out of his fingers. He walked on, and then he locked eyes with me. I felt his eyes look right into mine, and he didn't drop his gaze until he had walked by.

A huge grin filled my face. The memory of my dream with Baba came flooding back. I didn't care that everyone else was genuflecting and having a serious attack of D.D.D. I felt like laughing when I saw him, so I did. As he passed by, a huge black and white butterfly fluttered from his full head of hair. It flew back towards me, moving its delicate wings just enough to fly in circles above the area where I was sitting. I couldn't take my eyes off it. It was the size of a little bird. It finally perched on the enormous chandelier above me. I thought about the symbolism that Native Americans attribute to animals which cross their paths. I remembered that the butterfly symbolizes transformation.

By now, Baba had moved over to the men's side. He was chatting with someone who was kneeling at his feet. Baba stayed with him for a particularly long time before moving to the next person. After walking through the crowd, he climbed onto the low stage and stood in front of a group of men. In Puttaparthi, men are allowed to sit on the stage, which is actually more like a platform.

I heard the people he was talking to start laughing. They were having a long discussion with much interspersed laughter. I wondered what was being said, but I didn't really care. I was enjoying just being present. After a while, Baba went into the little chapel that was connected to the hall by a doorway at the back of the stage. After a very short time he came back out and went to talk to the same men again. I found out later that they were teachers at his college.

After a long time, Baba left the hall through a side entrance in the women's section. Taking more letters and stopping to talk along the way, he finally disappeared from sight.

Even though I had been sitting for over four hours on the cold stone floor, I did not want to move. I felt relaxed, much like I feel after having extended energy work done. I wanted to stay in that place forever, so I closed my eyes and waited for the crowds to disperse.

"Sai Ram. Sai Ram!" I heard around me. I assumed that someone was doing something that displeased the seva dals.

I kept my eyes closed.

"Sai Ram. No sitting. Sai Ram."

I opened my eyes and saw one of the women standing over me. The room had almost cleared out.

"No sit. Please. Sai Ram," she repeated.

It appeared that, in Puttaparthi, one isn't allowed to just sit still and soak up the energy. I wondered why Baba would discourage people from moving or talking after darshan and then allow the seva dals to throw everyone out as soon as he left the hall. It didn't make sense to me.

I walked out very slowly to the sound of the metal gates being shut behind me. I did not want to talk to anyone or go anywhere. I needed to move very slowly.

I noticed some monkeys jumping around the trees in the courtyard. I watched them playing and screeching, chasing one another. I stood still and looked at the elaborate building outside the main hall. Although it was tall, it had a very small footprint, and the roof rose in a step formation. It was all made from extremely intricate, detailed artwork. The final tier was a narrow ridge with a small pedestal-like, pointed tower on top. Perched on top of that sat a monkey.

Had it not been for the monkeys playing in the tree beside me, I would have thought that the monkey, so precariously perched on top of the tower, was part of the decor. He didn't move a muscle. He sat like a sentry and watched over the crowd below.

"Sai Ram. No stop," came a man's voice. A serious-looking male seva dal told me to move along. I was not holding anyone up. I was not in anyone's way, and, besides, I was not capable of walking faster. So, smiling, I looked at him and pointed up to the monkey. The man couldn't hold his serious attitude any longer. He smiled, too, and walked on, leaving me to enjoy my peace.

It took me about half an hour to walk around the building to the place where I had left John. I felt drugged, high on life. John was waiting for me, also feeling very peaceful.

"I was sitting right at the place where Baba was talking to those men. It was intense being so close for that long," he said.

"Is there somewhere pretty where we can walk?" I asked, not really wanting to be in the markets or traffic for a while.

"There's a place we could walk to up the hill," he said. "It has a beautiful view over the whole area, and there's a meditation wheel buried under a tree at the top."

We walked up the hill through the paths of greenery and flowers. The paths were tree lined and pretty.

"Baba took so many letters today," John said.

"Today was the first time that I could have handed him one," I said. "But I realized that there really is nothing to ask."

"If I was going to write him a letter," said John, "I would write, 'Dear Baba, I have been sitting on this hard stone floor, day after day, waiting for you to walk by. I have only one request Baba...please give me back the feeling in my legs.'"

We walked through a little metal gate and continued up a track, all the time heading uphill. Every ten metres or so, there was a sign with an inspirational message written on it about our relationship with God and the Universe. Some of them were really interesting and thought provoking with sayings like, "One hand in service is better than two hands in prayer."

We reached the meditation area. A lovely tree stood in the centre of a clearing surrounded by a circular stone wall. Its branches were spread out wide and fairly low. A couple of people were sitting beneath it, and a few more were sitting in the clearing beside it. I sat down and closed my eyes, enjoying the quiet and the stillness. I walked around the tree, and then we went to look at the view.

The surroundings were hilly. The whole area was arid but beautiful. The land glowed with a soft pinkish-orange hue in the last rays of the setting sun. The small village of Puttaparthi lay below.

We walked a little further up the hill to see the view from the other side. It was quite dark by the time we got there. The moon was almost full, hovering in the sky, throwing off a beautiful, soft feminine light. The only sound was the fast, fluttering wings of bats who zipped by us at a very rapid pace. They whizzed by so close that it seemed they would fly into us. I enjoyed having the butterfly of transformation and the bats of rebirth flying around my head on the same evening.

John pointed to a big building at the top of the hill.

"That's a really interesting museum. There's a display explaining the connection between religion and science. It explains the physics of energy and matter, and how it relates to spirituality and religion."

"I would love to see it. Do you think we'll have time in the morning?" I asked.

"We might. Or we could go and see Geta, Baba's elephant."

I remembered that we had arranged to meet Kathy and Bernado at six for dinner. We had made the arrangement before leaving Whitefield to make sure that we didn't leave India without saying goodbye.

"I looked out for them, but I didn't see them," said John.

We walked back down to the main area of the ashram. We still didn't see them, so we went back to the room to shower. I decided to wear shorts and a T-shirt, and break from the traditional garb for a change. It was still so hot that I didn't feel like wearing long sleeves and long pants.

Just as we were about to leave for dinner with John's friends at their hotel, there was a loud knock on the door.

"Who could that be? There's no room-service in this place," I said, opening the door.

The young boy who had helped carry our bags up the stairs earlier, walked into the room with a joyful "Sai Ram."

"Sai Ram," I answered.

"I carry you bag. Only other boy give money," he said, staring at us despondently.

"Oh, sorry! Here..." I said, handing him a tip.

It was as though someone with an instamatic camera had said "Cheese", as a wide smile transformed his expression.

"Could you order us a taxi for tomorrow morning after darshan?" John asked.

"Yes. I get very nice taxi," he said, seeing another few rupees in his future.

John gave him very specific instructions. He repeated several times that we wanted air conditioning, that the air conditioning needed to be operational, that it was a one-way-only ride, and that we needed the taxi to pick us up by eleven.

The boy left, closing the door behind him. Almost immediately, there was another knock. The bright shining face of the little boy who had rickshaw-napped us earlier that morning was at the door.

"Hello," I said, surprised to see him again.

"Hello. I come in," he said, walking into the room as though we'd been best friends for years.

"What's your name?" I asked him.

"Sheeva," he said.

"How old are you, Sheeva?" asked John.

John and I had discussed earlier that day how children in India looked much younger than they really were, perhaps because of malnutrition. I had guessed that Sheeva was eight or nine. John thought he was probably ten or eleven.

"Fourteen," came his reply.

"Really? You are fourteen?" I asked.

"Yes. I fourteen," he said again, smiling proudly.

"Are you still in school?" I asked.

"No! Finish school."

Sheeva seemed to be feeling very at home chatting with us. In fact, he felt so at home that he plunked himself down on our nice, clean white sheets. I could tell by looking at John that he and I were having exactly the same thought...lice...sweat, and that was the least of it! We burst into simultaneous laughter as the little street urchin began rolling around on our sheets, trying to change the speed of the ceiling fan to his satisfaction. Sheeva looked over at us, and he started laughing, too.

"We are going out now," I said. "Could you stand up? We need to leave."

"I close fan," he said, hopping onto the second bed to reach the switch more easily.

"No Sheeva. Leave it on," John and I yelled in unison, hoping to keep at least one of the beds clean.

Given the difficulty I had encountered getting the hotel owner to give me two top sheets for the night, I knew there was no way we would be able to get a change of sheets. Sheeva stood up grinning from ear to ear.

"You look happy," I said.

"Yes," he answered. "You give me more money?"

"Why would I give you more money?" I asked him.

"You give me more rupees," he said, smiling impishly.

"Sheeva, we gave you a tip this morning for finding us the hotel. I'm not giving you more now."

"Where you go?" he asked.

"We're meeting some friends for dinner," said John.

"Okay. I come," he announced, his white teeth still flashing a mischievous smile.

I turned off the lights and the fan, and we walked out the door. Sheeva followed. I struggled getting the key into the lock. Sheeva moved me aside and took the key. He turned the lock easily.

"There! I lock door for you," he said.

"I am not giving you a tip for that," I said, playing along with him.

We walked downstairs, and Sheeva followed alongside us. We passed our money-changing lady and went up the narrow street past the Chinese restaurant that I was still trying to forget. Sheeva never left our side. Walking three astride, we must have looked like a young family going out for an evening stroll. Sheeva kept asking for more money, and we kept saying no.

Finally he said, "Buy me rice."

"Okay," said John, "we will buy you a bowl of rice, but then you need to leave us alone, okay?"

"Okay," agreed Sheeva.

"Where do you want to get the rice?" I asked, looking at the road-side food vendors.

Sheeva pointed to a grocery shop across the street. There were large burlap sacks spread out on the sidewalk, laden with spices of intoxicating smells and colours. There were other sacks filled with lentils, dried beans, legumes and pulses of all colours. Huge closed sacks of basmati rice and long sticks of sugar cane leaned against the wall. Fresh pineapples, oranges, papayas, tomatoes, coconuts, small yellow bananas still attached to their stalks, bunches of fresh herbs, and other fruits and vegetables I couldn't identify were all displayed in colourful piles. An old-fashioned scale was balanced on a rickety wooden box at the entrance.

"I don't see any bowls of rice," I said.

"No bowl! Buy bag!" he said.

The sacks of rice he was pointing to had to weigh twenty kilograms. A family of four could eat from them for a couple of weeks and still have some left over.

"I'm not buying you that," said John, feeling like Sheeva was really pushing his luck. "Now please leave us alone. You need to stop following us."

It was useless. He wouldn't leave.

We found the hotel and went inside. Sheeva sat at the front door waiting for us. A gentle breeze blew through the restaurant, which was situated on the open flat roof. A thin, white, tarpaulin-like sheet was strung above most of the tables. It was probably used to provide shade during the day. Most of the tables were filled with Westerners eating and enjoying the cool breezes. We spotted John's friends sitting around a small table. The waiter quickly pulled over another table so that we could join them.

It seemed that the eighth member of their group had caught a virus the second day she was there and wasn't well enough to get out of bed. They had taken her to a doctor who prescribed antibiotics. Morning darshan had been canceled, and most of them had missed afternoon darshan because they hadn't left Bangalore until lunch time, so they weren't very happy.

John and I, on the other hand, were in a very good mood. We were enjoying a perfect blend of mind, body, and spirit, which had synthesized into the same experience. We ordered several entrees and juices, and we sat back relaxed. The others at the table asked us what we'd been up to since arriving in India. We started regaling them with some of the funny incidents that had happened along the way. We told them about our banana-leaf readings, about our midnight horse ride on the beach, and about the cobra lady who chased John around the parking lot.

"Then there was Pakua, the masseur," I said.

"I ordered a massage for Ilana in the hotel room in Bombay," explained John.

"It was a very unusual massage," I said, smiling.

"I thought I was doing her a favour," said John.

"John didn't realize there was anything weird about his massage until Pakua said to him, 'Now turn your head and cough!' Most people would have realized what was going on at that point, but not our John!" I said.

We both laughed as we recalled it. Everyone else looked quite shocked. A loud silence fell over the table.

I was surprised and somewhat amused by their reaction. If we can't have fun and laugh at ourselves and at life, then we are missing one of the best things about being human.

I remembered back many years before, when Clay and I were left sitting alone at his mother's Thanksgiving dinner table. His mother had cut out a little column from the newspaper, romanticizing the notion that Thanksgiving was a true joining of Pilgrims and Native Americans. Smiling, she'd handed the article to Clay and asked him to read it aloud. Being a lawyer, Clay was not about to read anything aloud without checking it first. He blanched, looking like he was going to toss the stuffed turkey and cranberry sauce.

"I can't read this," he said to his mother, handing back the paper. "Do you know what Thanksgiving really is?"

Now it was his mother's turn to blanche.

"What is it you mean?" asked his semi-deaf grandmother, who was so proud of her grandson that nothing he said could upset her.

"Columnists write these sugar-coated truisms, and people don't realize that, while it is nice to give thanks, we are ignoring the other side of it. It's a day of mourning for the Native Americans," he explained.

"In essence, it's celebrating the annihilation of a whole people," I continued. "It marks the beginning of the end for the indigenous people of this country."

"Look what has happened to them since the white Europeans arrived," Clay said. "They were tricked out of their land, they're living on reservations, and they're plagued with alcoholism. On Thanksgiving, they wear black and grieve. They are completely displaced."

"There's an excellent movie documentary called 'The Broken Rainbow' which explains it all," I added.

Clay's father, who always enjoyed a good debate, kept up the back and forth with us for a while, much to his wife's displeasure.

One by one, all the people sitting around the table got up and left. His grandmother probably would have stayed, but, being deaf, she thought the party was moving to the kitchen, so she followed the crowd.

"Well, I guess we won't be invited back for Thanksgiving dinner again," Clay said, as the two of us sat alone at the table.

And we weren't.

John and I decided to stop telling stories about our time in Bombay. Luckily, our food arrived, breaking the tension a little. Everything was delicious as always, and, having eaten very little all day, it felt good to eat again.

When we finished dinner, John was asked to give the sick member of the group a chiropractic adjustment. I decided to take a slow walk back to our hotel.

The streets were quite deserted. There was no bustling marketplace like the one at Whitefield. I kept looking out for Sheeva, wondering if he was still waiting for us. A few people tried to sell me stuff, but I kept walking without looking at their wares at all. I think the biggest intrigue for the people on the street was seeing a woman walking around in shorts and a T-shirt. I felt completely safe walking alone there, more so than in any American city at night.

I found a little street called Shanti Street. Shanti means Eternal Peace.

"What a lovely name for a street," I thought. Near Shanti Street was the little road that led to our hotel. Halfway down, I saw that the Internet-and-toilet-paper shop was still open. I remembered that many hotels in India didn't supply toilet paper, so I stopped off to buy some before they closed for the night. I took a roll from the pile on the sidewalk, and went in to pay for it. No one was using the computers, so I decided to check my e-mail. After trying for fifteen minutes to log on, I gave up and went back to the room.

John returned after a few minutes. It was late, and we were both tired. It had been another busy day, but nothing compared to what awaited us the following day. Darshan begins at about 4:30 AM in Puttaparthi, so I really wanted to get some sleep before our last one of the trip.

No sooner was I settled under the cool sheets than a dog started barking outside our window. It was not too bad at first, but then he started howling in a high-pitched tone that sounded like a bad soprano. Within minutes, a whole pack of dogs had gathered from all over Puttaparthi, and a midnight operetta began. There were many sopranos, several tenors and a few alto howlers. It was the funniest thing I had heard in a long time. They were howling at the almost-full moon, taking turns back and forth. It was so loud that other dogs, far in the distance, began calling back to them.

There was no chance at all of falling asleep, so I got up and looked out the window. There they were, every shape and size of stray mutt you could imagine. I closed the windows to mute the sound a little, but it was futile. All it did was stop the airflow through the already warm room. I reopened the windows and got back into bed. John and I were laughing so hard at that point that I thought I'd fall off my bed and land on the tiled floor below.

"This is why the room's so cheap! It's probably the hottest canine nightspot in town," I said, hardly able to speak.

John couldn't hear me with the cacophony going on outside. My belly ached from laughing. Even though I would rather have been asleep, it actually felt like a gift to have a good, spontaneous, belly-aching, uninhibited, unadulterated laugh about nothing in particular.

After about ten more minutes, I got up again and leaned out the window yelling, "Can you guys take the party somewhere else please? We're trying to sleep in here!"

Incredibly they did! I could still hear them howling as they walked off, far into the distance, oblivious to the disturbance they were causing along the way.

Within minutes of their leaving, I was asleep.

February 6

f

I woke up at about 3 AM. Other than a ray from a distant streetlight, it was very dark in the room.

A short while later, John woke up, too. He decided to do some push-ups and sit-ups, as he'd done the previous morning. At home, John works out every day. He was having workout withdrawal, so he started toning his muscles on the cold stone floor.

I feel like such a slob when people are exercising around me. I'm in good shape, and, when I'm home, I work out. But for the past few months, being on the road, it was difficult. We hiked in the mountains, swam and snorkeled in the ocean, and went for long walks, but the only weightlifting I did was lugging suitcases between taxis and airports.

After what seemed like a hundred repetitions, John was done. We decided to go to the ashram early because there was a pre-darshan meditation in the chapel, which John said was worth attending.

Everything felt special that morning, because I knew that it was the last of it for the trip. Even putting on my punjabi and silk shawl felt special.

We locked the room door without Sheeva's help this time and made our way quietly down the stairs. In the semi-darkness, we almost stumbled over a young boy who was asleep in the entrance way. In the dim light, it appeared to be the same boy who had come upstairs for his tip the day before. Apparently, he slept right at the front entrance to the hotel. He was fully dressed in the same clothes he'd been wearing during the previous day. Apart from the thin straw mat he was lying on, there was no padding between him and the hard, cold, stone floor.

We hadn't counted on being locked in the building!

"What should we do?" I asked, after John ascertained that the large wrought-iron gate was indeed padlocked shut.

"We'll have to wake him," said John.

"Excuse me, Sai Ram – excuse me," we said, timidly attempting to rouse him. He didn't even stir.

We called out again, this time a little louder and closer to his ear, "Excuse me, hello..." But that didn't work either.

John leaned over very close to the man's head and tried again to get his attention, but he didn't move a muscle.

"Do you think he's alive?" I asked.

"I think he's breathing," said John.

Then loudly he said, "Excuse me...hello!"

Still nothing.

"Imagine if we miss our last darshan because we're locked in by the sleeping night watchman," I said, thinking it quite an amusing start to our day.

John leaned over once again. This time he shook the man's shoulder. The watchman stirred, groaned softly, and rolled over onto his other side – dead to the world!

John shook the man some more, telling him rather loudly that we needed to get out of the building. Still nothing.

"If there was a fire in this building, no one would be able to get out, I said. "This locked gate is the only form of egress, and sleeping beauty is lying here unconscious."

We started laughing, not sure what to do next. Still, the watchman didn't stir.

John leaned over him again, shook him hard, and shouted right next to his ear, "Can – we – have – the – key. We – need – to – get – outside."

The young man finally stirred. John seized the moment and repeated his request. Incredibly, the sleeping man slid his thin hand into his pocket and pulled out a small key. John grabbed it immediately and tried it in the padlock. It was the right key – we were released! He put the key back next to the man, who didn't stir again.

"Sai Ram...thank you," we called and hurried out the front gate, leaving our comatose friend to his dreams.

The streets were empty as we made our way towards the ashram gates.

I heard crackling coming from a tall metal electrical post. I looked up and saw sparks jumping around in the air. It was coming from a couple of wires that were joined together like two twist ties.

"If this is the condition of the electrical wiring, it's lucky I didn't know we were locked in last night," I said, moving away from the sparking wires.

Given that it was still pitch dark, there was quite a lot of activity inside the ashram walls.

"Where else on earth would you find this many people awake and busy by 3:30 AM?" asked John.

"When I lived on a Kibbutz in Israel, we were at work by 4 AM. The work day was over by eleven o'clock because of the heat. It was nice, actually, because then we'd have the rest of the day to ourselves."

"I would like that," said John. "That schedule would suit

my lifestyle."

"It's like the siesta lifestyle. Sleeping in the middle of the day when the sun is at its hottest. I like that, too," I said, "but it wouldn't work in North America because it's too cold, and people drive so far to get to work."

We arranged to meet back at the front entrance after darshan, and we went to our separate areas. I wasn't sure how to get into the chapel for the meditation, but I saw a line of women, so I walked over to investigate. I couldn't find anyone with enough English to tell me what that particular line was for, so I left my sandals under a tree and sat down.

It was lovely sitting under the clear Indian night skies. The stars were twinkling brightly above me. One of the things I really enjoyed about being in Australia and New Zealand was being outside in the middle of the night, looking up at the brilliant skies. It was especially beautiful to see the Southern Cross twinkling brightly as it rose over the horizon each night.

I was invited to speak at a week long conference outside Sydney. I met wonderful people and really felt the warmth of the spiritual family while I was there. I was put up by a lovely woman, Colleen, who opened her home to me completely. We got up at five o'clock each morning, and at six we went swimming in the ocean. It was incredible. The air was very warm, even that early in the morning, and the ocean was a perfect temperature. We meditated on the soft white sand before immersing in the beautiful deep-blue waters. The rising orange sun wrapped me in its soft rays as I swam out beyond the waves. Swimming in the ocean, and playing under the waves at sunrise is as spiritual an experience as there is. I felt like I was in perfect synchronization with the vibration of the entire Universe.

Later, we'd shower and head off to the conference centre. At about two o'clock on the day I was leaving, I caught a ride to the airport to fly the five hours to Perth, where I was to give a talk a couple of days later.

The flight was delayed for two hours, so I didn't arrive in Perth until about nine o'clock at night. It felt like midnight to me because of the time difference.

While filling out the car rental agreement at the airport, the friendly guy behind the desk asked, "Where are you heading?"

"Dunsborough," I said.

"Dunsborough?" he asked, looking at me as though I was crazy. "That's about three and a half hours from here. That's if you know where you're going!"

I wasn't pleased that I still had such a long drive ahead of me, because it had already been such a long day, but I didn't really care.

"I'll be okay," I said.

"Actually, we can't let you have the car if you're driving that far out of the city. We don't carry insurance for that area because it's very dangerous to drive there at night. Kangaroos run across the roads, and many car accidents have been caused from hitting them in the dark. You'll have to spend the night in the city and drive down there tomorrow," he informed me.

"No, I'm going to do it tonight. I'll be fine; don't worry."

"But, Ma'am, we can't insure the car if you drive there after sunset."

"Then I'll take the car without insurance," I replied. "Pretend I told you that I'm going into the city. I'll be fine. I'd better leave because it will be really late by the time I get there."

It wasn't the most reassuring way to start a four-hour drive! Especially driving alone, on the opposite side of the road, in the middle of the night, somewhere in the Outback Down Under.

Getting to Dunsborough was quite an adventure. To keep awake, I turned up the volume on the radio. I listened to rock and folk music, dancing in my seat as I drove.

After about two hours of driving, however, the radio signals all disappeared, and the paved road turned to red dirt. There was significant road construction, so I was trying to avoid the potholes and keep on the path. There were no roadside lights, and it was so black outside that I could hardly see the dirt road, even with my headlights on high beam.

There were two things that kept me awake and happy as I headed south. One was the joy of knowing that I was doing exactly what I was supposed to be doing. I completely trusted that I was being guided through the whole trip, and that I had absolutely nothing to worry about.

The second awe-inspiring part of the drive was being led by the lights of the Southern Cross. I didn't have a map, but I could tell that I was heading south. Those five stars were in my windscreen the whole way, magnetically but gently drawing me towards them.

I realized that, in the old paradigm of living, it was entirely unusual to attempt the long drive alone at midnight and to show up at someone's house that I hadn't ever met before. I would arrive around one o'clock in the morning (if I found the house at all!) and climb into her guest-room bed. I had only ever spoken to my host when I called from the airport two hours earlier to say that the flight had been delayed.

Until then, Margot and I had only corresponded by e-mail. She had seen my photograph on my website. She said that a warm rush flowed over her when she looked at it. She felt as though we were closely related in a past life and ought to meet. I had no idea what to expect, and had no expectations about any of it. And so I found myself driving down there only because it felt right, and for no other reason. This way of living is an expression of The New Wave of Being.

Δ

Sitting under the twinkling Indian skies, I tried not to think about the marathon day looming ahead of me. I would still be awake twenty-four hours later, with a very long flight to London ahead of me.

I noticed that the lines behind me had filled up. Finally, we were led into another courtyard, where we were told to sit down again.

We waited for a fairly long time before being directed into the chapel. It was very small inside. The men were filing in from the other side and sitting on the floor. The interior was ornately decorated with gilded statues and brightly painted figurines. Photos of Baba and Shirdi were hanging up, and a red, velvet throne-like chair was positioned off-centre in front of the men's side. The walls and ceilings were covered in ornate Indian-style decor. There were many lit candles and lovely fresh flowers placed around the front stage area. When the last people had filed in, all the lights were turned off, and the room was bathed in candlelight. Out of the ethers, came the sound, "...OMMMMM..."

Everyone joined in, "...OMMMMMM..."

This happened twenty-one times (I found out afterwards). Sitting in the dark room and chanting in the middle of the night was magical. About halfway through, I started to feel lightheaded. I didn't know if it was the energy in the room, Baba's presence being felt so strongly, all the meditative chanting, or just being in a room with so many people and so little oxygen.

After the long, final, beautifully chanted "OM", the lights came back on, and the chapel quickly emptied. I made my way to the back of the building. The courtyard was already packed with endless rows of women. I sat down in a line. Within minutes, many more lines had formed behind me.

I heard singing and chanting getting closer and closer. I stood up and peered over the wall into the courtyard below. A procession of men was passing by. The men were chanting and singing as they circled the hall. Within seconds, a seva dal called, "Sai Ram, sit please."

A while later, I heard them approaching again, so I stood up and watched them go by. I ignored the calls of "Sai Ram, sit down." That kind of procession is not something I see every day, and it felt good to stretch my muscles. Apparently, no one had notified the seva dals about thrombosis, a medical condition caused by sitting in cramped positions for hours on end.

In the distance, I noticed that the first line was called. The women approached the metal detector as usual, but a large percentage of them were being turned away. Then several of the women started running down the aisles towards the exit where I was sitting. Five minutes later, panting and out of breath, they returned. I wondered what was going on.

At least ten women went through this routine until, finally, one of them, in her exasperation, said aloud to the seva dal near me, "I don't have anything in it except money. Why won't they let me in?"

I realized that they were all being turned away because they were carrying their little money purses. I wondered if the rules at Puttaparthi were even stricter than at Whitefield. Noticing my purse strap, the woman behind said, "You'd better go and check this in. They won't let you bring it."

I watched the steady stream of women being rejected for their little money purses. They were running up and down, visibly upset at having to lose their front row seats.

I intuitively felt that I would be able to walk through

without a problem, and I was excited to see if I was right.

Finally, my line was called. We made our way to the front, up the stairs, and to the metal detector. I saw a huge pile of cloth, plastic, crocheted, and leather purses piled up at the foot of the metal detector. Clearly, many women had decided to abandon their valuables rather than lose the opportunity of getting a good seat.

"Bag? Sai Ram, bag?" said the woman, wielding her metal detector at me.

"Yes," I said. "I have this purse under my shawl. It only has money and a passport in it, and I want to keep it with me."

She pulled it open, and looked inside.

I waited for her decision.

"Please, inside, Sai Ram," she said, pushing me past her.

I felt as though I had just won a prize! I was allowed to keep my purse.

I smiled as I looked around the crowded hall. I found a relatively open place to sit. "Relatively open" meant that I could shift position without landing in someone's lap. I sat for a long time, silently waiting for Baba to enter.

He arrived, walking down the same aisle as the day before. Bhajans played continuously as Baba made his rounds and went up to the stage.

Then he turned towards the entrance and held his hand up, almost as if he was calling someone. I watched carefully to see what he was about to manifest. His red BMW appeared at the stage seconds later. Either it was an incredible materialization, or the driver had been watching for a hand signal.

Baba climbed into the back seat of the car and drove off. I turned to a Swiss woman sitting next to me and asked if she knew what was going on.

"Baba goes to visit the hospital or the schools. He comes back at nine-thirty," she explained.

"Do people sit and wait for two and a half hours until he gets back?" I asked, noticing that very few people were leaving the hall.

"You can get breakfast and then come back. Just leave your pillow, and the seva dals will let you back in," she explained.

I sat with my eyes closed, meditating for a while, and then I decided to go for a walk. I left my pillow and made a mental note of where I was sitting. I walked back into the courtyard and tried to find my sandals. I couldn't remember exactly where I'd left them; everything looked different in the daylight. I walked around barefoot, retracing my steps. I looked against the walls and under the trees, where I eventually found them.

I decided to go back to the room to shower and get an apple. I didn't dare bring apples to darshan anymore.

The young night-watchman had woken up and was sitting on a chair in the hotel lobby. His straw mat was folded and stored under his seat. He was dressed in the same clothes, and he was ready for the day.

"Taxi come eleven-thirty," he assured me as I walked by.

"Thanks," I called back to him, wondering if he had any memory of the night's entertainment. It seemed hard to believe that someone could sleep that deeply on such a hard surface.

I felt better after the apple and the shower. I got dressed again and headed back to the ashram. It was still another hour before Baba was expected back, so I went to look for the food canteen to sample their breakfast. I walked around trying to find the cashier to buy coupons. I finally found the little blue kiosk. There was an arrow directing women to walk around the side, but a notice in the window said "Closed". I had missed breakfast by several minutes.

I headed back to the main courtyard, watching the monkeys jump between the buildings and the trees. I suddenly heard, "Hello, On the Mark."

I looked up, and there was Michael standing in front of me. I had almost walked into him. I was so immersed in my own monkey-watching world that I hadn't seen him. Not an easy feat, given that he's built like a football player.

"When are you leaving?" he asked.

"Today, after darshan," I answered.

"Sorry that I brought up the topic of your dream the other day. I didn't mean to put you on the spot like that. Kryshna only told me a little about it, and it sounded so interesting. I didn't mean to be pushy."

"Oh, I didn't think you were pushy at all," I answered. "I just didn't want to describe something so precious in front of a whole group of people that I hardly know. You know how the energy of something sacred dissipates when you talk about it in a flippant way. The dream was a big deal for me, but I didn't know that it would be interesting for anyone else."

"You're absolutely correct about keeping something sacred quiet," he said.

"I'll tell you now if you want," I said.

"I'd love that," he replied, "but we must move away from this area. Men and women aren't supposed to hang out together on the ashram grounds."

I followed him, staying a few steps behind until we found a quieter spot. Even so, he was not comfortable breaking ashram decorum. He stood a little bit away from me.

I recalled the whole dream while he listened quietly. He put his hands together next to his heart, and closed his eyes. When I was done, he said, "That is beyond incredible! Do you know how meaningful that is? That is the most rare and beautiful thing I have heard."

"Really?" I asked, knowing from both his tone and his body language that the words he spoke were true. He was genuinely moved.

"Ilana, listen to me. I have been coming here for many years, and I've heard so many stories about people's experiences with Baba. But I can honestly tell you that your interaction with Baba is off the charts. People can come here for forty years and never experience anything close to that."

"It's funny, because I'm not a devotee. I don't even really know why I came here," I said.

"Don't question it," he said. "You were called here by Baba. No one comes here without being called. I can see why you didn't want to talk about it the other day. You've been given everything you need. Don't pay attention to anything or anyone. You don't need anyone outside of yourself. Go within, and be very careful who you allow into your life. Just exist in the joy and the love that is yours. You have earned it. It's your good karma. It's the result of many lifetimes that you find yourself in this place. Baba doesn't want more devotees; he doesn't need them. He wants people like you to go out and be happy. Be Love. Listen to what I'm telling you, and don't doubt it. You'll be back for the second part when Baba calls you back here."

I stood silently and listened to Michael. I could feel the intense passion behind his words.

"Remember that you don't need anyone. You are it. You have everything you need. Now just enjoy it. I wish I could convey to you how special that experience was. Baba never appears to someone in a dream unless he is actually there. He orchestrates the dream. And that dream – what can I say – it's beyond incredible."

I was amazed by his response. The whole experience was very special for me, but I had no idea that Michael, who knows so much about Baba, would react that way.

"I shouldn't stand here talking to you anymore. It's considered very inappropriate to talk to a woman on the ashram grounds. I don't mean to be rude. Call me, if you want, when you get back to the States. I'll be back in a few more weeks, and we can talk. I'll explain more to you when we speak. I feel honored that you shared the dream with me. Thank you."

With that, Michael disappeared back into the crowd.

I felt completely washed over with an incredible warmth. Something transpired during that conversation that was very important for me. Perhaps it was the validation of the importance of my dream. Perhaps it was the tangible love that flowed through Michael in his listening and in his explanation of what it all meant.

I know that Baba never channels messages through other people, and that he disavows anybody who says they are channeling him. So, I knew that my interaction with Michael wasn't that. I did feel, however, that Baba sent Michael to talk to me, and that Baba's love was flowing through Michael to me.

It was perfect timing to get such a message. It was also a perfect preparatory talk for my re-entry into American life after three months away. We do have to go out into the world and share whatever it is we have and know, but at the same time we need to be discerning. That brief encounter would help me enormously.

Michael's words reminded me of Michelangelo's answer when asked how he was able to carve the masterpiece "David".

He said, "I created a vision of David in my mind and simply carved away everything that was not David."

I realize that I am doing the same for myself. I'm creating a vision of who I truly am, and I'm continually carving away all that is not really me.

In other words, we need only see our highest vision of ourselves. Then we need to undo and release all false beliefs and judgments. We need to let go of any view that we, or anyone else, has of us. What remains is who we truly are. It is that simple.

I felt filled with the type of peace that I feel after darshan. I floated back into the hall. I found where I had left my pillow, but the area was tightly packed, and my seat had been taken. I asked the Swiss woman, who had told me of the etiquette, where my pillow was.

"The seva dals came and took it. After eight-thirty, you can't save places anymore."

That would have been a useful addendum to the previous information she had given me, but there was no way I could have squeezed back into that tightly packed, very coveted space.

I didn't care. I went to another section further down and tried to sit there, but I was told that the space was being saved for seva dals. I found yet another area that had a tiny open space, but I was told that that was where sick people sat. Baba sometimes goes to that section to send them healing energy.

I was still so filled with warmth that I really didn't care where I sat. I went to the back row and sat down there. No one complained. Because of the layout in Puttaparthi, the side of the hall only has about seven rows. I blissed out for twenty-five minutes, sitting quietly with my eyes closed.

To everyone's delight and relief, the red BMW returned. Baba stepped onto the platform, and the bhajans began. After a while, Baba went into the little chapel behind the stage where we had been chanting the "OM" meditation that morning. I listened to the invigorated singing from inside and the crowds out in the hall answering back with the corresponding verses.

Later, Baba came out of the chapel and stayed on the stage for a while, conducting the energy and the music. Then he stepped off the platform and walked towards the side of the hall where I was sitting. He stopped a couple of times but didn't spend too long in any one spot. No one was behind me, so I could sit on my knees without being bopped on the head by anyone. I sat up tall and could easily see over the people in front of me.

Once again, it seemed as if Baba was looking right through me. He held the gaze for a long time as he walked by. I had exactly the same reaction as the day before. I burst into a spontaneous grin that filled my entire face. Baba left the hall, and people ran over to kiss the ground where he had just walked. There was a chalk drawing of the flower of life that people were kissing. They lined up to lie on the ground and kiss the centre of the flower where Baba had stood.

Personally, I have never been one to kiss the ground. In India, kissing the ground seemed more like a choice to commit suicide than to perform a religious custom.

I didn't want to get prodded by the seva dals, so I stood up and waited in the back until the last person had left. Then I walked into the pretty courtyard in front of Baba's large home, which was bathed in sunlight. There were two large statues of peacocks over his front door. I imagined that was why the peacock fans were being sold.

"The peacock must have some special significance in India," I thought.

I floated very slowly to the front of the ashram to find John. I would have liked to relax under a tree somewhere, but I knew we needed to catch the taxi at eleven. I spotted John talking to a tall woman in a straw hat. He introduced her to me, but I was so much in my own world that I didn't even catch her name. Although their conversation sounded interesting, I couldn't focus on it. In fact, I could hardly speak.

In The New Wave of Being, we don't need to experience a specific, dramatic happening in order to feel flooded with that other dimensional energy. It begins to wash over us as soon as we follow the Voice of our Souls. I'd felt it regularly in the preceding few months of travel.

Just then Kathy, Bernado and Chilita appeared, excited to have found us before we left. They said it took them hours to arrange accommodation at the ashram the night before, which was why we hadn't seen them for dinner. We said goodbye like old friends who had known each other for years.

When you begin to open your heart to the greater spiritual community, people that you only ever see once may feel closer to you than people you have known all your life. It's a different level of connecting that is so much greater than any type of connection made from the ego; it's a Soul connection.

We stopped at a restaurant for breakfast. I ordered a tofu dish which sounded delicious, but they didn't have the ingredients in stock. Puttaparthi was still trying to get in gear after Baba's surprise return the previous day. I had a fruit smoothie and a roll instead. John ordered apple cake and coffee.

"I had such a beautiful morning," John told me with a smile. "I was about to leave after Baba drove off because I thought he was done for the morning. So I got up to get breakfast and walked over to see Geta. Then I went back to sit in the chapel just a few feet from Baba's red chair. I sat there listening to the bhajans.

"Suddenly, Baba walked in. He came to sing with us in the chapel. It was so intense to sit and chant with him in the little candle-lit room."

In a past visit, Baba had blessed John's hands. I was pleased that he had had a special interaction again.

"Did you get into the chapel?" he asked.

"I did, but it was for the morning meditation. I didn't go back in there after Baba drove off. I went for a walk, and it turned out to be perfect."

I told him about meeting Michael and about locking eyes with Baba again.

We started walking back to the hotel. I saw a teenage boy

sitting in the street, rolling a small, white tube with tiny holes in it. As I watched, the chalk inside fell through the holes, forming beautiful little patterns on the tar. He picked up an identical-looking tube and rolled it next to the first pattern. A totally different, but equally pretty, pattern formed on the street. I pictured Nadi and Anna sitting on our driveway, looking in wonderment at the emerging patterns as they would roll the little tube.

"You like?" asked the boy, looking up for a moment.

"Yes, it's pretty," I said, knowing that the negotiations had begun, and that one way or another I would be leaving Puttaparthi with little white chalk-filled tubes.

"How much you want pay?" he asked.

"50 rupees," I said.

"No. No," he said resolutely.

I walked on, sensing him jump up.

"150 rupees," he called, running after me.

"No. This is a small piece of plastic with some chalk inside. It's pretty, but I'm not paying 150 rupees for it."

"How much you want pay?"

"50 rupees," I said again.

"No. No," he said, shaking his head.

I had lost sight of John, so I kept walking.

"100 rupees. Look at pattern. Very pretty, Madame." With that, he sat back down in the middle of the street, completely oblivious to the rickshaws and taxis skirting around him, as he started rolling out all the patterns for me to see.

"It's very nice. I will give you 50 rupees for it."

"No," he repeated. "How much you want pay? Best price."

"50 rupees is my best price."

By now, we were almost at our hotel. He had alternated between running ahead of me and sitting in the street rolling out patterns the whole way.

"Okay Madame. You buy all patterns, I give special price."

"I don't want all the patterns, I just want one."

"Okay. Best price. How much you want pay all patterns?"

This type of selective deafness would make an interesting case study. Was it simple denial, tenacity, or desperation?

"You know what? I don't think I'll buy any," I said, walking off again.

He knew I was serious. I wasn't in the mood for the game anymore, and it was getting very hot in the bustling street.

"100 rupees, three tube," he called after me.

"Okay. I'll give you 100 for three," I said.

He smiled broadly, and stood beside me, holding a little bundle of tubes tied together with a rubber band. I tried to find 100 rupees, but I didn't have any small notes. I needed change.

"I no change," he said.

I kept looking through my purse, which was filled with coins from several different countries, all coexisting peacefully, but I couldn't find the exact change in rupees. The boy went into a little shop behind us and asked for change for his notes. No one would help him. He went into a restaurant next door, but no one wanted to give him change there, either. He walked back up the street, looking for change in every shop.

I was tempted to walk off. He still had his tubes, and I still had my money. Why stand in the heat all day trying to make this deal? I couldn't walk away, though. It didn't feel right, after having finally agreed on a price, to walk off while the boy was running around trying to find change. I kept looking through my tiny purse. Suddenly, I pulled out a 100 rupee note which had slipped in between the pages of my passport.

I ran after him, holding the 100 rupee note in my hand. I must have looked like an Indian merchant's dream-come-true. A tourist chasing after the vendor, cash in hand! I found him almost back where we had started, and I handed him the money.

He gave me the little bundle, which felt very light.

"Where's the chalk?" I asked. "These are empty."

"Chalk extra," he said.

"Oh, please don't start that," I said. "You know it's included. These are no use to me without the chalk. You said it was included, and you have a whole container of it."

"You buy ten, I give chalk free."

"Okay, just give me back the 100 rupees, and I'll give you back the empty tubes."

"Here, I give you chalk," he said quickly, having no interest in returning the 100 rupee note. He put a little chalk in a small plastic bag and handed it to me.

I found John a little way down the street. I showed him my purchase as we walked towards the hotel. The landlord was sitting in the sun on the top steps.

"Sai Ram," he called out cheerfully.

"Sai Ram," we answered.

The young night-watchman, now fully awake, called out to us, "Taxi come eleven-thirty."

"You made sure the taxi has A/C, right?" asked John.

"Yes, very nice car," he replied.

"But it has A/C, right?" John repeated.

"Yes sir, car A/C. Eleven-thirty he here," he said proudly.

"Is the A/C working in the car?" I asked him.

"Yes, A/C work. Very good. Nice car, Madame," he assured us.

Having learnt our lesson several times already, John stressed the point one last time.

"If the taxi has no A/C, or if the A/C is not working, we will get a different taxi, OK?"

"Very good taxi – you very happy."

Certain that there was no room for a misunderstanding or for equivocation, we went upstairs. It didn't take long to get our things together.

"Should I pack the drum in my duffel bag?" John asked, showing me how much empty space he had.

It was magnanimous of John to make that offer, given how he felt about the drum and the guys who sold it to me.

"Okay. I will take it back at the airport because it might break with all the heavy suitcases thrown on top of it," I said.

While John was showering, there was a knock on the door.

"You ready?" the young man asked.

"Not quite. Is the taxi here?" I asked.

"No. No here," he replied.

I laughed, wondering why he had come upstairs to check on us if the taxi hadn't yet arrived. "Come and call us when the taxi arrives, okay?"

"Yes," he said and went back downstairs.

The room-service routine in India is very funny. I could never tell if they wanted a tip, or if they just felt like chatting. Maybe they were trying to be attentive, but I found the constant door knocking very amusing.

At 11:45, there was still no sign of the young man or the taxi. Finally, at noon, the young man knocked on our door.

"Is ready?"

"Yes, we're ready. Is the taxi here?" I asked.

"Yes. Is here."

A shiny white cab was waiting for us, with a thin young driver standing next to the open boot.

"You're taking us to Bangalore airport, right?" I asked him as he piled our bags into the boot.

"Yes. Bangalore," he said.

We climbed into the back seat, waved good-bye to the owner and his young helper, and set off on the long ride back through the Indian countryside.

"Can you make a quick stop so that we can see Geta?" John

asked the driver.

We stopped outside the high cement walls of Geta's home. I climbed up on a ridge in the wall and looked over to see a beautiful, gentle elephant standing in her huge cement enclosure. I'm sure that Baba treats her well, given his love for animals, but it hasn't ever felt right to me that animals, especially huge wild animals, are caged and tamed for the purpose of entertaining humans.

It was really hot back in the car.

"Do you have A/C?" I asked the driver.

"Yes A/C," he said.

"Does it work?" I asked.

"Yes, work, Madame."

"Well, could you turn it on?" I asked.

"No petrol for run A/C. Need first petrol," he said.

"When can we get petrol?"

"Seven kilometres more fill petrol."

It was very hot in the car, even with all the windows open.

We arrived at the petrol station, and he asked us for half the money. I handed him a wad of bills. With the petrol came the promise to crank up the cooling device.

We drove off. He still didn't turn on the air-conditioner, so I asked again.

"Close windows," he said.

I saw him push the magic button that illuminated the iridescent blue light – a sure indication that the A/C was on.

I was about to be shown the truth behind the old adage "Be careful what you ask for". The windows were all closed, the air was on recycle to keep out the fumes, and the A/C was running. I realized, however, that I couldn't possibly spend three and a half hours in the car like that. The car began to smell extremely bad. It was the smell of very old sweat. I put my T-shirt over my nose and tried to block the smell, but it hardly helped. The driver must not have showered in over a year. It was awful.

"How can I now ask him to turn off the A/C, and drive with the windows open after the big fuss we made to put it on?" I asked John, speaking through my T-shirt mask.

"No matter how hard we try to use A/C, something prevents it. It seems destined not to be," he said.

Even though I was breathing through the material, I was starting to feel like I would gag.

"I have to open the window. I can't stand it," I whispered to John.

I opened the window a little at a time, so as not to be too noticeable. The little bit of "fresh" air helped, if only psychologically.

Within a few minutes, though, the driver said, "Air condition on. No keep window open. Very much money."

I felt trapped. I didn't know what to do. I didn't want to insult the driver, but the smell was truly awful. Reluctantly, I closed the window.

The only question we hadn't asked was whether the driver had showered in the past several months. Who would have thought it necessary to ask that?

"Should we have him turn it off? Once we're in the country, there won't be so many buses and trucks. The air will be cleaner, so we can open the windows," John suggested.

"It's not just the fumes and the dust, it's also the heat," I said. "Still, I think I would rather be hot and inhaling diesel fumes than cool and breathing in this smell."

"You know, when you take a bus or a train in India, they pack people in so tightly that you are literally squeezed against the other people the whole way," John said. "Imagine what it must smell like in one of those trains."

"Maybe that's why so many people sit on the roof and hang out the windows," I said.

"First-class tickets are probably roof seats. Second class are hanging out the windows, and third class are the ones where you're sitting inside," John joked.

We started laughing at the thought that it could ever be preferable to sit on the roof of a vehicle rather than inside it. At that moment, I knew what I would choose.

I kept opening the window covertly to catch some fresh air, and the driver kept scolding me. Each time, he reminded me of the high cost of running an air conditioner.

After a long while, we stopped at a roadside restaurant.

"Would you like something to drink?" John asked the driver, remembering our dilemma on the way to Puttaparthi.

"I take cup tea," he said gratefully.

We brought him his steaming hot tea, served in a glass with a stainless steel handle wrapped around it. We also bought another two litre bottle of water, and an ice cream for John.

We waited in the shade of the building while the driver drank his tea. Once he was done, we set off again. The driver leaned over towards the cubby in the dash-board and pulled out a cassette tape. He popped it into the cassette player, and we had a party. This was the first car we'd been in that had any sort of stereo system, so we were very impressed.

I was still gagging from the smell. I couldn't tolerate it any longer, so I finally opened my window the whole way. The driver promptly flipped off the switch. I didn't care. I was pleased to be able to breathe again. I never thought the day would come when I would look forward to breathing in the dirty black smog that hung low in the air.

"Everything is relative – isn't that one of the laws of physics? The law of relativity," I mused to myself, listening to the Indian rock group on the tape.

A good song came on with a great beat. The driver cranked up the volume. I enjoyed the music. I had no idea what the words meant, but it was fun driving through India listening to rock-'n-roll. The driver was really enjoying the music. He turned it up even louder and started doing some great seat-dance movements. His hands were clapping and beating against the steering wheel, as he swerved around animals and potholes. He sang aloud as though he were alone in the shower, totally uninhibited by his inability to carry a tune.

Several times, I thought we would land in a ditch as we swerved hard around a scooter or a grazing cow. Each time, though, the driver quickly grabbed the steering wheel again and swerved onto the dusty soft shoulder. We just laughed; it was either that or scream. Enveloped in the spirit of laughter and music, I knew we'd be okay.

Δ

The roads became more and more congested, and the traffic steadily increased. I knew we must be entering the outskirts of Bangalore. We arrived at the airport right on time, unloaded our bags, paid the driver, and headed inside to check on our flight.

The flight was delayed by half an hour, so we went to the airport restaurant for lunch. I only ordered one entree because I thought we'd probably go out for a big dinner in Madras. We'd have about twelve hours to spend there before our flight was to leave. The food was good, although quite rich. After lunch, we walked across the tarmac to board the flight.

As we took off, we saw a completely straight line of smog across the sky. It was as if someone had carefully drawn a black line with a ruler.

"That's what we've been breathing every day," I said.

"It looks like a perfectly flat, black mountain," said John.

The flight to Madras was very short. Once we arrived, we collected our luggage and looked at each other with the question, "What should we do for the next twelve hours?"

John knew of an interesting church on a hill just outside the city. It is said that Jesus, Mary, and St. Thomas had spent time there. In fact, St. Thomas was killed up there. We decided to visit it.

We hoped to check our luggage in a little early so that we wouldn't have to carry it around for hours. John also wanted to change his ticket. He thought he would spend a night in London to break up the journey back to America. My friend, Sigal, was picking me up at Heathrow. I was going to stay in England for a while to visit my family and friends and to give a lecture in London.

Madras' airport is big, and wheeling the rickety cart from the domestic to the international terminal through the extensive construction wasn't easy. So I waited with the luggage while John went to investigate.

He finally came back, saying that British Airways wouldn't be open until midnight, so he couldn't get any of his answers. We noticed a sign that said "Sleeping Rooms", so we went to inquire.

After being sent from one office to another, we finally arrived at the Airport Manager's door. John went in while I waited with the luggage again. The air was hot and muggy, and the many vehicles going by made it noisy and smoky, too. This airport was cleaner than Bombay's, but it was not the type of place you'd want to hang around. It was sparse at best.

"They have rooms with a shower right here in the airport," reported John, coming out of the office. "Should we take a room and maybe get some sleep before we leave?"

"That sounds like a good idea. It will give us a place to leave our luggage, too," I answered.

John went back in and paid for a room. We followed the directions into the lift and up to the second floor. Off to the side was a rather dilapidated little kiosk that appeared to be the place to pick up the key.

A uniformed worker, who was reading a magazine, jumped up as we approached.

"We have a room for tonight," said John, handing him the receipt from downstairs.

"Okay. I give key. Third floor up room," he said.

John took the key, and we headed to the lift with our trolley, still laden with all our paraphernalia. A porter got into the lift with us. He smiled, and moved his head from side to side. (I had been practicing that movement for days, but I still couldn't get it right.)

He followed us down the very dingy corridor, which hadn't had a new coat of paint in decades. Each of the doors had a number, so we kept walking until we came to what should have been our room. The numbers had fallen off the door, so we checked the rooms to either side, deducing that it must be Room 312.

We wheeled the trolley into the room and looked around. The friendly porter followed us.

"Do you need something?" I asked him.

"I take key," he said.

"Why do you take the key?" I asked him.

"You call when go out – I lock door. When come back, I bring key."

That made no sense to me at all, but there he was, standing with his hand outstretched, as though it was perfectly normal to have the porter lock and unlock your room. After a quick laughing conference with John, I gave the man the key. He took it, but didn't leave.

"What now?" I asked him.

"Tip," he said.

"For what?" I asked, wondering if it was for following us in the lift, or perhaps for walking behind me while I pushed the trolley to the room.

"For take key," he said.

I suddenly understood why the key routine was invented. Now each time we wanted to get in or out of our room, we'd have to pay someone.

"Ohhhh, okay! I'll give you a tip," I said, looking through my purse.

He waited, smiling at his success.

"I only have ten rupees and big notes. John, do you have any small money?" I asked.

John looked through his money, but he only had big notes too.

I offered him my ten rupee note.

"Ten rupees no enough," he said, not moving.

"That's all we have," I said.

"No enough, more tip," he insisted.

"Well then, when we come back this evening, we'll give you a bigger tip," I said.

"So take the ten rupees now, or wait until later and get more," said John, laying out the options.

The man weighed the pros and cons.

"I back, get big tip," he said as he left.

The room was as basic as it could possibly be. There were two single beds that looked like the kind of cots you'd find in a jail cell. There was a piece of formica which served as a sideboard and a hard, uninviting vinyl couch.

"It's simple, but it's home," I said, as I laughingly fell onto one of the beds.

I pulled down the blanket and saw that the pillowcase had a big stain on it. I turned it over to use the other side. That side had what looked like a blob of old, crusty drool stuck to it.

"Which side should I put my head on? The side with the indefinable brown stain, or the side with the transparent drool?"

"I think I'd go with the brown stain. The drool looks newer," said John.

Life is wonderfully funny when you look objectively at everyday nuances. God must be laughing all the time, because we humans find ourselves in the funniest situations. We, however, miss the humour because we take ourselves too seriously. Life is incredibly funny when we slow down and enjoy the energy of each moment. Laughter is the expression of that joy.

I decided not to choose either side of the pillow. Instead, I pulled out my own faithful pillow and lay down on it.

"Should we go over to that church now?" asked John, looking like he wouldn't be able to move.

"Okay, let's go there while it's still light," I suggested.

Somehow, we got ourselves up. We went to the key kiosk in the lobby to tell them that we were going out.

We found a cab outside and determined that the driver understood where we wanted to go. We set off into Madras' rush-hour traffic, which was every bit as crazy as everywhere else we'd been. The roads were packed with cars going in every direction. After driving for less than ten minutes, the driver pulled over to the side of the road. He got out, leaving us sitting in the car with trucks and buses zooming by, inches from the side of our taxi. This was definitely not safe. I had no idea what he was doing.

There was activity all around us. We were stopped next to a street market with vendors everywhere, lots of food being prepared in little carts, and strange-looking things being cooked over small fires on the dusty sidewalks. We sat and waited, praying that we wouldn't get rear-ended. After a few more minutes, a man climbed into the driver's seat.

"Who is this?" I wondered aloud.

"Are you driving the taxi now?" asked John.

"I drive now," he said, starting up the car.

"Do you know where we want to go?" asked John.

"Yes, church on hill," he said.

"St. Thomas' Church," John clarified, making sure that we weren't about to be taken to some other, equally obscure, place in the hills outside Madras.

It was getting quite dark. Even though it's a big city, Madras apparently had the unwritten no-headlights rule, as well. We drove out of the city and came to a small road that led up the side of a hill. It was very steep, and the car almost slowed to a stop as it tried to climb the hill in first gear. It was completely dark by then, so I couldn't see much other than the lights in the distance. We pulled into a parking lot.

"This is it! Can you wait for us? We won't be too long," said John.

We jumped out of the car. From the darkness, a parking attendant appeared with a note pad. I gave him money for the taxi to park, and we went inside the little church. It looked more Mexican than Indian, with its brightly coloured stucco on the outside. The design was very simple and unpretentious, with an elongated oblong roof.

Inside, a little frame was hanging with a piece of human bone under the glass. The plaque said that it was a piece of St. Thomas' bone. It was carbon-dated to that period. There was also a framed drawing of Jesus, Mary, and Thomas that Luke had drawn and given them for a gift. Another glass frame housed a certificate stating that one of the Popes had visited the church. We walked around inside the church and then went outside to see the spot where the brutal killing of Thomas had occurred.

We stood silently, looking out over the city in the distance. It was lovely to see the twinkling lights below. Even though it was dark, it was still hot and muggy. John told me about the Gospel of St. Thomas, an unadulterated account of Jesus' life and teachings. This ancient manuscript, along with many other Gnostic texts, was unearthed in 1945 in Nag Hamadi, Egypt. Some of these manuscripts tell a very different story about the life of Jesus.

Apparently, certain texts claim that Jesus didn't actually die on the cross; his friends helped him off the cross and nursed him back to health. It's said that he learned yogic techniques that enabled him to transcend his physical body the way yogis do. After he was well enough, he traveled to India with his mother and Thomas, and he lived out his life in India.

There is a shrine in India where, it is said, Mary is buried. Another shrine, in Kashmir, marks the spot of Jesus' death. Thomas came to an untimely end on that very hill.

I was interested to hear that these stories were recorded. Ever since I was a child, I've intuitively felt that the traditional story wasn't accurate. I never heard the theory that Jesus was in India, but it all resonated with my belief. I've always thought the story to be exactly the way John said was written in the Nag Hamadi manuscripts.

We walked around the crest of the hill and found ourselves back in the car park. Our taxi was the only car left in the dark lot.

As we were driving away, the parking attendant came running after our car. The driver stopped, and the attendant put his head through my window.

"Pay parking!" he said to me.

"I already paid you."

He looked at me for a moment, said, "Okay," and waved us on.

We drove down the hill and back into the nightmarish traffic. It was unnerving to drive though heavy rush-hour traffic in the dark, with the majority of vehicles unlit.

After a while, the driver pulled over to the side of the road. Just like on the outbound trip, he got out of the car without any explanation and ran across the busy highway. Once again, we were left sitting on the side of a major highway, at night, with no lights on. I tried not to look as cars, trucks, and buses hurtled towards us, on all sides of the road. I realized that, despite having been in India for over a week, I still had no idea which side of the road they drove on.

After several minutes, the driver's door opened. The same driver (I think it was the same man, but, given how dark it was, I couldn't be sure) got behind the wheel. With screeching tyres, and a cacophony of horns, we weaved around the busy road and headed back to the airport.

Back at the terminal, we walked past the airport manager's office.

"I want to ask him what an appropriate tip is for the guy who unlocks the rooms," said John.

We walked in and stood in front of the manager's desk. John asked his simple question, and the man's face looked as though it would explode.

"Who ask you tip?"

"The guy in the hotel lobby wanted a tip for giving us the key," replied John.

"This no good! You pay room. No more money after that. No tip allow!" he said furiously, picking up the phone.

"Oh no," I said. "The poor guy's going to get fired."

"Excuse me, we don't want you to fire the man," said John, trying to get the manager's attention. "We just wanted to know how much to tip him. It doesn't matter – hang up – we won't give him a tip."

The manager wouldn't hear a word of it. For some reason, it really irked him, and he wanted to straighten out the breach of protocol immediately. He lambasted the person on the other end in Hindi. I couldn't understand the words, but I could certainly understand the message. Every now and then the manager threw an English word into the mix, which sounded very funny. Finally, he slammed down the receiver and composed himself.

"No more problem with this," he said, smiling broadly.

We thought it best not to show up minutes later in the lobby to ask for our key, so we went upstairs to a restaurant instead.

The restaurant was dark and grimy. The atmosphere definitely did not instill confidence in the kitchen's cleanliness. I was pleased to still be sated from lunch. I ordered a fruit smoothie. Unfortunately, there were no fresh fruit drinks, so I had to settle for an over-sweetened mango milkshake. It was nothing like the drinks we had been spoiled with at the ashram. John ordered chocolate ice cream. We ate slowly and then made our way back to the key-warden upstairs. He glanced at us sideways, probably surmising that we were the snitches.

He followed us up to our room and unlocked the door. This time he left us with the key, and without any discussion of a tip. I looked around the sparse room, and the song "We've got the bare necessities..." sprung into my head.

I showered and felt a lot better afterwards. It was about 10 PM by the time I fell onto the narrow bed. I set the alarm clock for 1:30 AM. In India, the airlines request your presence three hours prior to an international flight.

John was asleep in minutes, but I couldn't sleep.

I lay in the pitch-black room, the adventures of the past few days circling around in my head. I wondered how it would feel to re-enter my life back home after so much time away. What would I say when people asked me, "How was your trip?" Would I give a superficial overview or fully describe all the mysteries and craziness?

Each time we travel somewhere, we go on an inward journey as well. The person who left home is rarely exactly the same person who returns. When we rush the re-entry process and try to go back to what we were before the journey, we lose some of the spark and magic of the trip.

If I were to describe all the "magic" of the past three months, some people might think that I was crazy. I remembered a question I was asked on the radio one night.

"Where does a spiritual experience end and mental illness begin?"

I offered an analogy in explanation. If a little caterpillar told a group of his caterpillar friends, "I had an incredible vision! I was told to stay alone in a safe place and meditate for a couple of weeks. Then I saw myself flying, using beautifully coloured wings that were attached to my body. These delicate wings allowed me to soar up into the blue skies, rather than crawl around on the ground each day!"

The other caterpillars, having had no such vision, would certainly think their friend was mentally ill. If this caterpillar continued to hang out with his old friends, he might accept their diagnosis of his mental state. He wouldn't understand that what the others described as mental illness was just their inability to see his potential and recognize the transformation they all would eventually experience.

If, however, this caterpillar chose to hang out with his transformed butterfly friends, he would learn that his vision was a spiritual gift. It would show him his potential and his greatness. He would know that there was no cause for concern about his mental health or the physical changes he would need to endure in order to grow his wings and fly.

I thought about how society has historically decreed

some of our greatest visionaries insane. The Italian scientist Galileo was summoned to the Vatican to stand trial for heresy because he said the Earth revolved around the sun. The Roman Catholic Church said that belief in a moving earth was heretical. They sentenced Galileo to life in prison for making his wild claims, and ordered his books to be burned.

Ego-created reality is completely subjective. People accept certain outrageous claims while rejecting others. Claims of religious miracles, like a weeping statue or visions of Mary and Jesus, may draw thousands of devout adherents. People make pilgrimages all over the world to see a spot where Mary might have appeared to some children.

Are these claims any more believable than the manifestations of jewelry by Sai Baba, the appearance of Spirit Guides, or God's messages during meditations?

We need to ignore the assessment of others that we are misguided simply because our truth is different from theirs. We each have our own Truth; we must find it, speak it, and become it.

February 7

f

I think I might have dozed off for a few minutes, but I came around and wondered what time it was. I wasn't pleased that our departure from India was dependent upon my alarm clock working. The little alarm clock that I bought in Hawaii had been working pretty faithfully, but only when it was standing perfectly upright. It slowed down or stopped altogether if it was at any angle. The reason I couldn't leave it completely upright was that it had to be wrapped up in a towel or a blanket. That little clock ticked louder than any other clock I'd ever heard. Each passing second sounded like a drum beat. Lying in a dark, silent room emphasized the sound, making it seem more like a cannon firing. Also, given that it was full of sand from our nights of sleeping on different beaches, I wasn't sure how reliable the alarm feature was.

I imagined having to explain to John that the flight had left while he innocently slept, trusting that my alarm was reliable enough to rouse him out of his slumber. So, feeling entirely responsible for getting him out of India and back to America, I lay in bed trying to figure out what time it was without waking him. Finally, after silently debating my options, I crept over to his bed and tried to find his arm. I noticed that he had gone to sleep with his wristwatch on, so I thought I would try to take it off and check the time in the bathroom.

In the darkness, I couldn't see the outline of his body at all, but I did find his wrist. I loosened the watch strap, hoping that he wouldn't wake up. I started laughing to myself as I imagined John waking with a start, thinking that a taxi driver or hotel porter was trying to collect a tip.

I almost managed to loosen the watch the whole way when I heard, "What are you doing?"

Luckily, he didn't mistake me for an intruder.

"I need to check the time. I don't know if my alarm works."

He took off his watch and handed it to me. In the bathroom light I saw that it was 12:45 AM. There was no point in going to sleep for half an hour, so I lay quietly in the dark.

Δ

We wheeled our defective trolley into the lift and headed down the three stories. At the ground level, the lift door opened to the sound of a piercing alarm. Thick smoke quickly enveloped us. It was so dense that I couldn't see anything in front of me.

"John! The building's on fire!" I said in a panic.

"Let's go back upstairs," coughed John.

Neither of us was able to breathe.

"No. I don't want to be upstairs if the building's burning. Let's try to find the exit."

This was more frightening than the earthquake tremors in

Mumbai or any of the taxi rides through the dark streets. It was pure panic.

"What a way to end this incredible trip!" I thought, as I pushed the trolley into the corridor, trying not to breathe. I couldn't see in front of myself at all.

The high-pitched alarm continued to sound as the entire corridor filled with smoke. I moved in what I remembered to be the direction of the exit and finally slid through the glass doors, desperate for air.

"What was that?" I gasped, choking and coughing.

"I don't know, but the smoke didn't seem black enough to be a fire," said John.

Relieved to have exited the building alive, we made our way over to the International terminal. A uniformed security guard stood at the sliding entrance to the building.

"Tickets," he said tersely.

I handed him my ticket, using the same hand that was carrying the fans.

"What is that?" he asked, eyeing the fans.

"These?" I asked, thinking that it was pretty self-evident what they were. "They're fans."

"What you do with them?" he asked.

"I bought them for presents. I'm taking them home."

"You no take out India," he said sternly.

"Why not?" I asked.

"Peacock national bird India; no take national bird out country."

"These are not birds. These are feathers," I said.

"You give them me," he answered.

"No. I bought them. They shouldn't allow people to sell them if we aren't allowed to have them," I argued.

"You leave them," he insisted again.

"No. I'll ask immigration inside if I'm allowed to take them," I said.

Irritated, he waved us through the door.

"I didn't know the national bird was the peacock," I said, remembering the peacock statues on Baba's house.

"I thought it was the fly," said John.

It was completely chaotic inside the airport. It was filled to overflowing capacity, and it was difficult to walk around without banging into people. We waited in a very long line with hundreds of other bleary-eyed travelers. John went to buy himself some coffee, bringing me a cup of freshly squeezed lemonade. It was delicious – sweet and tart at the same time, with the consistency of a frozen slush.

I suddenly remembered a warning I'd read in a travel book about India: "Don't eat ice unless it is made from filtered water." It had gone on to explain that people pay attention to the water but forget about the ice, which is often made from regular tap water. I stopped drinking and hurried over to the little restaurant, where I was assured that the ice was supplied by a reputable company. I kept drinking the lemonade, but it didn't taste nearly as good after that.

We finally reached the front counter. I hoisted my luggage onto the conveyor belt.

"Where are the tags that show you've been through the x-ray machine?" asked the smiling British Airways woman.

"Where is the x-ray machine?" I asked her. "I didn't see it."

She pointed off into the distance, but there was such a crowd that it was impossible to see anything.

"You need to check through the x-ray machine before we can accept your luggage."

It didn't make sense that they would x-ray our bags, and then leave them in our care again until we checked in.

Back into the throng we went, finding our way to the randomly placed x-ray machine. We lifted all our bags onto the conveyor belt, including the delicate fans. I waited for the security guards to tell me that I wasn't allowed to put the birds through the machine, but they didn't say a word.

"This is why they tell you to be here three hours early," I said as we stood in line to reach the counter again.

Finally, back at the front, we checked our x-rayed luggage through and got our boarding cards. We passed through immigration, where we were officially stamped out of India. Still, nobody said anything about the fans. We followed the crowd up the escalator. At the top, another queue stretched so far that I couldn't see where it began.

We finally reached the hand-luggage checkpoint, only to be told that our boarding cards didn't have the required customs' sticker. Along with many other people who were also being turned away, we went back down the escalator in search of the sticker man.

After finding him, we went back upstairs and into the queue to be frisked. We displayed our stickers at the front of the line and were sent into separate cubicles. I was frisked by a female guard and scanned with a metal detector. Then she rummaged through my hand luggage.

No problems. I was waved through in full possession of my peacocks. The security guard did comment on how beautiful the fans were, but she didn't try to confiscate them. I wondered if the guard at the front entrance just liked the fans and wanted them for himself.

"That felt like getting into darshan," I said to John, as we met up on the other side. "They should employ seva dals to work at the airports."

"All they would need is 'seva dal' on their resume, and the

job would be theirs," laughed John.

The waiting room was absolutely packed. Many people were watching a TV movie which looked like a bad remake of "The Sound of Music". It featured a man and a woman running carefree through fake green mountain fields, stopping only to whirl around in circles and sing love songs to each other.

I found a seat as far from the screen as possible and waited for our flight to be called. I was getting really tired. Sitting under the stars in Puttaparthi seemed like much more than twenty-four hours ago.

Δ

I heard our flight being called. We boarded the huge Jumbo Jet and made our way to our seats at the front of the economy section. I sat at the window, with John next to me, and a middle-aged American man on the aisle next to him. It was 4:30 AM, and we had a twelve-hour flight ahead of us.

Just before take-off, there was an announcement that they were about to spray the cabin with some sort of chemical. They suggested that we all close our eyes. I remembered the spraying when I used to fly through African countries on my way to Europe, but I hadn't experienced it in years.

My eyes closed, I heard someone moving through the cabin with aerosol spray cans. It hurt my throat to breathe. I didn't want to even think about the toxic chemicals that we were being forced to inhale. My eyes were itching, despite being tightly shut, and I started breathing through my T-shirt again.

"Have you opened your eyes yet?" I wheezed, after what seemed like ages.

"No, and I'm trying not to breathe either," said John.

I waited for a long time and then opened my eyes.

"The good news is that you have no chance of getting lice now," I said. "The bad news is, you just tripled your chances of getting some horrible lung disease."

"Lice... or a horrible lung disease? Mmm...which one would I choose?" said John smiling.

"Do you think it was some sort of fumigation that was going on at the airport hotel?" I said, suddenly making the connection between the two smoky incidents.

"Maybe," said John, "but the smoke at the hotel was much denser."

We sat silently, each in our own thoughts, as we took off and flew into the night, climbing higher and higher above the Earth.

After a while, I heard the man next to John introduce himself as Reverend Bill. John started talking with him.

I heard Bill's voice get louder as he leaned over John towards me.

"John tells me that you host a radio and TV show. I didn't know I was sitting next to a celebrity."

I just smiled and said nothing; I was too sleepy to talk.

"What is your show about?" he went on.

"It's a spiritual talk show," I said. "A holistic, metaphysical, call-in radio show."

"How interesting," he said. "What kind of guests do you have on?"

"I interview a whole assortment of people. Holistic practitioners, artists, and authors – from unknowns to best-sellers. Anyone who's making the mind-body-spirit connection would fit."

"Would I have heard of any of the authors?" Bill asked

curiously.

"Possibly," I answered, too tired to think, let alone speak.

"Maybe you've heard of Deepak Chopra or the musician Kenny Loggins," said John. "They've been on her show."

"I haven't heard of them, but I would love you to recommend some books for me to read," said Bill.

"What were you doing in India?" I asked him.

"I come to teach the Bible in India fairly often. This time we also came over to distribute medical supplies to the earthquake victims. I'm here in the capacity of church leader. I'm with a group of my American parishioners, but for some reason I'm up front and they're all near the back."

With that, John, Bill, and I began what would become a ten-hour discussion about God, religion, the Universe, and spirituality.

Bill explained that he is a Baptist Minister. He got very excited when he found out that I'm Jewish. He told me that he loves Israel and the Jewish people, and that he feels so saddened by the trouble in the Middle East.

"Is your church evangelistic?" I asked him.

"Not really," he said. "They're more organized. They actively try to convert people to accept Jesus Christ as the Lord."

"So if you meet a Hindu or a Jew, you wouldn't try to convince that person that Jesus is the Lord?"

"Not exactly. Only if the topic were to come up," he said.

"What if the topic does come up? What do you do then?"

"I explain that real salvation only comes through accepting Jesus Christ as the Saviour."

Just then the screen in front of us filled with BBC news photographs of violence and destruction all over the world. I try not to watch the news too often anymore. It is too fear-based, and it spreads so much negativity and hatred.

A few years ago, I was walking along a beach near my house on a perfect summer's day with a friend. She said that she felt guilty walking on the beach in the middle of the week while everyone else was working.

"Don't feel guilty," I said. "You and I chose jobs that allow us to do this. We created this reality for ourselves. It actually benefits the world that there are people simply being happy, and spreading that happiness around without harming anyone."

It is also the G-string theory in action. When I walk around feeling the joy of life in my being, it resonates with the other people around me who are looking for permission to sound that same chord, but who haven't yet figured out how to do it. The ripple effect on the whole planet is huge. Sounding joy, happiness or love, so that others can resonate at that frequency, too, is a gift to the world that is as great as any work we could ever do.

Bill took off his headphones as violent images continued to flash in front of us.

"What hope do we have for peace in the world? Do you think there will ever be peace?" he asked, dejectedly.

"Watching this stuff feeds the fear frenzy," I said. "We have to continue to hold a vision of peace and to heal our own relationships with each other before we will ever see global peace. The work has to begin with each of us in our own homes, healing the relationship wounds that we have with each other. It is simplistic, but true, to ask how we can possibly expect to have peace between two nations, if we aren't speaking to our own mother or brother."

"I'm not sure how that could ever happen," said Bill.

I would love to see news broadcasters announce, "Today two people were seen walking on the beach looking very happy. We interviewed them hoping to find out the cause of their happiness." Then they would cut to a shot with people talking about feeling peaceful and connected with the Universe. Maybe they would film some people meditating and ask them what insights they have to share with the planet. That would be a news broadcast worth watching! That would inspire others to go out and express their Souls. It would encourage people to take some time to reconnect with the natural world. Society would be elevated to resonate at that frequency, rather than be dragged down by the dense energy of fear and misfortune. Unfortunately, the media's policy seems to be "If it bleeds, it leads".

I thought about an e-mail I'd received from a radio listener who wrote, "I get so excited and energized by your show....I finally understand that you are not interviewing your guests, you are connecting with them on a soul level....! And so many people join together at 7:30 to hear and feel words of love and hope (kind of a collective consciousness), which creates an energy that can be felt through the airwaves! I never thought of using radio that way, much less experiencing it that way before!! Ilana, you are a conduit for people to join together – what a joy to sit in my living room each week, and listen to someone talk about love and peace for an hour and a half!"

"Here are the three of us sitting next to each other, " said John. "You, Bill, are a Baptist, I'm a Catholic, and Ilana, one of my closest friends, is a Jew."

"So, if we can appreciate our differences and recognize that we are all one, that we are all searching for the same thing and ultimately talking about the same energy force when we talk about God, how could we hate each other?" I asked.

"It's only when we try to convince others that our God is right, or better than theirs, that we fill with fear and begin to hate each other," continued John.

"But how do you know what's right and what's wrong if you aren't following the word of the Lord?" asked Bill.

"There is no wrong and no right in the eyes of God," I said. "The duality of right and wrong, and the judgments that we impose, don't even exist outside of this human experience. Duality is something that is here for us to use as a tool for our human experience. On a Soul level we don't differentiate between up and down, hot and cold, right and wrong."

Bill seemed fascinated by the conversation we were having, although I suspected he thought we were a little crazy. Definitely unusual!

"If you believe in reincarnation, you begin to feel huge compassion for everyone, because you may have been Hindu, Buddhist, Jewish, or Pagan in a past life," I said. "How can we hate what we once were ourselves?"

"What do you think about reincarnation?" John asked Bill.

"I don't believe in it," he answered.

John explained to him that reincarnation is not only widely accepted by the majority of Eastern religions, but that it used to be part of the Judeo-Christian Bible as well.

"The emperor of Rome in the fourth century was named Constantine," I said. "He formed a committee that is known today as the Council of Nice. They removed many passages and texts from the Bible, and created a new version, which is the Bible we're familiar with today."

"Are you saying that's why reincarnation isn't part of the Bible?" asked Bill.

"Yes," I answered. "Reincarnation is, however, still a

central pillar of the mystical Jewish Kabbalistic teachings, although it isn't taught in mainstream Judaism. Similarly, the Gnostics were a mystical Christian sect. They followed Christ's teachings as they were originally taught. But when the Roman Empire began using religion to create fear and gain power around the world, the Gnostics broke away from them. Obviously, the mystical knowledge of the Gnosticism was seen as a threat to the power structure, so the Gnostics were scorned and disregarded by the Church to the point of oblivion."

Bill was incredulous.

John told him about the Gospel of St. Thomas, the church we'd visited outside Madras, and the tombs of Jesus and Mary in India.

"Apparently, one of the texts removed by the Council of Nice was the *Book of Mary*, which gives wonderful insights into Mary's life and her connection with Jesus," I said.

From the look on Bill's face during our discussion, I could tell that this information was quite revelatory.

"What do you do if someone comes on your show and speaks about these types of teachings, and you don't agree with their religious beliefs at all?" Bill asked me.

"I heard a Native American saying just before I started on the radio. I adopted it as a kind of a motto for how I would run the show," I explained. "It says, 'They drew a circle and excluded me, so I drew a bigger circle and included them.'

"I don't care if people agree with me or not," I continued. "I just offer my truth on the air. If it resonates with people, they can use it and learn from it. If it doesn't, they should let it go. All I can do is offer my truth as I experience it. Then I completely detach from caring if anyone agrees, disagrees or turns the radio off in disgust. I don't host this show to convince people that my way of life is the best way of life. I do it because it feels like the right thing for me to do. If I cared what people thought of me personally or professionally, I wouldn't be able to do the show at all."

"I hope the two of you don't mind me asking you all of these questions. I just find your answers so fascinating," said Bill.

"We don't mind," said John.

"Did you grow up in a religious household?" I asked Bill.

"Not really. My life was going nowhere before I found Jesus. I was drinking and gambling and didn't ever think about God," Bill answered. "Then one night at a party, I met a man who told me that Jesus really loves me. It's hard to explain, but something happened in that moment, and my life straightened out completely. Now I want to share that message with everyone. I want everyone to feel that same love from Jesus that I feel. I want everyone to accept Jesus Christ into their hearts."

"Why is it important that people relate to God in the same way that you do?" I asked. "Isn't it enough for you that *you* derive comfort and peace from your beliefs?"

"I want everyone to have the incredible experience of God that I have. I want everyone to know the happiness that I know and feel the love that I feel. This can only come through accepting Jesus Christ as the Saviour," he answered.

"Do you know what the opposite of love is?" I asked Bill.

"Is this a trick question?" he asked.

"No. What do you think the opposite of love is?"

"Hate," he said.

"I think that fear is the opposite of love," I said. "In God's world, only love exists. Fear only exists in the absence of love. When we are here having this human experience, we forget that simple truth and fill our lives with various expressions of our fear. These fearful expressions show up in many ways like hate, jealousy, shame, flattery, guilt, and doubt.

"We feel the need to prove that we are worthy of God's love. The irony is that everyone is worthy of God's love. God doesn't care if we pray ten times a day or tell Him how wonderful He is. Praying is for our own self-evolution. God doesn't care to hear twenty times a day from everyone on Earth that He is great. He knows He is. He wants us to know that, created in His image, we are too."

"But, don't you think it's important to pray and ask God for forgiveness every day?" asked Bill.

"I don't think that an all-loving, beneficent God would reject us or want us to roast in hell for eternity because we don't say prayers the right way, or because we eat meat on a Friday, or because we drive on a Saturday," I answered. "God wants us to be happy in the same way that we want our children to be happy."

"Excuse me asking – I don't want to sound rude," said Bill, "but where did you learn all of this?"

"We all know it, Bill. There is no school that can teach you how to love. There is no school that can teach you to be guided by joy and laughter. We can learn how to work in a trade or a profession that gives us the tools we need to share our love and joy with the world. I went to school to learn how to be on the radio and how to perform on stage and TV. As for the rest of it, it's simply waking up to who and what we really are and then sharing that information as enthusiastically and authentically as possible."

"Well, my wife and I have raised our children to be Christians. They weren't born knowing all this. They must learn about God somewhere," he insisted.

"Actually, young children are coming in these days already understanding their connection with God. They are called 'Indigo Children' or 'Children of the Blue Ray'. It doesn't really matter what they are labeled. What's important is that they are mostly Awake. They understand our connection with the Universe. They know that angels and fairies exist. They're bringing in a whole new vibration of pure Love and creating a transition out of fear. Their powerful energy is helping us move out of the Dark Ages and into the Light Ages."

"How do you know which children are from that group?"

"I've read that they're born after 1988. They tend to be vegetarians, they're very creative and artistic, they write beautiful poetry, and their senses are much more finely tuned than ours. The problem is that their parents and teachers don't understand this and don't know how to teach them. The children are accused of being daydreamers, hyperactive, and difficult to discipline, but they have so much to teach us. We have to encourage them to express themselves as openly and fearlessly as possible."

"Are there any books that prove all of this?" asked Bill.

"I'll e-mail you the names of some books if you want," I said. "You told us about that awakening experience when you moved from the gambling, drinking life-style into the arms of Jesus. I think that you're now on the verge of expanding to the next level."

"Why do you say that?" he asked.

"I can tell from the questions you ask, from your receptivity, and from your curiosity. Also, you were seated next to us, and apart from your group, for a reason. There are no coincidences."

Every few hours I got up, walked around, and sat back down. After about eight hours, I stood up and decided to remain standing. Sitting at darshan had been good practice for the long flight, but I really needed to move my muscles. I climbed over John and Bill and walked to the back of the plane.

I hung out there for a while, chatting with a Swedish flight attendant and drinking water.

I noticed that Bill was standing in the aisle, stretching his legs too.

"You know, if you don't mind me saying this, I find you so interesting," said the Reverend. "You have such a beautiful Soul. Your Soul will live forever."

Then he added wistfully, "I just wish that you could experience the joy and the love of Jesus that I feel in my heart. I want that for you."

"I already have it, Bill. I do feel full of love. I feel a Oneness with the Universe, and I don't need to accept Jesus as the Saviour to feel love. It has worked for you, and that's all that matters."

"Can you accept that Jesus Christ is the son of God?" he asked.

"I believe that we are all children of God. Jesus brought through a beautiful consciousness of a higher love, but the message that has been taught in his name over the past 2000 years is the complete opposite of what he was originally trying to say."

"Do you mean because of the changes that were made by that Roman council in the fourth century?" asked Bill.

"Not only that," I said. "Jesus was upset about the bureaucracy and the hierarchy in the Temple. He wanted to break that structure apart and teach us that we can all access God directly. Yet, today, the hierarchy in the Catholic Church is more rigid than ever. Look at the Vatican. The Pope wields so much power, both religious and political, through the church. Jesus brought through teachings of brotherly love, yet millions of people have been massacred in his name. He preached simplicity and walked around in simple robes, yet you could feed a whole country off the sale of the golden candlesticks, chandeliers, and artwork in the Vatican."

"The Catholic Church is far too powerful and wealthy an organization. It's very different in our Church," said Bill.

"I'm sure it is," I said. "There's a wonderful book called *Joshua* written by a Catholic priest. The premise of the book is that Jesus comes back and lives in a small town in America. He isn't accepted by the church and is practically excommunicated by the Pope. The Pope thinks he's heretical for preaching exactly what Jesus' original teachings were! Jesus would be appalled at what is happening today in the name of Christ."

"The bottom line is that Jesus died for our sins. He died so that we can be saved," said Bill.

"What sin did you commit as a newborn baby? What sin could you possibly have been guilty of at birth?" I asked.

"It's Original Sin."

"I think that the only original sin is the 'sin' of forgetting that we are Divine Beings," I said. "It's the 'sin' of forgetting that we are here as Souls having a human experience, and that none of this is real."

"What do you mean none of this is real?"

"Well, we know that everything on Earth is made up of electrons, neutrons and protons," I explained. "The electrons circle the nucleus. The amount of actual physical matter is minuscule. Most of what makes up any solid object is the space in between the spinning electrons and the nucleus. You are composed of exactly the same particles as the wall you are leaning against and the food you ate for lunch. But none of those things are 'real', because, if you were to take out the space between the electrons and the nucleus, there would be nothing visible left.

"I interviewed a scientist on my show who suggested that,

if the empty space found between the atoms of every single human on this Earth was removed, and the solid matter was compressed, everyone squeezed together would be the size of a baseball. All six billion of us would be the size of a baseball if we left only that which has actual weight or mass! Today quantum physicists are proving all this to be true."

"It seems impossible to believe," said Bill.

"From a Spiritual perspective, we know that nothing on this Earth is real," I said. "We come here as Spirit to experience ourselves as Love and to experience God's presence moving through our physical bodies. Everything else is a fabrication and a projection of our minds. Our egos go crazy when we realize this, and pull us deeper into fear. A good acronym for 'fear' is False Evidence Appearing Real."

"That's interesting, but are you saying that we are really nothing? Not real?" he asked.

"We are not real in the way we perceive reality. The Super String Theory is another revolutionary discovery. Scientists are suggesting now that we can take apart the smallest subatomic particles to a new level. On that level, we are revealed to be nothing but minuscule vibrating strings. According to this theory, we all vibrate at a certain frequency, and that's all we do, and all we are. Other prestigious scientists are suggesting that the whole Universe is just an enormous hologram – a projection of a reality that is far beyond our limited reality of time and space."

"I still don't understand what you mean when you say that we are not real."

"Do you remember what Shakespeare wrote? 'All the world's a stage and all the men and women merely players. They have their exits and their entrances, and one man in his time plays many parts.' That speech is so profound," I said.

"We're all part of this giant play, acting out our roles. The problem is that we've become so immersed in our roles that we've forgotten that it is only that – a role!

"When children watch a scary movie, they think it's real. They may scream or wet their pants or have nightmares afterwards because, to them, the movie was so real. They're unable to differentiate between their life and the movie. Adults, hopefully being a little more mature, know that a movie isn't real, and they don't have the same fearful reaction as children.

"Similarly, spiritual maturity is about knowing that none of this worldly drama that we act out every day is real. We might get frightened and caught up in the dramas in much the same way as the child does during the movie, but a mature Soul has perspective. The mature Soul can enjoy life and what it has to offer, while recognizing that our human experience is analogous to the child's movie experience. The spiritually mature person recognizes that, while matter appears solid and real, when it is broken down to its smallest subatomic particles, there is almost nothing there at all. It is all just energy."

"So where does God fit into all of this?" asked Bill.

"That's the huge paradox, because the space in between matter is nothing and everything at the same time. It looks like nothing. It has no form and cannot be measured, but it is the very glue that holds everything together. It is the innate, invisible force that is God."

"What about Jesus?" Bill asked. "You said you believe that he existed."

"He did exist," I said, "but only as you and I do now. He was a consciousness that seemed very real to the people in that 'play' at that time. You and I were probably around then, too. Jesus wasn't afraid to die because he was fully awake and he understood these principles. He understood that he couldn't really die because his Soul is eternal, and his physical body never really existed in the first place. His Soul brought a higher frequency of love to the human experience to help us all resonate with that frequency."

Δ

I went to my seat. After a while, Bill returned and sat down, too.

"I hope you two don't mind me taking up your time with all these questions," Bill said. "I just find you both so fascinating."

"We really don't mind. Besides, it's not like we have anything else to do," I said.

Turning to me, John said, "I think he's using the word 'fascinating' as a euphemism for crazy!"

"Bill, I want to ask you something," I said. "Do you believe that everyone who doesn't accept Jesus Christ as the Saviour is going to be eternally damned to hell?"

"Yes," he answered.

"Well, a few minutes ago you said that you think I have a wonderful Soul which will live forever. Do you believe that I will be damned to hell because I haven't accepted your belief system?"

"That is what the scriptures say. So yes, if I interpret them literally, I have to believe it," answered Bill.

"But do you, Reverend Bill, believe that in your heart?"

Bill looked down, gripping his hands together nervously. He seemed unsure how to answer. How could he very well tell this young woman he'd just met that she was going to hell because she didn't agree with him?

Finally, he said, "Ilana, you've really put me on the spot."

"I don't mean to put you on the spot, Bill. I just want you to look me in the eye and tell me, with all your heart, that you truly believe that I am going to hell because I don't agree with you. You don't have to worry about upsetting me. It doesn't matter to me if you think I'm going to hell. I don't believe that hell exists, so I have no fear of going there. I'm just curious to see how deeply your conviction about this runs."

There was a long silence as Bill sat in his seat, looking down, and wringing his hands. John and I sat quietly, waiting for his answer. It was as though the three of us were enveloped in our own little bubble outside of time and space. On some level, the simplicity of the question, and the answer it would receive, had a magnitude far beyond our immediate understanding.

"I – uh – don't think you are going to hell," Bill mumbled, tormented by his realization that, in uttering those words, everything he believed would be brought into question.

We were all silent for a while. Then I said, "It's very profound that you were able to say that, Bill."

"I'm only human," he said nervously. "That's why I have to look to the scriptures for guidance. I can't rely on my own personal interpretation. I have to get my answers from God."

It was interesting to hear a respected religious leader ultimately admitting that his own personal beliefs didn't jive with the doctrine. How many centuries have we followed some sort of religious doctrine just because that is what we've been taught? What Bill did in answering that question honestly was to drop the veil of dogma that clouds our personal knowing and truth, as he spoke his truth. He knows in his heart that the dogma isn't truth. He knows that, in spite of teaching it week after week, it doesn't ring true deep within his Soul.

The New Wave of Being is upon us. Now is the time for us all to become familiar with what our truth is. Our own personal truth that rings true, loud and clear. NOW IS THE TIME TO STOP CHASING AFTER OTHER PEOPLE'S TEACHINGS, TO STOP CHASING AFTER GURUS AND RELIGIOUS LEADERS. THE MESSIAH IS WITHIN EVERY SINGLE ONE OF US. THERE IS NO MESSIAH OUTSIDE OF US; THERE IS NO WORLD TO SAVE; THERE IS NOTHING EXTERNAL. THERE IS ONLY US ON THIS JOURNEY, WITH THE REST OF THE WORLD BEING A BEAUTIFUL MIRROR TO REFLECT OUR REALITY BACK TO OURSELVES EXACTLY AS WE ARE.

WE HAVE ONLY THE JOB OF WAKING UP TO OUR DIVINITY, OF SPEAKING OUR TRUTH, AND OF HELPING OTHERS AWAKEN AND REMEMBER WHO THEY TRULY ARE. GO OUT NOW AND SEIZE LIFE WITH BOTH HANDS. DANCE, SING, LAUGH, AND BE LED BY LAUGHTER, FOR LAUGHTER IS THE SONG OF GOD. THIS IS THE NEW PARADIGM WE COME TO ANCHOR IN. IT IS SIMPLE. IT IS LOVE. BE IT, SHARE IT, KNOW IT, LIVE IT. IT IS ALL THERE IS. I AM THAT. YOU ARE THAT. WE ALL ARE THAT.

EPILOGUE

f

A couple of weeks before this book went to print, a dramatic and transformational world event occurred. America was attacked on its own soil.

It happened on a Tuesday. The Sunday night just prior to the attack, I spoke on my radio show about the extraordinary energetic shift that was happening that very week.

I had read about a calendar which was found encoded into the Great Pyramid of Giza. The calendar began in 3999 BCE and ended September 17, 2001. This date coincided with the Jewish New Year (Rosh Hashanah). Incredibly, on September 17th a planetary alignment formed a perfect Star of David (the Jewish symbol).

Two nights prior to the attack, I explained on the radio that the upcoming week would be the darkest hour before the dawn and would end a six thousand year karmic cycle on the Earth.

We have just moved through that darkest hour, and we now stand at the threshold of a beautiful new cycle of light.

I decided to add this epilogue because I felt this book would be incomplete without welcoming in the beautiful new LIGHT energy.

When the world witnesses huge destruction, it's extremely difficult to avoid being drawn into fear, but we must not get pulled into the fear that usually accompanies profound Earth changes.

If we look at this from the First Wave perspective, America was brutally attacked by an external, dark force. America must now retaliate against the Taliban with even greater force to rid the world of evil.

Ironically, the Americans helped the Taliban gain power in Afghanistan because, at the time, the evil Russian empire was the enemy of the West.

Retaliation is a key word of First Wave energy. Safety and protection are brought about by spending billions of dollars on weapons, and by declaring war on the enemy. People buy flags and sing anthems in preparation for war.

This paradigm cannot bring about peace because the enemy is also hiding within each of us. Until we can bring our own deepest, darkest shadows into the light, we will always perceive and hunt down an external source of darkness.

Whether or not war is waged in retaliation, nothing will change until we end the war we wage within ourselves, the war we wage to remain separate from God, and the war we wage with our friends, families and neighbours. Only then will we see an end to the wars which are waged on this planet.

Throughout history, people have been killed in the name of God. During the time of the Crusades, and during the darkness of the Middle Ages, thousands of people were forced to convert to Christianity, or they were killed. Recently, the Catholic IRA and the Protestants of Northern Ireland have been at war over their religious beliefs. In the Middle East, it's Jews and Moslems. In Bosnia, it's Moslems and Catholics. The Germans created the Holocaust against the Jews while the Vatican stood by in silent complicity. In Tibet, the Chinese waged war on the Buddhists, and in India, it's Hindus and Moslems.

We cannot continue to kill in the name of God. The god that we've decided wants other people killed in his name is a fabricated god projected from a frightened ego mind.

Great civilizations have come and gone throughout history. The Mayans were eradicated by the Spanish Conquistadors who wanted to convert them to Catholicism. No one knows what happened to the Minoans, a highly sophisticated, peace-loving civilization from Crete. Ancient empires like the Romans, the Greeks, and the Egyptians, who dominated the world for thousands of years, are now relegated to historical monuments and exhibits in museums. Yet we continue to believe that we are immune from the patterns of history.

At some point every group has been the enemy, yet we continue to search for an enemy outside of ourselves to avoid finding the darkness dwelling within.

Our separation from our Souls is the real human tragedy. We have forgotten that beneath the illusions and beneath the appearances we are magnificent beings of light.

Just as we each have our own dharma, so every country has its own dharma. America has a huge dharmic responsibility during this time. America has been gifted much light and many resources. It is imperative to be in harmony with Universal energy, and not misuse these gifts of abundance and wealth. Compassion for the Earth cannot take second-place to our personal desires and comforts.

We each need to take personal responsibility. There is no more room for blaming an outside force. There is no more room for finger-pointing and revenge. We cannot continue to flood the TV, the movies, and the media with violence, and then get shocked that there is so much violence in the world. We co-create our world, and if violence is accepted viewing, it becomes an acceptable element of society.

The specific buildings which were destroyed show us that we cannot look outside of ourselves for protection and safety anymore. The collapse of the Twin Towers symbolizes the collapse of duality, financial security, and the material world.

The Pentagon, a building which houses the world's most powerful military system, represents physical security. In the wake of the September 11th terror, we realize that we cannot rely on anything within the earthly realm to serve as our protector. There is no place left to go, but within. To find true peace, we have to make that inner journey. That is what we most resist, but our reluctance to go within locks us into a state of fear.

We hear many Second Wave prophecies and predictions pointing to this time period. We decide to act from love rather than from fear. We meditate and send light and healing to the planet. This is a far higher vibration than going to war, but it still implies duality. It implies that there is something outside of ourselves to send light to, that there is someone outside of ourselves to heal.

The entire Universe was created with absolute perfection. Everything on this Earth, when left alone, is a mirror of God's perfection. When we begin to manipulate energy, sickness and disorder sets in. Attachment, greed, and fear all disturb the equilibrium and the perfection.

Terrorist organizations are analogous to cancer cells on a potentially healthy Earth. Cancer can be radically treated in the traditional way, by surgically removing and burning it out. It can also be healed by using Second Wave alternative therapies. In the Third Wave, we recognize that everyone we encounter is merely a manifestation of our projected mind images, and that we are already whole and healed.

We need to vigilantly hold this New Wave of Being vision of ourselves, identify with the infinite realm of our Souls rather than the limited scope of our egos, forgive ourselves for our self-imposed separation from our Source, recognize that everything is within us, fully embrace our darkness and our light, trust the magnificence of the Universal plan, and *experience* the "I am" consciousness that, until now, we have only intellectualized.

In other words, in The New Wave of Being, it's not enough to pray for peace or to send thoughts of peace; we have to feel the experience of peace deep within our Souls. We have to *become* peace. True peace has to start within and radiate out; it cannot be brought in from the outside.

When I am Peace, I don't have to look for peace outside of myself. If I simply resonate at that frequency, everyone I encounter will be able to resonate from deep within their Souls at that vibration of peace, too. This is the application of the G-string theory.

When we step into the Third Wave we realize that we can't fight to make a better world, we can only stand still and allow God's world to become our earthly experience. We experience God when we feel the fullness of our Souls.

Part of the Third Wave energy is admitting "I don't know" while quietly standing by to witness how the greater Universal plan unfolds. We cannot understand or judge mind-numbing atrocities from our human First Wave perspective.

The concept "We are all One" is taking physical form. We see this in the outpouring of community support in New York and in cities all over the country. We see it as the Western World steps up to America's side. These First Wave shows of support are mirrors of the Third Wave's emerging unified consciousness.

The message, written in capital letters on the last page of this book, is more pertinent now than ever before. We have been handed a blueprint by which to live.

When our light shines, we, along with this planet Earth, ascend into Oneness. The Oneness is a full integration of the physical with the spiritual. It is the synthesis of Heaven and Earth. This synthesis is our collective Third Wave dharma.

f

Ilana has been the host of weekly live radio and television shows for several years. Her show "On the Mark" is a live call-in talk-show which is devoted entirely to bringing through The New Wave of Being.

Ilana has moderated television debates of local and national political candidates. On the radio, she has interviewed hundreds of healers, authors, and musicians, in addition to sharing her own Universal messages with listeners.

Ilana has also been a guest of national and international radio and television shows. She is a certified Reiki Master and travels frequently, visiting many sacred areas around the world.

Δ

To order additional copies of this book, ask about bulk discounts, schedule Ilana Marks for workshops, or find out about talks in your area:

Write
ilana@ilanamarks.com
or
Ilana Marks
P. O. Box 197
Scituate, MA. 02066

Visit
www.ilanamarks.com

For appearances & book orders only
Call tollfree: 1-866-768-7664